True
Canadian Ghost
Stories

Other Books by John Robert Colombo

Many Mysteries

Ghost Stories of Canada

Weird Stories from 19th-Century Canadian Newspapers

Ghosts in Our Past

Mysteries of Ontario

The UFO Quote Book

Three Mysteries of Nova Scotia

Marvellous Stories

Haunted Toronto

Ghost Stories of Ontario

Close Encounters of the Canadian Kind

Ghosts Galore!

Personal Accounts of Hauntings in Canada

Singular Stories

Strange Stories

Voices of Rama

The Mystery of the Shaking Tent

Dark Visions

The Little Blue Book of UFOs

Windigo

Mackenzie King's Ghost
And Other Personal Accounts of Canadian Hauntings

UFOs over Canada

Mysterious Encounters

Extraordinary Experiences

Mysterious Canada

Colombo's Book of Marvels

True Canadian Ghost Stories

John Robert Colombo

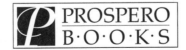

PROSPERO
B·O·O·K·S

National Library of Canada Cataloguing in Publication

True Canadian ghost stories / edited by John Robert Colombo.

ISBN 1-55267-414-2

1. Ghosts—Canada. I. Colombo, John Robert, 1936–

BF1472.C3T78 2003   398.2'097105   C2003-905862-X

This collection produced for Prospero Books.

Key Porter Books Limited
70 The Esplanade
Toronto, Ontario
Canada M5E 1R2

www.keyporter.com

Cover design: Peter Maher
Electronic formatting: Jean Lightfoot Peters

Printed and bound in Canada

04 05 06 07 5 4 3 2

To Matthew James Didier and Jennifer Krutilla,

who care for the ghosts among us

The knowledge that you can have is inexhaustible, and what is inexhaustible is benevolent. The knowledge that you cannot have is of the riddles of birth and death, of our future destiny and the purposes of God. Here there is no knowledge, but illusions that restrict freedom and limit hope. Accept the mystery behind knowledge. It is not darkness but shadow.

Northrop Frye, address,
Metropolitan United Church, Toronto,
April 10, 1988

Contents

Part V: Warnings and Whatnots

Preface

Have you ever seen a ghost?

Have you felt something that might be described as a spirit?

Have you ever witnessed a poltergeist-like effect, that is, a door opening or closing all by itself, sounds that have no point of origin, cold spots, objects levitating, appearing or disappearing for no apparent reason?

I am willing to bet that there is a twenty-five percent chance that you have had one of these experiences. In other words, one-quarter of the readers of this book will admit to some sort of eerie event or experience. I am willing to wager, further, that in three cases out of four, you know someone else, a relative or a friend, who attests that he or she witnessed just such an episode. Therefore, three-quarters of the readers of this book have heard of such an odd episode from someone close to them. If I win my bet, everyone wins because it makes for some wonderful stories!

It also makes for a lot of goosebumps, brows with beads of perspiration across them, bated breaths, heads and arms with raised hairs on them, pumping hearts, a welter of emotions, frights that border on alarms and panics...all symptoms of our deep-seated fear of and for the unknown!

Reports of uncanny experiences and mysterious events are common and widespread. They come in from all parts of the world, in the past as well as in the present, and presumably in the future as well. What to make of them is the question, one that I will discuss here.

But first, here is a description of the contents of this collection of ghost stories. There are more than seventy-five stories here and most of them are first-person accounts. Most of the encounters with the spirits of the unknown are recalled in the words of the witnesses themselves, and they derive from personal correspondence. Others are third-person descriptions of the weird things that have happened to other people, and these come from newspapers and journals as presented by reporters, researchers, interviewers, or investigators. Of the two types of stories— first-person and third-person—I prefer the former. They sound real! But both types make good reading.

The stories in this collection cover more than a century and a half of Canadian history. A number of the tales are classic stories. But most of the stories date from the late 19th and early 20th centuries and were first told in the columns of daily and weekly newspapers. Added to these are stories that I have collected from living informants. All of them convey mankind's fabled "sense of wonder" when faced with the challenges of the unknown.

I am pleased to acknowledge the assistance of researcher Alice Neal and librarian Philip Singer. Fellow investigators who are ever-helpful include Dwight Whalen, W. Ritchie Benedict, and David Skene-Melvin. I discussed a number of the subjects of this book with Dr. Cyril Greenland and Dr. David A. Gotlib. Matthew James Didier and Eric McMillan provided answers to pointed questions. Tony Hawke has always been of great assistance, and my wife, Ruth Colombo, remains ever-supportive. The idea for the book, as well as its title, were the inspired suggestions of Anna Porter of Key Porter Books, and the manuscript is all the better for the editorial talent and fine effort of Janie Yoon.

I continue to collect reports of strange events and experiences in Canada. Readers who wish to share their accounts with me for future publications are invited to write to me care of the editorial department of the publishers. I may also be reached through my website, *www.colombo.ca*, and my email address, *jrc@ca.inter.net*.

J.R.C.,
October 31, 2003

PART I
PHANTOMS OF THE SEA

Ghosts are associated with old houses and older graveyards. But they are not bound to such sites, for they are known to board ships and sail the Seven Seas. The stories of ghost ships are legion.

In this section we will encounter a fleet of phantom frigates, spectre brigs, fire-ships, doomed vessels, and voodoo ships. Savvy seafarers were said to eschew such jinxed vessels.

Canada has its fair share of doomed ships, including the *Mary Celeste*, the most famous "mystery ship" of all time. The twin-masted brigantine was jinxed from the day it was launched, June 10, 1861, at Spencers Island, N.S., to the day it was discovered adrift and crewless, its cargo intact, near the Azores, December 4, 1872. No one theory seems to account for its "accident." Under new ownership, the unlucky vessel sailed again but went aground off Haiti in 1884. No one knew where the site was until in 2002 some of its remains were located.

Seamen traditionally see mermaids and mermen. Could these be ghosts or spirits? Could they be projections of fears and favours? This section includes a couple of these strange, mainly marine creatures. Then there are sightings or visions of lake monsters and sea serpents. A few of these are included too. Finally, we have the phantom vessels themselves.

That Monster of
a Merman

NICOLAS DENYS

Nicolas Denys (1598–1688), a colonist and promoter of the fisheries and the fur trade throughout Acadia, was born in Tours, France. He worked as a merchant at La Rochelle from 1632, and died at his trading post at Nepisiguit, Acadia. He is the narrator of the account of the sighting of "a Merman" that follows.

Denys' account appears in his book *The Description and Natural History of the Coasts of North America (Acadia)*, translated into English from the original edition published in Paris in 1672 and edited for the Champlain Society by W.F. Ganong in 1908. The passage that is of cryptozoological interest appears in the "Collateral Documents" section of Ganong's edition; it first appeared, not in the original French edition, but as an interpolation into the Dutch translation of Denys' book, first published in 1688.

Did the mariners of Acadia of the 1650s believe in the existence of a race of mer-beings, creatures that are half human and half fish? Whether or not they did, they reported seeing at least one such creature.

◆◆◆

I must here make a little digression in order to relate a matter which deserves special notice and of which there have been eye-witnesses enough so as not to bring the truth of the same into doubt. While in the year 1656 three ships were lying on this coast for the sake of catching cod, the men of Captain Pierre Rouleau, lying farthest away from the shore, noticed some distance away in the sea a peculiar commotion that was not caused by anything which had the form of any known fish. They stared at it for some time without knowing what to make of it. Since the opinions about it were very much divided, as it usually is among men who have little knowledge, they rowed in the boats to the ship to get a telescope. Then they saw clearly that this fish, or to say better, this monster, which still retained the same appearance, seemed to take pleasure in the beams of the sun (for it was about 2 p.m. and very clear and fine weather); it seemed to play in the gently undulating water, and looked somewhat like a human being. This caused general astonishment and likewise great curiosity to see this strange creature near by, and, if possible, to catch it. Upon the order of the Captain they therefore kept very quiet, in order not to drive it away by any noise, and descended quickly into the boats with ropes and other things, by means of which they thought they could most easily get the monster alive into their hands. But while the men of the Captain named were thus engaged, those also of the other two ships, although they had lain farther away, had caught sight of the same object, and being extremely curious to get a nearer acquaintance, had betaken themselves to their boats and had taken the oars in hand. Captain Rouleau, who was himself in one of his boats, rightly understanding that in this way they would by no means attain their end, but, on the contrary, would by untimely noise drive away the monster, beckoned all these vessels together and gave command to row out a long way on both sides, in order thus unforeseen to fall upon it from behind. This was done in all quietness, but it came to pass that one of the sailors, or the fishermen, throwing out overboard away from the boat, cast a rope over the head of the Merman (for it was in fact a Merman), but since he did not quickly enough draw it shut, he shot down through the loop and away under water, presenting in his lowest part, which became of the quick movement could not well be made out, the appearance of a great beast. At once all the boats gathered round in order to catch him in case he should come up once more, each one holding himself ready for that purpose with ropes and cords. But instead of showing himself there again above water, he came to view farther out to sea, and with his hands, whereof the fingers (if indeed the things were fingers that stood in the place of fingers) were firmly bound to each other with membranes just as those of swans' feet or geese feet, he brushed out of his eyes his mossy hair, and which he also seemed to be covered over the whole body as far as it was seen above water, in some places more, in others less. The fishermen distributed themselves again, and went a long way around, in order to make another attempt; but the Merman, apparently noticing that they had designs on him, shot under water, and after that did not show himself again, to the great dejection of the fishermen, who many a time went there to be on the lookout, and incessantly racked their brains to invent stratagems to catch him.

I am sure this digression has not been unpleasant to the reader, yet one might have wished that the trouble of the fishers had had better success, and that they might have gotten that monster of a Merman into their power. Now let us take up again the broken thread of our story.

A Mystery of the Gulf

The Gulf of St. Lawrence has taken its toll of ships and men. It presents pilots and navigators with peculiar sailing difficulties and atmospheric anomalies. One of the latter is the appearance of "phenomenal lights."

Were mystery lights responsible for the wreck of the fleet above the ramparts of Quebec? Are such lights the cause of the "burning ships" seen in Maritime waters?

"A Mystery of the Gulf" appeared in the *London Daily Advertiser*, London, Upper Canada, later Ontario, September 1828.

◆◆◆

A Mystery of the Gulf
What the Phenomenal Lights
Seen in the Lower St. Lawrence
Portend to the Canadian Fishers

Miramichi, N.B., August 27:—The mysterious lights in the Gulf and the Lower St. Lawrence, those sure precursors of a tempestuous fall with grievous shipwrecks, have been unusually brilliant this season. The light off the Cape Maria Cascapediac has blazed almost every night since May 15. In the Baie des Chaleurs, the Point Mizuenette light has been seen nightly by hundreds of people from the settlements of New Bandon, Grand Anse, Caraquette and Salmon Beach. The *habitant* says they are supernatural manifestations marking scenes of wreck and murder, or warning the sailor of great tempests; while the English settlers think they are the will-o'-the-wisps of the ocean. Whatever they may be, it is a fact established by the experience of a century that when they blaze brightly in the summer nights the fall is invariably marked by great storms. One would think on looking at these mysteries from the shore that a ship was on fire. The heavens behind are bright and the clouds above silvered by the reflection. The sea for half a mile is covered with a sheen as of phosphorous. The fire itself seems to consist of blue and yellow flames, now dancing high above the water, and then flickering, paling and dying out only to spring up again with fresh brilliancy. If a boat approaches it flits away, moving further out, and the bold visitor pursues in vain. At the first streak of daylight it vanishes in the form of a mist, and is seen no more until darkness again sets in. These lights are brightest when there is a heavy dew, and are plainly visible from the shore from midnight until two in the morning. They appear to come in from the sea shoreward, and at dawn retire gradually and are lost in the morning fog.

Paradis, the French pilot who took charge of the British fleet under Admiral Sir Hovenden Walker when it sailed up the St. Lawrence from

Boston to seize Quebec in 1711, declared he saw one of these lights just before the armada was shattered on the 22nd of August; in fact, he said it danced before his vessel, the *Neptune*, all the way up the Gulf. Walker's squadron comprised the flagship *Edgar*, 70 guns; the *Windsor*, 60 guns; the *Montague*, 60 guns; the *Swiftshire*, 70 guns; the *Monmouth*, 70 guns; the *Dunkirk*, 60 guns; the *Humber*, 80 guns; the *Sunderland*, 60 guns; the *Devonshire*, 80 guns; the *Enterprise*, 40 guns; the *Sapphire*, 40 guns; the *Kingston*, 60 guns; the *Leonard*, 54 guns, and the *Chester*, 50 guns; with no less than seventy transports, of which the *Despatch, Four Friends, Francis, John and Hannah, Henrietta, Blessing, Antelope, Hanna and Elizabeth, Friend's Adventure, Rebecca, Martha and Hanna, Johannah, Unity* and *Newcastle* were from New England ports. On leaving Boston Sir Hovenden drew from Governor Dudley rations for 9,385 Englishmen, seamen and soldiers, and 1,786 colonists on board the fleet. On the 20th August when they lay off Egg Island, on the north shore of the St. Lawrence, having just cleared Gaspé Bay, a dense fog fell upon them. The Admiral ordered the vessels to keep together, and soundings were taken every half hour, but the land gave no bottom. On the night of the 22nd Paradis lost his head and signalled for the fleet to close upon the shore. While they were moving slowly a dreadful gale arose and as Sir Hovenden said in his journal which was published in London in 1720: "We soon found ourselves amongst rocks and small islands, fifteen leagues further than the log gave, when the whole fleet had like to have been lost." "But by God's good providence," he goes on, "all the men-of-war, though with extreme hazard and difficulty, escaped. Eight transports were cast away and had I not made the signals as I did, but continued sailing, it is a great question whether any ship or men had been saved." After the wreck the roster showed only 8,878 survivors. The Labrador shore, says the historian Charlevoix, was strewn with the bodies of at least a thousand soldiers, including two complete companies of the Royal Guards and many more of Marlborough's veterans, whose corpses were easily distinguishable by their scarlet coats. It was suspected that

Paradis had willfully cast the fleet away. In his defence, as found in the writings of Mère Juchereau, he pleaded that he saw the moving lights when they first made Gaspé Bay and told some of the high officers that heaven had ordained a terrible catastrophe, "so clearly and with such vividness did the celestial fires burn not only by night but often when there was a fog throughout the day." The disaster saved Canada to France for the time being, and the pious colonists reared many churches in gratitude to Notre Dame des Victoires. The court of Queen Anne went into mourning, and Sir Hovenden exiled himself to South Carolina, where, as a French writer quaintly said, "he wrote humorous apologies for the disaster with which God had been pleased to visit the English fleet." The flagship *Elgar*, with 470 men, blew up at Portsmouth on her return from the Gulf, which was "further evidence of God's displeasure at the invasion of New France."

Every great wreck that has taken place since Sir Hovenden's calamity has been preceded, if tradition is to be believed, by these mysterious lights; or rather they have warned the mariner of the fatal storm. When the Gulf gives up its dead there will be a vast muster. In 1797 the French war-ship *La Tribune* was lost, with 300 souls. In 1805 the British transport *Nacas* went down, with 800. In 1831 the emigrant ship *Lady Sherbrooke*, from Derry to Quebec, was lost, only 32 out of 273 passengers being saved. In 1847 nearly 200 Irish emigrants were lost with the big *Carrick*, and 240 more on the *Exmouth*. Two hundred and twenty-five souls perished in the wreck of the *Hungarian* on the 19th February, 1860; 35 on *Canadian* on the 4th of June, 1861, and 237 when the *Anglo-Saxon* was lost in a fog off Cape Race on the 27th April, 1863. How many fishing boats and coasters have gone down with all hands, leaving no sign, it is not safe even to guess. This fall, if the lights are to be believed—and the Gulf fishermen say they cannot lie—storms of unexampled fierceness will rage from the autumnal equinox until the winter is past. Should this augury be fulfilled perhaps it may be worth while for meteorologists and seafaring men to inquire into the source and origin of these strange watchmen of the deep.

A Mermaid in the Gulf

S ailors have been seeing mermaids and sirens on the Seven Seas throughout recorded history. Now and then landlubbers report the unexpected sight of these creatures. The creatures themselves are usually as surprised to see humans as the humans are to see them.

This news story is reprinted from the columns of the *Victoria Daily Colonist*, July 1, 1863. Neither the newspaperman who wrote this story nor Mr. Graham, who reported seeing this "mythological marine animal," attempted to relate what was seen to a known species of marine life. Instead, the creature is related to previous sightings by natives and to their beliefs.

◆◆◆

Mr. Graham, who is erecting a saw mill on Burrard Inlet, has just given us an interesting description of one of these mythological marine animals which he saw on Monday week in the Gulf of Georgia, about midway between the Inlet and the mouth of the Fraser. It was about 6 o'clock p.m., when he saw it gradually rise above the surface of the water within about 30 yards of where he was, showing the entire bust, in which position it remained for the space of five minutes looking in the direction of the boat in which he and two Indians were sitting, when it slowly sank into its native element. The Indians evinced considerable alarm at the strange phenomenon. Mr. Graham describes it as having the appearance of a female with long hair of a yellowish-brown tinge drooping over its shoulders, the color of the skin being a dark olive. The Indians have a legend that if this animal is seen and not killed, those by whom it is seen will pine away and die, and relate an instance of the kind as having occurred amongst the Squamish tribe. Hence the alarm of these Indians at the sight of the one alluded to.

They also state that many years ago one was killed on Squamish river by an aged Indian.

The Spectre Brig

Here is a robust account, a story within a story, of the voyage of a mysterious vessel. It is written with vigour and it may not be farfetched to say it recalls the sea tales of Joseph Conrad. The newspaper account is reprinted from the columns of *The Examiner*, Charlottetown, P.E.I., January 26, 1863.

◆◆◆

The fall of 1853 saw me on board the bark *Swordfish*, bound from New York to Yarmouth, Nova Scotia, thence to Liverpool and a market. I cannot imagine what odd freak decided the owners of the bark to give her a name so inappropriate, for the swordfish is known to be of uncommon symmetry, and moves with the quickness of light, while its ungainly namesake was tub-built, blunt-bowed, short-sparred, requiring four men at the wheel in a gale of wind to keep her within six points of the compass, and then she would make more lee-way than a Dutch galliot.

However, she proved to be a tolerable sailer, despite her unpromising appearance, and the fifth day out, we made the Seal Islands, in the Bay of Fundy, and a few hours later were moored alongside the wharf at Yarmouth.

Here we were informed that our cargo would not be in readiness for several days, and as but little remained to be attended to aboard the vessel, I concluded to take a cruise over the city and surrounding country.

The city has a gloomy and antique appearance, looking as though the blight of ages had fallen upon her buildings in a night. The houses are of a style and architecture in vogue half a century ago, being built still earlier by Tory refugees, who fled from the Colonies during the Revolutionary War.

Many of these were offshoots of noble families in England, and clinging to their sovereign with fanatical blindness, they fled to this and adjacent provinces, where their descendants have managed to keep up a dingy show of gentility in their old tumble-down tenements.

Their hatred of republicanism, a hatred gathered and intensified through many generations, until it has become almost a passion, is only equalled by their love and veneration for their sovereign. The poorer class, mostly Irish and Scotch, are ardent admirers of republican institutions, and are outspoken in their sentiments.

Between them and their more aristocratic neighbours exists a bitter feeling of partisan hostility which increases in intensity with each succeeding year, and must, ere long, break forth in a rougher shape than a mere war of words.

The Home Government is fully alive to this and accordingly grants every indulgence consistent with its dignity. But still the people are dissatisfied. They feel that there is a lack, a moral blight that deadens their enemies and clouds their prospects.

They know their country to be rich in mineral wealth, yet it remains undeveloped. Rich in its fisheries, yet they are unprofitable.

One day, while taking a stroll on the high ground bordering the bay, and watching the tide as it came in from the sea, rolling in the solid wall thirty feet in height that reared and rumbled like distant thunder, I chanced to hear some remarks made by a group of persons near me, that drew my attention. Not wishing to play the part of listener, I was turning from the spot when the foremost speaker of the party exclaimed:

"I tell you, gentlemen, it is no illusion! There is not a person for miles around who has not heard or seen the 'Spectre Brig.'

Furthermore, if you will remain a few days longer, you can satisfy yourselves of the truth of my statement, as it is nearly time for her annual visitation."

Being interested by these strange remarks, I turned and joined them. During the conversation that followed, I referred to the above and requested to be enlightened as to its meaning, addressing myself to the person who had attracted my attention. He looked at me as though surprised at the request, but seeing I was a stranger, he replied:

"Certainly, sir; with pleasure if it will be of any interest to you."

Seating ourselves, he then proceeded to relate the story, as nearly as I can recollect as follows:

"Fifty years ago, the brig *Yarmouth*, commanded by Capt. Bruce, and manned by a crew from this neighborhood, sailed from this port to the West Indies. Days and weeks went by, and the time for her return came and passed. Apprehensions began to be felt for her safety as the days went by, and daily an anxious crowd of women and children might have been seen gathered on the headlands that overlooked the bay, straining their eyes seaward in the faint hope of catching a glimpse of the missing vessel that had borne away a husband, a brother, a father, or son. Each night only witnessed a deeper disappointment, and at last apprehension had become almost certainty, and people began to speak of her as a thing of the past.

"A year had just passed away, when one night, as the watchman was going his rounds among the wharves, he chanced to look seaward, and was surprised to see a vessel covered with canvas from truck to kelson, standing boldly into the harbour, although it was blowing a living gale sufficient to swamp the strongest craft with half the amount of sail. On she came, plowing before the blast like a thing of life until she had reached within a cable's length of the shore; when suddenly her main topsail was backed, her anchor dropped into the water with a splash, followed by the rattling of the chains as it ran out through the hawse-hole. At the same instant her tacks and sheets were let go, her sails clowed up and furled, and in less time than it takes me to narrate it she had swung round with the current and was riding quietly at a single anchor.

"As she swung broadside to the wharf the astonished watchman recognized her, and started up town with a tearing rate. 'The *Yarmouth* has come.' The glad cry ran from house to house and street to street, and in a few minutes a crowd of people had gathered upon the wharf making the air ring with their cheers, while wives, mothers and sisters were kneeling and with streaming eyes returned thanks for the wanderer's return.

"As yet not a sound had been heard or an object seen aboard the brig to denote that a soul was near her. Every one recognized her as she lay silent and dark, rising and settling with every wave.

"Finding their efforts to arouse the crew to be of no avail, they procured boats, and in spite of the violence of the wind, put out to board her. Bending stoutly to the oars with a hearty good will they soon found themselves within a few yards of her, when they were surprised to hear a hoarse voice exclaim, 'Keep off! Keep off!' Hardly believing their senses, they returned to the shore, which they had scarcely reached before a thick black fog, peculiar in that land of fogs, swept in from the sea and enveloped everything in an impenetrable veil. Surprised and terrified at what they had seen, the people returned to await the morning, hoping, yet scarcely daring to believe that with daylight everything would be explained. The gale still continued, and as morning broke, the vapor raised for a few moments, but not a vestige of the vessel of the preceding night was to be seen.

"Another year went by and the phantom vessel again appeared under nearly the same circumstances, and all attempts to board her resulted as before.

"'Thus,' continued my narrator, 'nearly fifty years have gone by, and still she makes her annual visit at just such a period of each succeeding year. Of late no attention is paid to her whatever, her arrival being hardly noticed, as she comes in invariably at midnight, and disappears within an hour.'"

Here the story concluded, and thanking my informant for his kindness, I arose, bid the party good-bye, and returned to my vessel and retired to my berth, as it was getting late.

I felt feverish and restless, and lay tossing about for several hours. Not being able to rest, I got up, dressed myself and went on deck, where the night air soon cooled my heated blood, and I was about to go to my stateroom again, when my attention was arrested by hearing a loud splash in the water, followed by the rattle of a chain as it was rapidly paid out. Looking out into the harbor, I saw, to my astonishment, a large, old-fashioned full-rigged brig lying quietly at anchor, with sails snugly furled and everything in ship-shape style. I was at first considerably startled, as I knew it would be impossible for any sailing vessel to come in and anchor when not a breath of wind was stirring. Not believing in anything of a supernatural character, whether it be ghost or ghoul, hobgoblin or witch, I resolved to pay the strange craft a visit, feeling confident it was the "spectre brig," whose history I had heard a few hours before.

Going to the forecastle, I turned out two of the men, and ordered them to lower away the boat, throw out a pair of oars, and jump in, which they promptly did. I followed them over the side, and taking the tiller, sat down to wait the result.

In a few minutes we were within a dozen yards of the stranger, and rising in the boat I hailed:

"Brig, ahoy!"

No answer.

"Brig, ahoy!" I again shouted, with all the force of my lungs, but still no answer.

The third hail resulted as before.

There she lay, grim and dark, her sides covered with barnacles and clothed with seaweed. Not a sound could be heard, not even the creaking of a block, or the rattling of a rope.

Determined to board her at all hazards, I directed the men to pull with all their strength, and lay the boat alongside, while I grappled the rigging.

Bending themselves to the oars they sent the light boat seething through the water like a dart; but when, apparently with an oar's length of her side, the stranger craft began to grow indistinct, like a vapor. One moment her outline could be plainly seen, stamped against the sky, and the next she had vanished wholly, without a sound, without a sigh.

A thick fog soon set in from the bay, and we were compelled to grope our way to the shore as best we could, feeling awed and perplexed at what we had seen.

In vain I have tried to explain this phenomenon, but without success, and at last I am forced to the conclusion that it must remain one of those secrets that must continue until the Last Great Day, when the "heavens shall roll away like a scroll, and the mysteries of the universe stand revealed!"

The Monster of Lake Utopia

T he lakes and rivers of the Maritimes are the domain of innumerable "monsters," and the Lake Utopia Monster is among the best known, if only because of the sound of its unlikely name! "The Monster of Lake Utopia" appeared in the *Summerside Progress* of Sunnyside, P.E.I., August 19, 1867. It was contributed by the correspondent of the *Saint John Globe* of Saint John, N.B.

◆◆◆

A correspondent of the St. John, N.B., *Globe*, writing from "St. George, Aug. 6," gives the following account of a monster in Utopia

Lake, in addition to that which he contributed some time ago to the same paper, and which we then transferred to our columns:

Agreeably to my promise that should any further be developed respecting the strange monster in Lake Utopia, I would write you, I now beg to say that it has been seen by a number of persons since, in different parts of the lake, and on Wednesday, July 24th, by thirteen persons, some of whom are of the most reliable character. I would have written you sooner, but being rather sceptical about it myself, I waited to get the correct accounts from the lips of the individuals themselves; and I now have no hesitation in saying that some huge animal of fearful aspect exists in the waters of Utopia. To the north and east of Lake Utopia, there is a small lake well known to the sporting fraternity, which connects with the larger waters by a stream, perhaps 400 yards in length. About midway on this stream, between the two lakes, Messrs. H. & J. Ludgate have a saw mill in operation. The deals when sawn are floated down the stream to the deep water in Utopia, where they are made into rafts to float down to St. George. On the day before alluded to, a number of men engaged in rafting, had their attention drawn to a violent agitation of the water, about 100 yards distant out in the lake, which continued for a time, and then, there appeared distinctly above the water a huge bulky object, variously estimated from 20 to 40 feet in length, and from 4 to 10 feet across the widest part. The men describe the skin as presenting a shaggy appearance, not unlike a buffalo robe, and of a reddish brown color. It created a great quantity of foam which drifted up to the shore in huge flakes. At no time could they see the head of it; but at a distance of 20 or 25 feet in rear of the large mass, could be seen what they supposed to be a tail from the movements. The man called H. Ludgate, Esq., who was at the mill, and he and his son, together with others, ran down and witnessed the evolutions of this strange creature. Mr. Ludgate told me himself that it agitated the water to a perfect boiling, seething state, and threw up in its course edgings and mud from the bottom, occasionally rising itself to the top; a dark cumbrous body—not unlike a large stick of timber—disappearing again almost instantly. It finally moved off, and they could trace its course down the lake by the foam it created long after it went below the surface. Later in the day Mr. Thomas White, his two sons, and a hired man haying in the field, saw it *seven different times*, and Mr. White says it came up at the outer end of the raft, quite close to it; the men at work at the inner end being turned away did not observe their acquaintance of the morning.

Mr. White's description of it is about the same. He being farther off could not describe the skin of the animal, but says that when most exposed it resembled a large rock left bare of the tide, 10 feet across; and he further states that he can safely swear he saw 30 feet in length of it. His statement is corroborated by his sons, and by all of the thirteen persons who saw it the same day. Now, Mr. Editor, heretofore I could scarcely believe in the existence of such an animal and unprecedented inhabitant of our lake; but when I heard men of the character of H. Ludgate, Esq., Charles Ludgate, Charles Mealy, Thomas White, Robert White and many others say *positively* that they saw it as described, and when I take into consideration the destruction of fish which must take place in Utopia every year—otherwise it would teem with splendid trout, perch, cusk and smelt, and together with these the tradition of forty years—I must say that in common with the majority of our citizens, I firmly believe that a monster of vast dimensions and formidable appearance is located in the lake. Two of our most enterprising citizens, Mr. H.A. Smith, and Mr. W.W. Shaw, have had hooks made and attached to lines buoyed in the lake for some time, but so far without any satisfactory result. It is the opinion of many that a large net will be required to capture the creature, and I understand that a movement is on foot quietly, to make the attempt, which I hope will succeed. The people living in the vicinity of the lake are really afraid to cross it in boats; and if you could only hear some of the oldest settlers who saw this "thing" tell the story with fear and trembling, you would be fully impressed with the truth of their assertions, and consider them justified in their fears.

Phantom Ship

Here is another account of a phantom ship, one that suggests hearsay rather than eye-witness evidence. "New Brunswick's Phantom Ship" appeared in the *Newfoundland Evening Telegram* (St. John's, Nfld.), 18 Jan. 1886. Apparently the account was reprinted from the *Halifax Herald*, Halifax, N.S.

◆◆◆

New Brunswick's Phantom Ship
A Queer Tradition Lingering about the Bay of Chaleur

Annapolis, Dec. 18:—Some years ago, while on a visit to the Bay de Chaleur, I had an opportunity of learning a little about the celebrated Phantom Ship spoken of in the *Herald* of the 17th inst. A man named Harper, living at Little Shippegan, informed me that the Phantom Ship generally appeared on the Bay about the 22nd or 23rd of November, and stated that he had seen it several times. Some years ago, he said, a vessel belonging to the firm of Robin & Company, doing business at Paspebiac, on the opposite side of the bay, was given up as lost. One hazy afternoon, after all hopes of ever seeing the vessel again were abandoned, the fishermen living in the vicinity of Point Miscow were surprised to see the vessel (a small brigantine) enter the bay and cast anchor between the point and Shippegan. The news spread like wild-fire, and soon the beach was alive with a joyous throng, assembled to give a welcome to the supposed lost ones. A boat was soon launched and five men got on board and rowed off to the vessel. The people on the shore watched them eagerly as they climbed on the brigt.'s side. Now the vessel was enveloped in a heavy mist or fog and the watchers patiently waited for the mist to clear away. The mist, however, hung on till near 5:00 o'clock, and when it raised nothing was to be seen of the vessel or boat.

This is the story as given by an English resident and one who firmly believes it to be true. The French seem to be a little mixed as to the origin of the delusion. A Frenchman at Port Daniel said that it was the Devil's ship coming after the fish, and the French in general believe that the summer following the visit of the Phantom Ship will be an unlucky one and consequently they do not exert themselves, as they do not believe in wasting energies. As far as I can learn the story of the ship coming into the bay, and the men beaching her, is quite correct. But that it was Robin's vessel is another matter.

A man named Campbell, a magistrate at Shippegan Gully, said he believed the vessel was looking for men and sailed away with the visitors on board. It was his idea that she was a pirate. Nearly every "old inhabitant" of the Bay has seen the Phantom Ship. It is very often seen near Gaspé Rock. During the equinoctial gales the French keep a regular watch, and someone generally manages to work up his superstition to such a pitch that he imagines he sees the ship, and exclaims: "Grand Dieu! I see the ship!" The report then spreads that the vessel has been seen, and nearly everybody believes it.

A Spectre of the Sea

"A Spectre of the Sea" appeared in the *Calgary Herald*, January 16, 1890. The article was apparently reprinted from the *Examiner* (San Francisco, California). It is one of the few accounts to locate in the seaways of the New World the legendary Captain Vanderdecken, the master of the mysterious *Flying Dutchman*, whose brigantine is doomed to travel the Seven Seas until the Day of

Judgement. The legend served as the basis of Richard Wagner's opera and also the Hollywood movie *Pandora and the Flying Dutchman*, which starred Eva Gardner as the temptress Pandora, who falls in love with the doomed mariner played by James Mason.

◆◆◆

A Spectre of the Sea
The Bark that Sails by the Shores of the Unshapen Land
Canvas Set, But No Time at the Helm
Skirting the Crushing Pack and Dodging the Crumbling Bergs
How John Hansen Was Shocked

Stout John Hansen, wrapped up in furs, stood at the wheel of the bark *Reindeer*, a whaler of the Arctic seas. It was night, and the vessel was working along the ice pack with Cape Smythe just looming in the distance. The biting wind twirled about Hansen's feet, catching up the light snow and sending it swirling across the darkling water. There was a brisk breeze and the night was too cold for comfort by reason of the proximity of the floe; but Hansen cared little and cheerily whistled the tune of a folklore song he learned while a child sporting on the shore of a Norwegian fjord. He seemed as strong and fearless as one of his Viking ancestors when they faced the unknown Atlantic until "cloud-like they saw the American shore stretching to leeward."

Suddenly, right out of the pack came another bark, bow on. Her mizzen was gone and she veered and yawed strangely, but her sails were set and she was making fair headway. Hansen could hear the swish of the wind in her shrouds and the swash as she munched the bone in her mouth. In an instant she tacked and bore away. Then, before going 100 yards, she came about and made straight for the *Reindeer* again.

Hansen hailed her. There was no answering hail. His voice rang hollow and strange as the wind took it up and seemed to make of it a mocking echo. Then he hailed again. No return.

Hansen's lips grew white. His knees shook. He put his helm hard over and made for the open sea. Then he muttered a prayer which had not come to him since a ship burned under his feet in the southern ocean way back in the '60s.

He had seen the spectral ship, the *Flying Dutchman* of the frozen ocean. The phantom came so near that he could see the glisten of the salt spume frozen on her rigging and the icicles which hung from her spars. There was ice upon her deck, and upon her wheel, and upon her battered hatches—ice, and nothing more.

Her decks gave back no echo of footsteps. Her sailing lights were out. She was so low in the water that she seemed almost awash—but she kept on into the darkness, reeling, staggering, unsteady, but on and on and out of sight.

John Hansen came into port. Death sat watching by his bedside. He chattered and gibbered, and stared with straining eyeballs. For no man may look upon the phantom ship and live.

But what John Hansen saw in the depths of that July night was not a spectre of the seas; nor was it the grim vision of a fever-stricken brain. It was something far more dangerous than an airy phantom—a derelict of the deep. It was the wreck of the *Young Phoenix*, which since the 5th of Aug., 1888, has been sailing through ice and gale, breasting the crushing pack, dodging the toppling bergs, guided by an unseen hand, and sailing for no known port. No one may say she has not touched the northern pole. No man may tell where she will be seen again.

On Aug. 8 of that year the whaling fleet was riding between Point Barrow and Cape Smythe, waiting for the ice pack to clear, when down came the southwest gale, beating the sea into ridges and tossing the stout ships like the paper argosies of children. Down went the bark *Fleetwing* that had outlived many an Arctic storm. The *Mary and Susan* strained, plunged and foundered. The sea's great maw took in the schooners *Ino* and *Jane Gray*.

Things were lively on the *Young Phoenix* then. Both anchors were let go and the men were ordered to the pumps. She was leaking badly and the heavy seas swept clear over her. With the night the wind shifted to the west and came in stronger gusts. One after the other the cables parted and the bark drifted. Then an effort was made to get to sea, but the vessel fouled the *Triton* when trying to get over the bar. Her rudder, stern post and jib boom were carried away and the leaks were started freer.

The crew of thirty-seven men stuck by the bark until Aug. 6. By that time the water was at her lower deck. Her mizzenmast had been cut away. It was not thought that she could float more than an hour or two longer. The sails on the fore and main masts were set or partially furled when Capt. Millard ordered the men to the boats, and the *Young Phoenix* sailed away, rudderless and undirected, to meet whatever fate might come.

She was not seen again that year, and it was supposed she had foundered or been squeezed between the floes. But she kept on her erratic course, buffeted by the winds, caught by the currents, lonely and forlorn.

On May 5, 1889, she was seen again and boarded by Mr. Leavitt, manager of the whaling station on Cape Smythe. She was then close to shore, some sixty miles from where she had been abandoned. A few relics were taken from her, and the next morning she was gone again. She was little changed, and though water-logged, made good headway.

This abandoned craft is probably the phantom whose ice-sheathed shrouds and silent decks loomed upon the startled vision of big John Hansen that chilly night in July, and gave him that shock from which he may never recover. For nearly a year she had roamed the chartless sea, touching at no port, piloted by no hand, answering no hail, purposeless, silent and alone.

The Phantom Re-Appears

Phantom ships forever plough the Seven Seas. The archetypal phantom ship has to be the one that was or is captained by the Flying Dutchman, Captain Vanderdecken. He cursed the Almighty when foul weather made it impossible for him to "round the Cape." God in turn cursed him to live and sail the Seven Seas till the end of days. His spectral ship, complete with its ghostly crew, is spotted from time to time, during especially stormy weather, and will be... until the captain is redeemed through the love of a woman pure in heart.

The coastal and inland waters of Canada have been visited by at least one phantom vessel, according to this account, which appeared in the *Victoria Daily Colonist*, September 6, 1899. (The account has been slightly re-edited, and the list of the passengers of the *Willapa* has been dropped.)

◆◆◆

The Phantom Re-Appears
Mysterious Barkentine Now Reported from Hesquoit
Away for Dawson

Somewhat after the fashion of another famous ghost, that of the late Mr. Banquo, that phantom barkentine reported several times recently from points along the West Coast, resolutely refuses to be laid. It was thought that the last had been heard of it when Mr. Thomas Earle's manager at Clayoquot gave the denial to the previous reports to the effect that there was no sign of life on board. He said that he had seen men walking about the deck, and it was then concluded that the mysterious craft had only got a little closer inshore than safety would warrant, and had at the first opportunity stood out again. The *Willapa*, returning from the Coast yesterday, brings another report, however, which would indicate something serious amiss, if not on this same barkentine, upon some other and very similar craft afloat in the waters skirting the Vancouver Island coastline. This time the news comes from Hesquoit, considerably farther up the Coast than Clayoquot. John Goltz, a prospector, giving the information that he saw a barkentine, or at all events a three-masted vessel appearing to be barkentine rig, on the afternoon of August 20, or for a week later than the vision had appeared out of the fog to the Clayoquot folks. At this time the weather was clear, and the unidentified craft rode within two miles of the shore, with sails partially set, and unpleasantly close to Sunday Rock. Goltz distinctly made out a flag in the rigging and apparently reversed—in any event a signal of distress, and he would have gone out to learn more of the ship and her people but for the fact that the water was too rough to think of venturing on it in a small boat. He could not see any movement of people on board, nor recognize the nationality indicated by the distress flag. It seemed, however, darker than an American flag would be. The winds since the 20th ultimo have been westerly, which would carry the ship to the southward in the event of her rudder being carried away, which is supposed to be the case. Aside from this supplementary news of the phantom barkentine, the *Willapa* brought little specially interesting information from the Coast.

Mr. Extry Man

Some ghosts are menaces, others are helpers. Here is the story of a spirit that returns from the dead to help the crew of a vessel in distress. The spirit turns up as an extra hand when one is needed, even though his death was caused by the mate. The story is told in nautical language by Horace Johnson of Port Wade, N.S. The language was wonderfully preserved by the collector Helen Creighton in *Bluenose Ghosts* (1957), but it is not necessary to know the meanings of all the sailor's terms to savour the tale's salty tang.

◆◆◆

About fifty years ago when my brother was captain of the *Vesta Pearl* I sailed with him as mate. The captain takes care of the after end of the ship and the mate the forward end. Well, this vessel was built in St. John, and that's where we bought her, and after we got her they said she was a hanted vessel. One old fellow said, "You can't run her, she hanted." So I said, "If she's hanted now she's hanted so bad she's got to keep moving." (The word "hant" is often used here for haunted.)

The crew didn't want to stay aboard after the word got around. Someone told them the last captain had been knocked overboard when she was new and on her first trip and that he'd been drowned, but none of us knew the whole story. All we knew was that he was always around. He'd be there in a gale of wind when we were reefing the sails. If four men were reefing and one was at the wheel, there would be one man at the wheel and five men reefing, but you had to be at the wheel to see him.

He didn't bother us until we'd been out four months. We got caught in an easterly wind going to Boston and we were bobbing in the sea and when we went to reef, there was Mr. Extry Man. My brother called me to come and take the wheel. He said, "I'd rather go and help reef," but he didn't tell me why. It was then I found out about the extry man. I saw him for myself.

One time when we were in Annapolis we got rigged up (dressed up) and went ashore. It didn't take much to dress you up in those days. On account of the tide the boat was high up in the water and we figured out the tide to see what time we should come back. Tides are mighty high here and when it was out we could walk right out to the boat but it would be muddy going. Then you could climb up the ladder and on to the ship's deck. If we stayed ashore too long we couldn't walk back to her.

I had my rubber boots waiting on the shore and when I got back I put them on and made my way to the ship. The tide was getting pretty well up to the vessel when I got there, and I figured that the other men wouldn't be able to get back without a boat till the next tide. I shook my feet to get the mud knocked off my boots, and scraped them on every rung of the ladder.

It seems that anybody going to sea, it makes no odds whether they've had their supper or not, because when they come aboard they always have to have a mugup, hot or cold. This night I was the only one aboard and I was having a mugup. Tea, it was. They had a lot of salt horse (salt beef) aboard this vessel and I was quite hungry because I'd gone without eating from six to eleven.

Well, I was having my mugup and salt horse when I heard another fellow coming stomping same as I did and, when he reached the deck, he seemed to go forward. So I says, "My gracious, he just made it," because the tide was pretty well around the vessel. I could tell because while I was setting there the ship riz and I could feel her come up out of the mud. I said to myself, "Who's that come aboard?" because after I heard him stomping I didn't see no more nor hear nothin', but I'd heard him all right because he scraped his boots off the same as I done. So I took the lantern to see where he walked because I knew the mud would show his tracks, but nothing showed.

Well, the watch had gone off when I come aboard and I knew I was alone and I don't know whether I was frightened or not, but it was a little bit of a strange kind of feeling. I thought somebody might have gone overboard but I couldn't see nothin' with the lantern and, when the others came back, I asked, and it hadn't been them. So it must-a been him—The Extry Man....

Later we were told the reason for it all. It seems that when the company was building this vessel they didn't know which of two fellows to give it to and, after they finally made up their minds, the fellow who lost went as mate. He was steering the wheel when the captain went over. He was probably working on the deck when the wheelsman gave it a sudden turn and sent the captain over the side. It was always thought he done it a-purpose.

What the Mermaid Saw

"Comic relief" are the best words to describe the item that follows. It is an early instance of an "infomercial," for it offers the unsuspecting reader a combination of editorial content and advertising matter, all of this in the guise of a news item. It no doubt entertained readers of the *Saint John Daily Sun*, Saint John, N.B., December 20, 1902.

◆◆◆

What the Mermaid Saw in the Canadian Lakes
A Message to Canadian Women

Being a Mermaid of the Canadian Lakes, I only know Canadian women as they can be seen from my watery bed in the vast depths. I often wonder if up there in the sunlight you have pretty dells, mountains, and sandy wastes, such as we have in dear old water-land. I don't know about your mountains and your dells, but I do know you must have wastes; for every day, and particularly on one day of the week, you send down to us more waste than you know of. When your soap suds flow into our pure water, we have the power of sight to divide in the water the true from the false; and we find that in your soap suds there is a mixture that you cannot see, a mixture of silicates, ground glass, and adulterations that never dissolve in water, and consequently must be useless for washing purposes. You must waste money in buying such concoctions, you waste time in using them, you waste your clothes in rubbing them in. Alas! there is a lot of waste up there in the sunlight; but there is no waste in Sunlight Soap. Where Sunlight Soap is used by any of you, I find no leading refuse, no adulterations coming down to me in my home in the deep. Sunlight Soap reduces expense in the wear of clothes, and you don't waste money on loading mixtures, such as I have seen in common soap suds.

Please, dear Canadian women, don't send down any soap suds but those of Sunlight Soap. Have respect for your dear Canadian waters, and your purses, is the message of the Mermaid of the Canadian Lakes.

The Phantom Ship

The Phantom Ship of the Bay of Chaleur exists in story and song. This sighting, which comes from the unpublished files of the late Edith Fowke, was originally collected by Catherine Jolicoeur, who began to amass ghost ship legends in 1960 and compiled over a thousand sightings of such vessels from all over the world. Jolicoeur wrote, "People who see the Phantom Ship are not just imagining things. They certainly see something. One theory is that it's a kind of mirage; others think it's a marine phosphorescent manifestation."

The Bay of Chaleur lies between Quebec and New Brunswick. This account reproduces the words of Mrs. Joseph Comeau of Carleton, Gaspé, Quebec.

◆◆◆

In June 1912, when I was twelve years old, after three or four rainy days...one foggy morning near a sandy shoal called Larocque Shoal I had the sudden impression of seeing an enormous ship coming between two rocky capes and moving. I cried, "Papa, look at the ship run aground there near the shore, scarcely three hundred feet from us."

My father said to me after a long silence, "That, my child, is the fireship, look at it well." It was indeed the shape of an enormous vessel with dark grey sails flecked with white. You could distinguish the masts, the sails, large and small. I saw no rudder or bow, it was all a big mass. I didn't see any people but instead some black shadows overlapped each other; they resembled bodies or barrels. I was thrown into confusion. It passed very quickly. After a good ten or fifteen minutes the famous ship advanced into the Bay of Chaleur with bigger waves, broke up, disintegrated, as though the hull, the sides, were eaten; finally it all disappeared from our sight, carried away by an enormous wave. My father seemed frightened by the apparition of the Phantom Ship.

We spoke of it at dinner. I recall that Papa spoke like this: "The first time that I saw it was the year that my father died; and another time, my brother died in the Klondike. This time I don't know what will happen within the year." In the month of October the same year, a little sister died....

July 1914, after a stormy night...my brother and I saw a mass of black smoke, which seemed to have a long broad opening surface plunging into the most extensive of the two springs whose surface resembled a layer of water fifteen to thirty feet around. The rest of this mass was high, resembling a little mountain, taking different forms, swelling like sails. One would have said an animal whose sides moved in breathing. We were like jellyfish through fright, holding our breath. After quite a long time, at least half an hour, the black mass, as though satisfied, began to move, rocking, doubtless drawn by the sea, took the form of a great ship, releasing the sails, which we believed to be of smoke, and quietly launched itself into the sea between the two rocky capes....Concerning this sight of the Phantom Ship we weren't allowed to tell these stories of the abnormal sights we'd seen; we had to keep the secret lest we be taken for superstitious people.

The Phantom Lake Steamer

ROWLEY W. MURPHY

T he "mysteries of the seas" are legion. One of the best-attested mysteries is the appearance of the phantom lake steamer on Lake Ontario off the coast of Etobicoke, west of Toronto. The vision was witnessed by Rowley W. Murphy, retired seaman and marine historian. According to Murphy, the event or experience took place in August of 1910. At the time Murphy was still a youth, but he was not alone in experiencing the vision, or apparition, for it was simultaneously observed by at least ten other experienced sailors and seamen.

Murphy recalled the experience in considerable detail in his two-part article "Ghosts of the Great Lakes," published in the journal *Inland Seas*, Summer 1961. Even a half-century after seeing the vessel, the vessel that should not be there, he was still of two minds as to the nature of the ghostly lake steamer.

◆◆◆

Experienced Great Lakes seamen have, like the writer, seen curious and extraordinary sights which remain clear in the memory. Could not some of these members record impressions of strange or wonderful occurrences which they have seen afloat, and yet appeared to be outside the boundaries of fact?

Another appearance from the past was seen by the crews of three yachts one beautiful night with full moon (like cool daylight) in August, 1910. My father, a cousin, and I were on a holiday cruise around the west end of Lake Ontario, and as we were late getting underway from Toronto Island, and were running before a light easterly, decided to spend the night in the quiet, sheltered and beautiful basin at the mouth of the creek, spelled "Etobicoke"—but always pronounced "Tobyco" by old timers. (This seems hard for present residents of that area to tolerate, as they insist on trying to pronounce each syllable.)

In 1910, the Tobyco Creek was really a small river which made an abrupt turn westward and widened into a small lake, with a good beach held by poplar trees, between this harbour and the Lake. There was perfect shelter in this excellent harbour from wind from any direction, though in a hard easterly, it was not easy to reach Lake Ontario through the narrow harbour entrance.

At the date of this cruise, there was one brick farm house westward of the harbour entrance and no buildings at all among the walnuts and oaks on the lovely grassy banks of the creek, except one ancient landmark, known as "The Old House," from the veranda of which Lieutenant Governor Simcoe is said to have shot a deer in 1794. This house was in good condition, when a few years ago it was torn down to increase parking space for a supermarket! The whole area is now completely built up, but in 1910 the beautiful grassy plains contained no buildings from Lake Ontario to the Lakeshore Road, except the landmark mentioned.

Our cruising yawl, with a larger sister of the same rig and a still larger Mackinaw (one of several "fish boats" converted to cruising yachts with great success), were the only occupants of the harbour this perfect night. The crews of the three yachts numbered eleven in all, and as is generally the case, after dinner was over and dishes done, gathered on deck in the moonlight to engage in the best conversation known to man.

All hands turned in earlier than usual, there being no distractions ashore, and by midnight were deep in happy dreams, helped by the quiet ripple alongside. At what was about 1:30 a.m., the writer was wakened by four blasts on a steamer's whistle. After waiting for a repetition—to be sure it was not part of a dream—he put his head out of the companionway.

There, flooded by moonlight, was a steamer heading about WSW—at about half speed, and approximately half a mile off shore. She had a good chime whistle but not much steam—like *Noronic* on that awful night of September 17, 1949, who also repeated her four blasts many times.

But who was she? On this amazingly beautiful night, with memory strained to the utmost, it was difficult to do more than think of who she was not! She was considerably smaller than the three famous Upper Lakers, *China*, *India*, and *Japan* (about this date under Canadian registry, known as *City of Montreal*, *City of Ottawa*, and *City of Hamilton*). She was not as small as *Lake Michigan*, but like her, did not appear to be of all wooden construction. However, there were many in the past, of quite related design and size. The vessel seen had white topsides and deckhouses, and appeared to be grey below her main deck, like the Welland Canal–sized freighters (at this date, the big wooden steamers of the Ogdensburg Line of the Rutland Transportation Company). *Persia* and *Ocean* were like her in size and arrangement, but were all white and came to known ends, and of course *Arabiana* was of iron, and was black.

In this appearance off "Toby Coke" (a variant of spelling), the starboard light, deck lights and some other lights seen through cabin windows, had the quality of oil lamps; and her tall mast, with fitted topmast, carried gaff and brailed-up hain-sail. Her smokestack was all black, and she had no hog beams—but appeared to have four white boats. Her chime whistle was a good one, but was reduced in volume as previously mentioned, and was sounded continuously for perhaps ten minutes. Very soon all hands now watching on the beach decided that something would be done. So a dinghy was quickly hauled over from the basin, and, with a crew of four made up from some of those aboard the three yachts, started to row out with all speed to the vessel in distress, to give her what assistance might be possible.

As the boys in the dinghy reached the area where something definite should have been seen, there was nothing there beyond clear and powerful moonlight, a few gulls wakened from sleep—but something else, impossible to ignore. This was a succession of long curving ripples in a more or less circular pattern, which just might have been the last appearance of those caused by the foundering of a steamer many years before on a night of similar beauty. In any case, the four in the dinghy returned in about an hour, reporting also small scraps of wreckage which were probably just old driftwood, seldom seen with any fresh breezes blowing.

But something more there was. This was the appearance to the visual and audible memory, which those on the beach and those afloat had seen and heard, of something which had occurred in the more or less distant past, and which had returned to the consciousness of living men after a long absence.

Whatever the cause, the experienced crews of the three yachts mentioned were of one mind as to what had been seen and heard. At least eleven lake sailors would be unlikely to agree on the character of this reappearance without good reason! And the reason was certainly not firewater working on the mass imagination, as no one of the three yachts had any aboard. So, reader, what is the answer?

PART II
WHATEVER COULD IT BE?

The term "ghost story" covers the gamut of narratives that range from those described as *supernatural* to those described as *paranormal*. Supernatural tales turn on physical impossibilities, whereas paranormal accounts require powers or forces inexplicable because as yet unexplained. In other words, a supernatural tale is a legend and never happened, whereas a paranormal account just possibly might have a basis in some natural force yet to be explained by some advanced wing of science in the future. Lying between these extremes of impossibility and improbability are tales of occurrences that are grotesque, eerie, or weird. All of them remain quite out of the ordinary. They belong in *The Twilight Zone* or in the *X-Files*.

So in this section you will find native bogeymen, wild children, madmen, relics of ancient beasts and prehistoric creatures, and even the remnants of petrified human beings!

An Indian Tradition

It would be possible to fill this section and even this book with nothing but accounts of aboriginal beliefs and practices. The Native Peoples have a rich tradition based on the interaction between the known and the unknown worlds, yet the stories of the Indian and the Inuit are quite unlike ghost stories in intent. They are "just so" stories that offer an imaginative explanation of why things are the way they are, or they are cautionary tales that seem to say "Don't tempt the spirits" or "Even if you don't believe in the spirits, respect them."

"An Indian Tradition" appeared in the *Victoria Daily Colonist* Victoria, B.C., October 6, 1860. The identity of the correspondent J.D. is unknown. The author refers to the Sim-moquis, which seem to be "wild men of the woods," that is, real human beings, not hairy Sasquatches, which are said to be ape-like creatures.

◆◆◆

An Indian Tradition
The Sim-moqui

Having a little leisure time, one fine evening in the spring of 1853, I started out for a few hours' ramble on the banks of the Camas-sau (the Indian name for the Victoria arm or slough). As I walked along, I met a Cowichan Indian, and understanding the language perfectly, I entered into conversation with him. He commenced telling a heap of stories about hob-goblins, ghosts, etc., and after I had listened some time, he asked if I had ever heard of the Sim-moquis? I replied I never had. "Well," said he, "sit down a bit, and I'll tell you a story about them."

I obeyed and, sitting down, listened to his tale, which ran very much as follows:

"By the side of a lake amongst the highest mountains of this Island, where the crack of a rifle has never yet been heard and the deer and bears roam all unacquainted with the smell of the deadly gunpowder, lives the terrible Sim-moquis. From these mountains the daring hunter, who ventures to pursue the game to their fastnesses, seldom returns to tell the tale of his wanderings. No berries in the whole world are so large, or so sweet, or so nourishing, as the berries in the Sim-moquis country; yet who dare gather them besides their terrible owners?

"The Sim-moquis are a tall, strong, athletic race, with heavy black whiskers and matted hair. They are totally without knee or elbow joints, and depend upon staffs to assist them in rising from recumbent attitudes, or in sitting down. They never rise but leap with the aid of their staffs to a great distance. Like the deer, whose wide-spread antlers would seem to be a hindrance to its rapid progress through the forests and thickets, the Sim-moqui never miscalculates the distance he has to spring, or the space allowed him in which to leap. His eyes are large and red, and shine like a torch; his teeth are black; his hands and feet are webbed like a water-fowl. They have canoes and hunt with bows and arrows made from the bones of dead Sim-moquis.

"The unfortunates who chance to visit their country are immediately seized upon and led into captivity. If they happen to be men, they perform all the drudgery; if women, they take them to wife, to try if they cannot introduce the fashion of knee and elbow joints into the race."

"Did you ever see any of those strange people?" I asked my companion.

"No," he replied; "but my father did. It was one time when some of the Nanimooch (Nanaimo) Indian women went out berrying, and wandered far up the side of a very high mountain. The farther they went, the larger and the better the berries became, and as they gathered them into their baskets, they wondered at their size and excellence. Higher and higher they went, alternately filling their baskets and pouring them out upon the ground, only to fill them again with still finer *olallies*. At last they reached the top of the mountain, and there their wondering eyes gazed upon a sight which caused them to cry aloud. Berries grew everywhere as large as their baskets; the air was filled with the fragrance from the many-coloured flowers that adorned the green carpet at their feet. The trees, too, were mighty, and their tops were lost to view among a few fleecy clouds that were wafted by a gentle breeze through the air high above them.

"As they stood and wondered at the strange sights above and around them, the sun suddenly sank to rest behind a still higher mountain in the west, and then they felt their danger. The 'Sim-moquis!' burst from their pallid lips, and they seized their baskets and swiftly prepared to descend. But, alas! they had not bent the twigs of the saplings as they came along, and they had no mark by which to guide them back to their homes. They sought for a Sim-moquis trail; but those people leave no trail. As I said before, they leap, by aid of their staffs, over the closest thickets and through the densest forests. After searching for a long, long time in vain for the way down, the poor women threw themselves upon the ground and wept bitterly. Tears dropped like rain, and the ground at their feet was moistened by the crystal drops that fell from their eyes. They thought of their homes and of their little ones, and bemoaned their sad lots in accents of grief and despair.

"Suddenly, while they were seated thus, they saw two lights in the distance, and heard a rushing sound through the air (as of a limb of a tree falling to the ground). The poor creatures started to their feet and essayed to run; but, too late! A Sim-moqui leaped with the swiftness of an arrow shot from a bow into their midst, and motioned them to stay. The affrighted maidens obeyed, and examined the stranger critically. He was tall and straight; his hair was blacker than the features of the blackest raven, and it was neatly combed too. His features were regular and handsome, and half concealed by the flowing whiskers and moustaches that adorned his face; but his colour was much darker than that of any Indian ever before seen. His limbs—who shall describe them?—were straight and appeared strong, but were thin as that sapling" (our friend here pointed to a young fir tree about six inches in circumference). "His arms, too, were straight like sticks, and as he extended his hand as a token of friendship towards the unfortunate girls, they saw that the stories which their grandparents had often told them of the absence of knee and elbow joints among the Sim-moquis were indeed true. His red eyes glistened and shone in the dark like a lantern, and were the lights which had first attracted the women's attention. After they had sat some little time in silence—for the Sim-moqui language was strange to them—their visitor rose, by means of his staff, and placing his hand to his chin, opened his mouth, and uttered a loud, piercing cry. In an instant a commotion was heard in the bushes, and in a few seconds lights glanced in all directions, and soon huge, unwashed, unjointed Sim-moquis leaped into the open space in which the captives stood. The light from their flaming eyes fell upon the maidens, and objects in the immediate vicinity became as clear as noon-day. No need for torches where the Sim-moquis live," continued the narrator. "Every Sim-moqui is provided with two torches—that is, his eyes. If a fire be needed, dry sticks of matches are not required—his eyes start the wood into a blaze; if his hands be cold, he raises them to a level with his natural torches and warms them.

"The newcomers held a short consultation with the Sim-moqui who had first joined the unhappy women, and then, at the word of command, six stalwart youths approached, and each seizing a woman threw her over his shoulder and commenced leaping through the air, on their way up the mountain. The rest of the party followed, singing a war-song, and so they went on during the night, toiling up the mountainside, until the first dawn of day. Then they sat down by the side of a running brook, prepared a hasty meal of dried venison, and coiling themselves up like hedgehogs, went to sleep, after binding their captives securely. I might here remark that the Sim-moqui never travels in the daytime, as he is as blind as a bat while the sun is shining.

"When the night came, and the women did not return, the lodges of the Nanimooches were in a state of excitement, and a solemn council was held. The unanimous opinion was that the Sim-moquis had carried their females off. For some time, no one ventured to go forth and attempt their rescue, such was the dread in which the mountain savages were held by the coast Indians. At last my father, who was a chief, addressed them in tones of eloquence—pictured the distress which the poor creatures must feel, and the horrible treatment they would receive. At the conclusion of his speech a dozen braves started up, seized their rifles, and prepared to follow my father in search of the lost ones. It was midnight when they commenced to travel up the mountain side, but they walked briskly, and by daylight reached the top of the mountain, the beauties of which had so charmed their countrywomen the evening before. They were so astonished, and wished to remain a short time to feast their eyes upon the wonders of nature. But my father urged them to continue their search, and after a brief rest, they commenced to climb another high mountain—the same over which the Sim-moquis had passed with their captives a few hours before. Night was coming on apace when the pursuers reached the summit, and throwing themselves upon the ground, after a hasty meal, sought repose.

"My father, however, could not sleep, but lay wrapped in his blankets for a short time musing upon the lost ones and the probabilities of rescuing them. At last, he rose from his couch, and was walking up and down in front of the camp, when his eyes suddenly detected the glimmer of a light at some distance to the north. Awakening his companions, they stole, gun in hand, towards the light, and soon came upon the band of Sim-moquis, who had encamped for the night on a grassy knoll. They were all asleep; and to the utter amazement of my father, he discovered that the light he had seen came from the eye of a sentry, perched upon a high rock. Levelling his gun at this sentinel, my father directed his followers each to pick his man. This having been done, a dozen rifles cracked at once, and a dozen Sim-moquis bit the dust. The rest, owing to the absence of joints, were slaughtered before they could rise to their feet. The captives were unloosened, and they threw themselves sobbing upon the breasts of their rescuers. My father, before he left the spot, examined the body of the sentry, and discovered

that one of his red eyes was still open; the other was closed tightly. The
party, after securing all the valuables they could find, started down the
mountain and reached home the next day."

"And are there any Sim-moquis now-a-days?" I asked the narrator,
as he turned to leave.

"Oh, yes," said he as he walked away; "lots of them. They live by the
side of a lake on a big mountain, and the shores of the lake are covered
with gold."

I walked home in the dark, Mr. Editor, musing on what I had heard,
and after seven years' lapse have committed it to paper for your especial benefit. If you believe it, publish it; but if you are at all sceptical on
the subject, commit the document to the flames.

A Ghost in Thorold

A spirit is often believed to be the guardian of a person or the
warden of a specific site. Religious traditions are rich in
"guardian angels," not to mention devils, demons, and satans.
This article appeared as "A Ghost in Thorold" in the *St. Catharines
Journal*, C.W., October 23, 1863. It recalls a tradition of the area
around the town of Thorold, a tradition that today has all but disappeared from this historic region of the Niagara Peninsula.

◆◆◆

Last week the bridge-tender at the bridge over the Canal entering the
village from the North resigned his position, and a gentleman of the
Irish persuasion from the town took his place. It seems that at some
indefinite period a man was drowned near the bridge, whose shade

remained perfectly invisible until Thursday night last, when Andy was on duty. On that night Andy saw a man with a lantern, or a lantern without a man, approach the bridge, and apparently inspect it very closely. Andy went toward the object, and said, "It's a fine night then," but received no answer. This incivility on the part of a stranger irritated Andy, who raised his foot and made a kick at the lantern, hitting a shabbing post. He repeated this operation several times, and with a like result each time. Before he would kick, the lantern would seem to be between him and the post, and after doing so, it would appear on the other side. This puzzled him, and caused his toes and conscience both to become sore, and he retired to his shanty, locking himself in. On Friday night the same interesting programme was performed. On Saturday night Andy swore he would not stop alone, and when three boys came along, he impressed them and detained them until 2 a.m., and then let them depart, the

Witching hour of night,
When church-yards yawn,
And graves give forth their dead,

being over. On Monday he resigned, and refuses to go near the bridge.

P.S.—Since the above was written, a new version of the ghost has appeared. It now comes in the shape of a dog, with six legs and six lights, one being in its mouth. The story has thoroughly alarmed the boys and women of the village, and they will not pass that bridge alone on any consideration. In our opinion, it is the duty of the Canal Superintendent to suppress this ghost, as it may interfere with navigation. If he would inquire very closely of the remaining bridge-tender a solution might be obtained. It may be that somebody is anxious for the situation.

A New "What Is It"

We still experience fright at the thought (not to mention the sight) of the strange creatures who are said to wander the woods at midnight. Many stories and movies exploit the *frisson* of fear that affects the man or woman or a child who is abandoned and all alone in a forest. Here is a story about such a fear...and such a fascination. "A New 'What Is It'" appeared in the *Daily Sun*, Saint John, N.B., October 7, 1882. It was credited to the New York *Correspondence*.

◆◆◆

A New "What Is It"
From the Woods of Northern New Brunswick

The transition may be somewhat sudden, but I saw the "Bear-Man" at Brighton the same day. He reminded me of Quilp, only he was less intelligent and consequently not as capable of being a villain. A sort of a lair is partitioned off in one corner of the museum for him, where he is concealed from view except when the spectators are allowed to pass through and look at him. When we went in he was sitting quietly on a raised platform which was carpeted and railed in. This was a special privilege given by his keeper, a weak-looking man with a long brown beard. On seeing us the wild man sprang forward and snapped his jaws like a dog. His head is abnormally large, and is covered with long, curly brown hair. His eyes are gray, very small and shaped something like those of the Japanese. From his broad forehead his face tapers to a pointed chin, on which there is a tuft of fine hair. There is a suggestion of the pig in his lips, when they are extended as they are when he snaps. The neck is thick and strong; the chest and shoulders broad in proportion to his height, (or rather length, as he does not walk erect), and his arms are thick and muscular between the shoulder and elbow. The muscles of his arms are at the back instead of on the anterior surface. His forearms are smaller in proportion than the upper arms, but his hands are large and fat. Each hand has a double thumb and six fingers. They are stubby and callous on the palm, like the paws of an animal. His knees have the appearance of being double-jointed, and his legs below the knees are without the usual muscular development. There are six toes to each foot, which is broad and flat like the hands.

While he was being inspected, "Heddy," as his keeper called him, sat with his legs drawn up, much as a tailor sits when at work on his bench, playing with a string of beads. Occasionally he picked a few loose beads from a box and added them to the string.

"He is always doing something," said the keeper, "just like a bear. He can't keep still."

"I must do something," said Heddy, looking up.

This remark was a revelation to us, as we had been informed that the bear-man could understand a few words, but could not talk.

One of the doors swung partway open.

"Shut that door, Jack," said the man-bear, addressing the giant.

The monster kept up his snapping at intervals. Once he snapped at me and made me jump back involuntarily, striking my elbow against the iron railing. When he perceived that I suffered pain he appeared to be very sorry for me.

"You made me do that," said I sharply.

"No, I didn't," he replied, as if he meant he didn't intend anything of the kind.

When several spectators came into the small enclosure, Heddy jumped down upon the floor and made at them. He hopped along upon his hands and feet after the manner of a toad. The crowd retreated perceptibly. A man whom he seized by the leg shook him off and slammed the door shut.

The keeper said that he captured the bear-man in the woods in the northern part of New Brunswick. He was in the nude state then, and lived on what he could pick up around lumber camps. His mother was an intelligent woman, but the monster was supposed to have received the physical formation of the bear, from the fact that the mother was frightened by a bear before his birth. The man-bear, he said, had a tail, which was not a prolongation of the spinal column, but a tail like that of an animal. This was his story, and he looked like a man who was lying. Of course he was.

When the time came to admit the crowd, a wisp of rope was tied around Heddy's belt loosely. A chain, which was fastened to the wall, was snapped into this, and the wild man was fast. As each person passed before him, he jumped at them as a chained bulldog would, grinding his teeth and growling. Women screamed and shrank from him, and almost went into hysterics. The very nervous persons were warned against going in. The man-bear knew enough not to jump too hard. If he had he would have broken the rope. This creature, divested of all humbug, is a queer animal and makes one feel a trifle uncertain about one's ancestry.

Chased by a Wild Man

The motif of the Wild Man of the Woods is a staple of folklore; it is encountered in many if not all of the world's cultures. In Europe it takes the form of the Feral Child who has been denied the benefits of modern civilization. In the tales told to kids in summer camps across the country, it takes the form of the Hermit in the Bush. In Western Canada, watch out for the hairy wild man, or the ape-like Sasquatch. Some of these "encounters" are pranks, pure and simple, attempts to scare children or entertain adults. This account was published in the *Winnipeg Free Press* (Winnipeg, Man.), October 8, 1887. The account is apparently reprinted from the *Brandon Sun* (Brandon, Man.).

◆◆◆

Chased by a Wild Man
The Weird Adventure of Two Manitoba College Students

About a week since, two young gentlemen, Messrs. McEwen and Mulvey, who are teaching school some distance southwest of this city, were on their way to Brandon to attend the convention of teachers. They left the place at which they were staying very late in the evening, and were accompanied part of the distance by some young friends, who had a dog with them. Taking leave of their friends they started northward. They had not gone far before they entered a wheat field, and were somewhat surprised to see an apparition in the shape of a man spring from behind the shocks, and run towards them. They were not frightened at first, thinking it was one of the party they had left playing pranks upon them. The figure approaching nearer, though, gave them a close and better view, and they discovered that it was a man with nothing upon him but a breech cloth, his hair, long and dishevelled, flying in the wind, and was foaming at the mouth. The man was coming towards them at a rapid gait, and they ordered him to stand back. At this he commenced to bark, and the young men to run. It was a test of fleetness. There is no question that the wild man, for there is no doubt that the man was fairly wild, would have caught them. His bounds are described as being leaps such as they had never seen a man take. His barking caused the dog that was with the young men to bark, and hearing this, he immediately turned and ran in the direction of the noise. In a few minutes he caught up to them; but the dog giving him chase he ran, and ran so swiftly that he soon outfooted the dog, and was soon lost in the distance. The time was about one o'clock in the morning, and the night well lighted by the moon. The neighbours turned out to follow, but he had either hidden himself or got far away before they turned out. No one else in the district has ever seen him that we have heard of, and his appearance is shrouded in the mysterious.

An Ancient Mammoth

Mammoths are those elephant-sized beasts that roamed the polar world during the Pleistocene Epoch, the 2.5-million-year period that lasted until about 10,000 years ago. Paleontologists unearth their fossil remains in the geological record. As well, carcasses of woolly mammoths, preserved in permafrost, are now and then exposed, thawed, and eaten by dogs and other wild beasts. The chronicler Alexander Solzenitysn once described how starving prisoners in the Russian Gulag came upon portions of the carcass of a frozen mammoth in the permafrost and hastily unthawed it and ate it.

"Dawson Prospector Says He Has Found Ancient Mammoth" appeared in the *Dawson Daily News*, 22 July 1915. R.A. Fox's tale may very well be a tall tale. The "mammoth steak" could be asbestos fibre.

◆◆◆

Dawson Prospector Says He Has Found Ancient Mammoth

"Waitah, bring me a mammoth steak!"

Such may be the cry in Dawson within a few days if R.A. Fox has just what he thinks he has. Fox blew into town today from up the Yukon with a gunnysack filled with what he declares is the steak of a prehistoric mammoth.

"Have I got it? Well, I should say I have," declared Fox today.

"Just wait a few minutes," continued Fox, "and I will bring you some of the mammoth with the fat clinging to the sides of the meat."

Fox was gone a short while, and returned to the *News* office with several slabs wrapped in a gunnysack. Unwrapping it in the presence of several who had not been informed what the material was supposed to be, Fox said:

"Now, see here, what is it?"

A sourdough miner stepped up and looked through his glasses carefully as he turned over the strange substance.

"Why," exclaimed the sourdough, "that's asbestos. Sure thing. I've seen it in the raw state, and I've seen the finished product."

A veteran "print" who had called on the *News* dropped in and was asked what it was.

Feeling the material carefully, he declared, "Why asbestos, of course. Wish I had plenty of that for future use."

In ambled a third man, who was shown a piece, and asked his verdict. "Well, it looks like wood fibre," declared he cautiously.

A cheechaco from Tacoma walked in and was shown the samples.

"What does she look like, Mr. Cheechaco?" said the discoverer.

"You don't get me on that," said the cheechaco. "I've visited Seattle in my day, and I have nothing to say."

"Well, now just let me tell you fellows what it is you are looking at," said Fox. "That long, white, stringy, slabby stuff is nothing more or less than the flesh of a prehistoric mammoth reduced to fibre. That whiter portion, which is less marked by strings, is the residue of the fat. The real grease evaporated."

"Where did you shoot that mammoth?" piped a fellow in the crowd.

"Well, maybe you boys think you have it on me," rejoined Fox, "but let me tell you I did shoot him, and I shot him on the Yukon river bank above Dawson, and the carcass is now there."

All the fellows opened their mouths with astonishment. Everyone was from Missouri.

"But it's the way," said Fox. "I shot him while he was lying compressed under a million tons of rock, and where he had been resting for two hundred million years.

"As I was coming down the Yukon river in the canoe the other day, I put over to the right limit of the river below the mouth of the Sixty Mile River.

"In a secluded bend in the river, where it was almost a cove, I observed in a cliff about thirty feet high a singular whitish object projecting a foot or so from the regular face of the rock. I got closer to it, and on inspection found it was the end of a mammoth tusk. I took a shot at it with my rifle and brought down a part of the ivory. That confirmed my first suspicions. I had done ivory carving in Dawson for years, and I know mammoth ivory from mastodon ivory quite well. The mastodon ivory is checked like a crocodile hide, and yellowish, while that of the mammoth is whitish and has a long grain.

"After securing the sample of the tusk, I got several sticks of dynamite, and placed them in the face of the bluff just beneath the point where the tusk protruded. There is where I shot the mammoth. Those several shots of dynamite disturbed enough of his prehistoric majesty to afford me these samples. The dynamite explosions freed a cap of rock along the face of the bluff so that the mammoth remains were exposed. The strata is two feet thick and twenty feet along the exposed edge. I did not have time to drift in on the proposition, but I feel assured the bones are there unless absorbed or done away by leaching of the water and the chemical action in the rocks.

"Now, it is only a matter of recovering the rest of the fibre. I believe that the mammoth was caught under the heavy rock from above, which crushed him against the other rock beneath, and, being encased hermetically, the fibre was preserved. I threw some of the white fibre to my cats, and they gnawed on it. Since it did not hurt them, I have eaten some, and I think mammoth steak is all right. Of course it is a little drier than jerked beef, and lacks the salt, but we can get plenty of salt.

"Dr. Alfred Brooks, the American geologist, will be here tomorrow on the Dawson, and I shall call the mammoth discovery to his attention, and get his views on the matter. When Dr. Cairnes, the Canadian geologist, arrives here later this season, I shall ask him to go up and examine the find, and he may tell me just how to remove the big fellow."

Mr. Fox has samples of the mammoth at Nick's place, on Queen Street. Mr. Fox has been prospecting and following other pursuits in Yukon several years.

Several years ago he had a thrilling experience in a cabin on Quartz Creek, where a miner, who had been killed by an accident, reappeared at night in the corner of the cabin and operated a rocker and held a conversation with Fox. At the end of the conversation the phantom form disappeared suddenly.

The Petrified Woman

BONNYCASTLE DALE

Premature burial...Egyptian-style mummies...the Transylvanian vampire's power to rise from its day-long stupor...the resurrection of the body...the corpse of the saint that is said to be incorrupt...ghosts who will not die...such facts (and fancies) continue to fascinate children, teenagers, and adults. As a species, we draw ever closer in our emotions to dying and death. The subject holds us in its power, subjects us to its unearthly spell.

"The Petrified Woman of Mud Island" appeared in the *Herald* (Calgary, Ont.), November 23, 1929. Bonnycastle Dale, the writer, has an old-fashioned literary style. His news story records a local tradition in a way that is more characteristic of the last half of the 19th century than it is of the first half of the 20th century.

◆◆◆

The Petrified Woman of Mud Island

While we call Sable Island, 150 miles seaward, "The Graveyard of the Atlantic," we call the reefs and submerged islands—past the "Devil's Limb" and "Limb's Limb" westward to the "Noddy," twenty miles out—"The Hospital." On the jagged spears of these foam-streaked rocks, many's the stout bark, the tall creaking ship, the wallowing, smoke-spurting tug and collier have crashed—all now rusted, sea-wracked, torn and riven hulls, some that we ourselves saw wrecked, others for half a century back, others like the unknown bottom that struck on Mud Island (Big Mud) sometime in the dim past, so long ago that only this odd story survives it for three-score years and ten.

As you go westward around Cape Sable, Nova Scotia, past "Seal" and "Noddy," you come to the far outlying Mud Island. It is in the twenty-five-fathom line and subject to the mighty tides that sweep and scour the Bay of Fundy. (Imagine, my mid-continental readers, the great Lake Ontario—twice—filled and twice emptied every twenty-four hours, and then you can glimpse the power and fury of the fifty-six-foot tide which sweeps on and up to the end of "The Bay.")

The distressed vessel with its human burden was swept thus far up the great bay and struck on "Big Mud," and the next tides the pitiful bodies of Negroes and whites were swept ashore on the flood. The great bay was not girdled by lighthouses as it is today, and the story spread but slowly. We know that the boat was a packet—steam and sail—and that not all the bodies which came ashore were dead; in one, a white girl, life still lingered. But, notwithstanding all the few lobster fishermen gathered there could do (so my informant, the light-house-keeper, told me), she died, and was given Christian burial.

Big Mud Island was then used mainly for summer shanties for the lobstermen of the Mud Island Lobster Company, and soon the wreck and the few lonely graves lay unnoticed, a nine-days' wonder passed by. The lobster pots were set, drawn, the season passed, and the island lay almost deserted. Year after year, every March, these lobstermen, and at times their families, too, returned for the short spring season, and one day, in an idle moment, a visitor with that fiendish lust for curiosities dug down into the shallow grave of the shipwrecked girl. The spot where it had been buried was right in the seepage run of a tiny creek, full only in the early spring melting time.

Soon the rude shelf which enclosed the body was reached and torn asunder and the digging tool struck something which sounded like stone. The visitor sent out a call for assistance, and soon the petrified body of the poor drowned girl was exposed to the glare of the spring sun. It was as hard and as unyielding as marble. The lime contents of the underground seepage had thoroughly filled each cavity and vein and artery, soaking in and replacing its natural contents with the filmy deposits which, once they dried out as the summers advanced, were stone-like in their formation.

This story, sent abroad by word of mouth in the early seventies, spread like wildfire, and the result was that visitors poured in daily to see the strange sight of a body marble-like in its consistency but faithful still to its human form in every line, shrunken though some of the once fuller parts were. Merciful people reburied the poor body, but the next few hours saw fresh visitors feverishly digging up what should by all our precepts be hallowed ground. Nor were the ghoulish excavators careful.

The fingers of the petrified body were especially brittle and were broken off and some were carried away to the great scandal of this most peaceful people, for, though the waters of Fundy writhe and tear along, sixty feet deep of continual ebb and flow, and the winds thrash the seas, and these Acadians and Nova Scotians, French and British, all good neighbours now, daily snatch a living from this confused sea, they are a most simple hospitable people.

The priests and the clergy and the councils took up the tale, and orders were sent to Big Mud Island to bury the body deeply and put up a headboard. This, too, was thrown over and the body again exhumed. Now the real governors of the island, the Mud Island Lobster Company, took a hand, and they wrote to the man who lived there all the year, shepherding the half-wild sheep (which also snatched a living from the sea, a precarious living on dulce and laver and kelp), ordering him to take the poor abused body and secretly and at night convey it into the woods and hide it and to bury it deeply.

They also bade him make a sketch of the exact spot where the body lay. So at last the harried remains rested securely hidden from the clutching fingers of the ghouls. So well did the island shepherd do his work that not a trace of the body can be found today.

You can get this tale from the mouths of the older people all along that shore. Go by motor-boat, from Wedgeport via Calf Island, Bald and Inner Bald direct to Mud Island. See Gannet Rock, if you pass outside Spectacle Island. If ever the body comes to light again, I trust that a fund will be raised for cement block interment and a suitable headstone erected.

I thoroughly believe the story, as it was told to me by a man so faithful in his work, so trustworthy, so hospitable to us during the two years when we dwelt in the little cabin by "The Light," and we also heard it repeated by many mouths for miles along Fundy's rude shores.

A Headless Man

LOUIS SOUCIER

T his account concerns the apparition of a "headless man." It is not to be confused with the story of "the headless horseman" in Washington Irving's celebrated story "The Legend of Sleepy Hollow." Headless figures are surprisingly common in myth and legend; they are less commonly found in personal, eye-witness accounts. Yet in Quebec in the past, the figure of a decapitated man would be equated with the *loup-garou*, the shape-changing werewolf. In Quebec, such tall tales are known collectively as *contes*.

Despite the fact that the story is told in the first person, as a true account, it has all the earmarks of a legend. The narrator is identified as Louis Soucier, a lumberjack who once worked in The Pas in Northern Manitoba. At the time of the telling he was a resident of Ottawa. His tale first appeared in the *Ottawa Evening Citizen*, June 11, 1932.

◆◆◆

This happened to me in July, 1880, between La Passe and Fort Coulonge. I was twenty-two at the time. I had been working for Damase Gervais near La Passe, helping him with his crop, and I was on my way back from Fort Coulonge, two and a half miles away, where I had spent the weekend.

It was eleven o'clock on a Sunday night. My route lay over a sandy plain which was skirted by a pine bush. The sandy plain was hard walking and I was going along with my head down to make the walking easier. But something caused me to raise my head. There, three feet ahead of me, stood a man.

It was dark at the time, but the man was so close I could easily distinguish what he looked like. He was dressed in black clothes and wore a white stiff shirt. But horror of horrors! He had no head!

My hair rose on my head and I became frozen with fear. I sidestepped to let the man pass. But as quickly as I moved, the headless man followed me and stood before me again—only this time a foot closer.

Living as I had done with shantymen, rivermen, and old-timers, I had heard many times of people "seeing balls of fire in the sky," "people who walked ahead," "headless men," and "*loups-garous*," but I didn't believe such things and certainly never expected to see any of them. But, here on a sandy plain at dusk I was experiencing the worst of all—a headless man. What was I to do?

Instinctively I struck out blindly at the creature before me. I then saw blood on the man's white shirt front, and immediately appeared before me the familiar form of one of the best-known men of La Passe. He was a *loup-garou* and the drawing of blood had freed him from a nine-year curse.

He then told me that he had committed a serious sin, having some years ago sold himself to the devil for monetary gain, and every night after that, according to his agreement with the devil, he was forced to walk the roads of La Passe. If, while haunting the roads, he were killed by someone, his soul would go to the devil. But, if somebody should only draw his blood, he would be freed from the bargain he made with the devil.

The man begged me not to reveal his true identity and this I promised.

Five Mysterious Events

GRAHAM CONWAY

I received the following letter on December 10, 1992.

Dear Mr. Colombo:

Having read two of your recent books on Canadian mysteries, I thought the story of a personal experience seventeen years ago may be worth adding to your collection. The enclosed copy was in the form of a letter sent to a friend. Feel free to publish it if you so desire.

Yours sincerely,
G. Conway

Graham Conway, who lives in Delta, B.C., kindly enclosed with his letter the one that is reproduced below. He added to it a footnote that places its contents in the larger context of the experience of seeing phantom skiers in an isolated valley. The letter, written some ten years earlier, has been slightly edited for presentation here.

But that is not all. In addition, here are accounts of four of Mr. Conway's even eerier experiences, which occurred between 1950 and 1983. These come from his subsequent letter dated January 25, 1993.

◆◆◆

1. The "People" Appeared to be Solid

Dear Paul:

You asked for a detailed report on the two people who "vanished." Well, here we go.

In January, 1976, I think it was on the 2nd, I had taken three of my children, each with a friend, on a short holiday to a Youth Hostel, located in a fairly remote valley near a town, called Chilliwack, in British Columbia.

Our purpose in going was to engage in some cross-country skiing. The valley is very much a one-way street, in so far as it is a "dead end," so to speak. Steep mountains, thick forests on the slopes, and snow capping the summits. The end of this particular valley is a lake, then the border, although no official crossing point exists. Our intention was to use the seldom-travelled logging roads on the valley floor for fun skiing, as none of us was an expert skier.

The day we arrived it snowed all night, depositing about six inches of powder snow. After breakfast we equipped ourselves ready to go. Knowing the teenagers wouldn't appreciate having an "old," fuddy-duddy parent along, I read the riot act on safety first and on staying together. Then I took off in the opposite direction.

My objective was Chilliwack Lake, about 1½ miles from the Hostel. As I headed southeast, I found the temperature was rising and the snow was becoming wet and impeding my progress. On arriving at the lake, I had a short rest and enjoyed the spectacular scenery. Then, looking at my watch, I realized that I was not going to be back at the Hostel by my noon deadline. I decided that I would make faster time on the return journey if I carried my skis and walked back.

Shouldering my equipment, I began the return journey using the same route I had taken. Coming down a short steep hill from the lake, I rounded a bend and had an uninterrupted quarter-mile view of the logging road ahead of me. Approaching in the distance, to my right, were two youngsters who appeared to be skiing. Gazing at them, I concluded that one of them was my eldest daughter, the one who is quick to worry should things not go according to plan. My assumption was that becoming concerned about my non-arrival she had persuaded her friend to accompany her on a search for me. As they approached, they appeared in the distance to be engaged in conservation.

A few minutes later the road dipped slightly and I lost them from my field of vision. I regained my previous viewing level in time to see the two teenagers begin to cross the road to my side, so that we were now facing and approaching each other. By this time we were closer and I had to revise my assessment. Although still unable to clearly identify the couple, I now felt sure it was my youngest son and his friend, but I now decided they were not skiing, but were walking and still engaged in earnest conversation. Before they had come close enough to enable positive identification, the two figures left the road, which was raised, crossed a shallow fire-break ditch, and entered the young forest that bordered the road. At this point I assumed they were answering a call of nature.

Continuing my steady walk along the deserted road, I was rather surprised when they did not emerge from the trees again. Having mentally marked the spot where they left the road, I knew that no path existed at that location. The only entrance that existed, in fact, was a driveway to a cottage, situated a short distance from the point where I turned off this particular road to go to the Hostel. Any attempt to walk through such bush in summer is difficult, even when you can see the obstacles. In winter, when the snow covers branches, rocks and holes, it's a formidable and quickly exhausting task. Only a fool or a desperate man would undertake such a useless trip. The only place to go was the river, and crossing that would also be a major undertaking.

In a short period of time I reached the place I had mentally noted, and then I began to casually look for the footprints in the snow that bordered the forest. Continuing my pace I was surprised to find my judgement had been greatly in error, as no sign of entry appeared. My amazement increased as my progress brought me to the driveway of the cottage. Arriving at that spot I was dumbfounded to find an unbroken snow surface. Slowing my pace, I carefully continued to my turn-off but still I saw nothing.

By now, unable to understand how I could have possibly missed them, I turned round and slowly and carefully retraced my steps. Deer and rabbit tracks were all I found. Nothing else left the road-edge that I had walked. Then I had a brilliant idea. Crossing the road to the opposite side, I traced the route that I had walked to the lake that morning. Now without difficulty I found my earlier tracks, snowmobile tracks, *and that's all I found!* Not a single solitary footprint, and only the track of my own skis.

I returned to the hostel in a daze. Finding my brood of youngsters all present and accounted for, I explained my late arrival, and ate my lunch. I said nothing to them about my experience, other than to ask if anyone had been concerned enough to go out to search for me that morning. The answer was, as I expected, *no.*

Unable to believe my eyes or senses, I returned that afternoon to the scene and again retraced the route. *Nothing.* After a good night's sleep, I repeated the exercise in futility. Still the same result.

Now, I may have imagined all this. I had not been drinking. Weather conditions were close to ideal for long-distance viewing. Yet the "people" appeared to be solid. I am convinced it was a "real" experience, if for no other reason than I had the two figures in view for a period of at least ten minutes.

As a footnote....

I have told this story a number of times. On one occasion, a listener said, "How do you know they were engaged in conversation?"

I answered, "Because I could not see their faces, their heads being down, I presumed."

"Perhaps they were wearing opaque helmets," he replied. "How did you know they were skiing? Did you see the skis or poles?"

"No, I saw no signs of equipment. My belief is based on the arm and leg motion."

"Possibly they were actually floating above the ground and moving in a robotic manner," was his suggestion.

A very reasonable explanation, I thought.

Over the years I have had a number of odd experiences, not including about a dozen UFO sightings.

One was in Ontario of two "ball-bearings" that I had under observation for 1¼ hours close to the Bay Ridges nuclear plant. Another here in Vancouver was of an object that I and several witnesses watched for forty-five minutes that looked like a hot-air balloon, but which for a variety of reasons I think not.

Should you have any further questions, feel free to ask.

Yours sincerely,

G. Conway

2. The Gate

Sometime around 1950, I was working in a hotel as a bartender in Peterborough, England. My duties required that I work every second weekend. Consequently, I got every other weekend off. I would take the train home to Sheffield.

To make the stay at home as long as possible, I could catch the early train back to Peterborough on Monday morning. As public transportation was not available at that hour, I had two alternatives. I could take a taxi or I could walk. For a period of two years, I walked the five miles to the city railway station. I was twenty-four and I enjoyed the challenge.

I took the same route through a residential area, a good part of which consisted of houses that had been built at the turn of the century. They were stone-built houses, with large gardens, high stone walls with glass fragments garnishing the tops to deter potential thieves. Naturally each formidable wall included an equally formidable wooden gate. Often these gateways were shaded on both sides by large chestnut trees.

One night I entered this older residential area. It was peaceful. There was a full moon, no wind, no intrusive noises. Suddenly, with no apparent signs of warning, I came to an abrupt halt. I have no idea what made me stop. But I do know that I was suddenly cold with fear. The hair was literally standing up on my neck. I *knew* that up ahead something lurked in the shadows that the trees were casting over the gateway. I also knew that whatever it was could best be described as evil. My heart was pounding so loudly it almost deafened me. If you had piled all the gold in Fort Knox alongside me, I would not have walked another inch forward!

The alternatives that were available to me were to retrace my steps and go the longer route, or to pass this spot on the other side of the road. As time was a factor, I chose the more dangerous alternative. I thanked my lucky stars that the road was a very wide one. Although I carefully scrutinized the gateway as I hurried past, I could detect nothing in any way out of the ordinary. No apparent form or presence. No light, noise, sound, or smell. What lurked there, I have no idea. Nor did I wish to know.

Many times afterwards, I took the same path. I always exercised great caution at that spot. But never again at that location did I experience that overwhelming feeling of horror.

I was brought up on the perimeter of the city. I was very familiar with everything that the countryside had to offer at night. In my youth, I and my friends would delight in walking from point A to point B, through fields and woods, over walls and across streams. The darkness never bothered us. We felt no threat there. Our satisfaction lay in traversing difficult country without compass or injury.

I mention this simply to illustrate that darkness alone did not make me fearful. Certainly it never served to conjure up wild imaginative feelings or visions.

3. The Lady in White

In October 1963, I was a patient in a hospital in Ajax, Ont. I was recovering from pneumonia. I was the sole occupant of a room with four beds on the ground floor.

One night I awoke. I awoke fully alert, as is my custom. I have no idea what caused me to awaken. To my surprise, I saw a lady standing alongside my bed. She was dressed in a long, white gown and she appeared to be very tall. I was lying flat on my back. She stood to my left. She looked down at me, smiling. How long I observed her, I have no idea. At the very most the period lasted for two minutes. During that time I found myself, for some reason, conducting an analysis of the situation. I felt no fear, only peace and caring. She was not a nurse.

Dawn was breaking. Outside, through the window, I could see the bushes and the trees that bordered the hospital's walls. However, I could not see through her. She was not luminous. She did not radiate energy. What usually happened was that I woke up to the "background" noises that are heard in a hospital. On this occasion, my senses reported total silence. Nothing out of the ordinary was present in the way of extra-body sensations. There were no unusual aromas or scents. The lady did not dissolve. She just vanished. I promptly fell asleep.

Maybe she was my guardian angel. I like to think so.

4. Mark Twain

For a period of twenty years, we lived in a house that was old by Canadian standards, having been built in Delta, B.C., circa 1902. Every family member agreed that it had "character." That is a nice way of saying that it was expensive and a pain in the ass!

The house was haunted, or so we were frequently told. I readily admit that some rather unusual things took place during the period we lived in it. But those happenings did not meet my personal criteria for that particular label. For me, the house had a friendly feeling.

The incident that I am about to relate took place around 1980. I had come across a recording in the library of the school where I was a teacher. It was of the American actor Hal Holbrook, who impersonated Mark Twain. Not only did he dress in the style of that period, he recounted anecdotes in the manner of Twain. The recording was very entertaining. In fact, I enjoyed it so much I brought it home for my wife to hear. The cover showed Mr. Holbrook dressed like Mark Twain, smoking a cigar.

While we were listening to the recording, my young son came into the room. What were we listening to? Who is this guy, Mark Twain? Not wanting to allow an educational opportunity to slip by, we stopped the recording, then provided a brief historical outline with the capable assistance of Funk & Wagnall's. Then we listened to the rest of the recording and he went to bed.

The time was now 11:45 p.m., and dreamland was calling us. My wife had some sewing to do before retiring, so I decided to make some hot chocolate for the two of us. Our kitchen was a large one, with the small cooking and preparation area adjacent to the more spacious eating area.

As I reached over the stove, out of sight of my wife, I was suddenly overwhelmed by the strong odour of fresh cigar smoke, seemingly alongside me! It was so strong it almost made my eyes run. I looked around for the cause but was not able to find it. Puzzled, I looked around the doorway to where my wife sat facing me at the table at the other end of the room, about fifteen feet away. To my surprise, she had her head up in the air, sniffing.

"Don't tell me," I said, "you can smell cigar smoke?"

She nodded before answering. "Yes, it's so strong, it almost makes me want to cough," she replied.

Now, the room in which we were in had four doors off it. They were all closed. Our forced-air heating system was located in the basement-cellar; therefore the only way such an aroma could enter this space was from downstairs.

We searched the whole house. There was nothing. Our four children were all asleep. We even went outside and checked. Nowhere other than in the kitchen could we detect that very strong odour. It remained for a period of about twenty minutes.

Who knows? Maybe Mark Twain had called upon us that autumn evening.

5. The Knock at the Door

Around 1983, we invited a group of friends to our home in Delta, B.C., with the intention of trying to assist a lady who was puzzled by an incident that had taken place during her return from a holiday in the Chilcotins. She, her son, and a male companion had been approached by a red ball of light while driving along a road. They had lost all memory of events from that point on, until quite some time later.

The purpose of our get-together was an attempt to recover, through hypnosis, the unrecalled events "lost" during the UFO-like encounter. I was present along with my wife, an Ojibway friend, the lady who had experienced "missing time," and most important of all, our experienced hypnotist friend.

The subject stretched out on our chesterfield. I knelt by her head, holding the microphone for the tape recorder. The hypnotist was facing the subject and positioned near her feet. My wife and our friend sat facing the subject. Our red setter was locked in the kitchen.

Initially the hypnotist followed an established routine to set the subject at ease. Then he commenced his countdown to obtain a positive response from the subject. The lady responded in a predictable manner. After some time passed, the hypnotist suggested that she would return to a possible previous-life existence. Her response to this was to provide a description of events that suggested a frightening episode in the Middle East during an earlier century.

As the hypnotist was bringing her back from this event to an already agreed-upon "safe" location, the lady looked up to her right, where only a window was located, and said, "There is a man here, he is telling me not to be afraid...." She was visibly shaking.

Further questioning revealed that "he" was tall and dressed in a dark blue scuba-diving-type suit. As her fear was clearly apparent, the hypnotist make valiant efforts to return her to the haven of safety and bring her out of her hypnotic state. For some time, she seemed not to hear him or chose to ignore him. Needless to say, these events created a degree of tension within the living room.

Suddenly, without any warning, there was a thunderous knocking at our front door. Everyone jumped about a foot into the air! The dog started barking. The only person who was apparently not startled was the lady on the chesterfield.

My wife went to the front door to see who was there at this late hour. I should explain that our house had a steep staircase to the front door. It was slippery in the perpetual wet weather of British Columbia. Consequently, we very seldom used it ourselves, and we discouraged others from doing so. Alternatively, we had a paved path to our back door, with good illumination from the driveway. This was our regular route into the house. During the twenty years we lived in this house, only two people had ever come to the front door. This was one of them!

On opening the door, my wife was faced with a youngish man. He was dressed rather inadequately, she thought, for the damp, cold fall weather. He was seeking directions to a street number that we knew did not exist locally. She suggested that he try farther down, although it was not likely to be productive. With that he renegotiated the dangerous steps and set off down the garden, even though my wife called out after him that he could not get out that way, as it was fenced off. He appeared not to hear her and continued into the darkness. Then she closed the door.

By this time our hypnotist friend had brought the frightened lady back to the present. She seemed none the worse for her adventures. We all proceeded to discuss the night's events.

Some time later, we played back the tape. We could hear all that had taken place up to the "arrival" of the man in blue. That was not on the tape. Nor could the thunderous knocking on the door be heard, despite the fact that my microphone was only ten feet from the front door. However, we could quite clearly hear our dog barking twenty feet away, despite the closed door.

On reflection, it is interesting that the stranger arrived at the exact moment that we were seeking information about the man in blue and the circumstances of his presence. Talk about synchronicity!

Not only did this interruption serve to upset our quest for further information, we were never able to convene again to uncover those "missing time" events.

The Car Started to Rise Up

GLENN THERENS

The following letter was addressed to me by Glenn Therens, who lives and works as a cook in Moose Jaw, Sask. He wrote the letter on June 14, 1990, in response to my request for "ghost stories" which appeared in the *Moose Jaw Times*.

I wish I could deserve Mr. Therens' thanks. I have no idea what caused his moving automobile to tip to one side while he was speeding along a highway. The experience was a profoundly moving one, one that has been recalled in detail more than one-quarter century after it happened.

◆◆◆

There is nothing "ghostly" about what I'm going to write about, but it sure is mysterious.

It happened on July 6, 1964, at about 2:00 p.m., about four or five miles southeast of Weyburn, Sask., on Highway 39. It was very hot, 90 to 95° F, and there was absolutely no wind. I was with my wife and our two sons, five years and three years. At the time I was thirty years old and my wife twenty-eight. I was driving. My wife was beside me. The three-year-old was standing on the front seat between us. The five-year-old was in the back seat of our car.

Our car was a 1953 Pontiac in mint condition. It was kept in top-notch condition by my father, who was a garage operator. We were going home to Moose Jaw, after visiting my sister and her husband at Carlyle, Sask. I was driving approximately 60 m.p.h., about four or five miles southeast of Weyburn, with no traffic ahead or behind me. I slowed down to about twenty-five or thirty miles per hour. Why? I don't know.

All of a sudden, very, very slowly, the right side (the passenger side) of the car started to rise up, and we were driving on the two left tires. The car continued its rise up until, even with my left arm bent at the elbow, I could have extended the palm of my hand and it would have rubbed against the pavement. The highway was in very good, very smooth condition.

The first person to speak was our older son, who was in the back seat. He asked, "Hey, what's going on?"

I spoke second, and yelled to my wife, "Grab hold of the kid," referring to the one standing between us, "he's gonna fall out of the window!"

I had my hands on the steering wheel all the time, but I was definitely not in control of the car. We travelled approximately one hundred yards in the proper lane, then the car started to right itself again, very, very slowly. Then we were driving on four wheels again.

I came to a stop and got out of the car. Still there was no traffic on the highway. I got back into the car and proceeded again. I was about to speak when my wife actually put into words what I was going to say, which was, "I don't think we should tell anyone about this. They'll think we're both crackin' up."

At the time neither of us drank alcohol—we couldn't afford it!

Some years later, on radio station CKRM in Regina, there was a man on a talk show who explained, or tried to explain, unexplained happenings. I tried to phone in, but the lines were busy.

I hope this will be of some use to you for your book. If you could enlighten me as to what may have caused this situation, I thank you.

All of this that I write is true with God as my witness.

That, Too, May Be Sheer Coincidence

DONNA ENGLUND-PRICE

"There you go," wrote Donna Englund-Price. "If you think there is merit to this story, perhaps you'll want to use it." Mrs. Englund-Price wrote to me on June 17, 1990. She sent me an account of a series of unusual—and heart-wrenching—experiences. There is much suffering here; also a sense of resolve or resolution. It is difficult to know what to make of the premonitions, birth, deaths, and apparitions. Yet one lesson is clear: One has to accept rather than reject anomalous experiences, and seek to incorporate them into one's everyday life.

◆◆◆

In the year of 1968, I was pregnant with our daughter, Barbara Ann. My husband David's mother had been dead for several years, and the course of her life had never been smooth. It was for that express reason that we decided to make our about-to-be-born daughter her namesake, in the hope that we could provide her with a better life than her grandmother had enjoyed.

My husband had described in some detail how his mother had died. He also described the events leading up to the death of her father, my husband's grandfather. On that particular day, a clock struck twelve, only my husband insists that it struck thirteen. For some unexplained reason, my husband had experienced a premonition that his grandfather had succumbed to heart failure. That insight unfortunately proved to be correct, as, indeed, he had passed away.

Several years later, in the summer of 1968, our beautiful daughter Barbara Ann was born. In an almost total repeat of his grandfather's death, my husband went to check our daughter after the clock struck 12:00 p.m., Thanksgiving Day, 1969. Our daughter had died of crib death.

No matter how much those around us tried to reason with me, I insisted that I would bear the same daughter again. Like some incredible coincidence, our daughter Sherrilee was born the following Thanksgiving Day.

There are pictures of my late mother-in-law and other pictures of my second daughter that show an uncanny resemblance. That, too, may be sheer coincidence, but there is more. I am not at all sure how what I am about to describe fits into this scenario. But I sense that it does.

Our son was four years old at the time of his sister's death. Some time later he told us that the night before our daughter died he had seen funny, frightening faces looking and laughing at him from outside the window. This may not be an unusual occurrence for a young child, but that was the first occasion on which we had ever had to reassure him that he must have been asleep. Until then he had never been afraid of the dark.

Also, during the time prior to our second daughter's birth, a very vivid apparition appeared before my eyes. It was the face of a beautiful man, typical of the way men are depicted in the pages of biblical texts. The most outstanding feature was that the apparition appeared to be standing sidewise, not straight forward.

The birth, death, and apparition all occurred during the period when we lived in St. Catharines, Ont. Several years later, when we lived in Toronto, I was alone in our townhouse. I decided to lie on the couch to rest until my husband returned home. Suddenly, I felt almost a whisper of a touch. At first I thought that our cat had jumped up beside me and that I was feeling her tail. Then, without knowing why, I knew it wasn't our cat at all. I am not sure whether I said, "Can I turn over?" but through words or thoughts, I knew that I could. Upon turning, the same apparition appeared to me, but this time it lingered longer. I experienced the most sensual feeling I had ever known. The man smiled at me and, after perhaps thirty or forty seconds, faded.

I remember thinking how strange it was that I felt no fear, only amazement. Suddenly I felt completely drained and turned back around to face the couch. There was a swirling pattern of illumination all over the back of the couch and I literally passed out.

I've never seen that face again, but I often wonder what all of this was about.

Until these events took place, I'd never even heard about the theory of reincarnation, and I'd laughed at other people's ghost stories. Now I am convinced that I have had paranormal experiences. I rarely talk about them to anyone, except family members and close friends, and even then I find it a little embarrassing.

Things that Twitch in the Night

DEBBIE RIDPATH OHI

I have never met Debbie Ridpath Ohi, but I know that she lives in Toronto and that she is the author of this brief memoir. It was written in 1995 and reads like fiction. By that I mean it reads so smoothly it feels more like fiction than it does fact. But it is a memoir.

I wonder about the answer to Ms. Ohi's question. I wonder if she will ever be able to answer her own question.

◆◆◆

When I was six years old, my babysitter and her friend told me about the giant rabbit who lived in the forest near our house.

"It eats children," Rebecca told me solemnly.

I was horrified, of course. My parents had never warned me of the monstrous predator in our vicinity, and had even taken me for walks on the trail. Perhaps they didn't know.

"Everyone knows about it," added Rebecca. "Three kids have been eaten, just this year. All that were left were their bones and their hair."

My lower lip trembled. "I don't believe you," I said, even though I did.

The next day Rebecca and her best friend, Genevieve, took me for a walk.

"What are those for?" I asked, apprehension stirring. Both Rebecca and Genevieve had a carrot in their hands.

"In case we run into the rabbit," Rebecca said matter-of-factly. "So he'll eat the carrots instead of us. I would have brought you a carrot except my mom only had two."

"Anyway, you said you don't believe there's a rabbit," added Genevieve. I didn't like Genevieve very much.

She was right, though; I had expressed disbelief in the existence of their giant child-munching rabbit. So I didn't say anything and pretended not to be scared to death as we started on the trail.

The trees rustled with the wind as we moved deeper into the forest, and I struggled to keep my eyes on the trail, away from the shadows beneath the trees.

"What was that?" Rebecca gasped.

"I don't know. Maybe it's following us," Genevieve spoke in a whisper.

Panicked, I strained to hear. "What? What?"

"Ssshhh," whispered Rebecca, and we kept walking. I was numb with fear, and I kept looking around behind us.

The giant rabbit knew I was here! I pictured its huge pink nose twitching malevolently as it caught my scent. I wondered how long it had been since it had eaten.

A few minutes later, Rebecca and her friend stopped. I was not happy about this, of course. All my instincts were screaming at me to run home as fast as my little legs could carry me.

"We've got something to show you," said Rebecca mysteriously.

They knelt, and motioned for me to come closer. I did, and glanced down at where they were pointing.

It was a giant rabbit footprint.

I gasped and took a step back.

"See?" said Genevieve. "Rebecca told you it was real. You didn't believe her."

Panic-stricken, I started looking around us, my head turning in jerks. "I wanna go home." It was here, I could sense it. Somewhere in that shadowy forest lurked an evil child-devouring monster with a twitching nose and pink-rimmed eyes.

Then I screamed.

To this day I swear I saw something, behind a clump of trees. What exactly, I cannot say. It was more a fleeting glimpse, a flash of raggedy fur perhaps, a single twitch of a giant whiskered nose. Whatever it was, the glimpse galvanized me into action.

Without waiting to consult Rebecca or Genevieve, I ran down the path towards home, screaming at the top of my little lungs all the way.

Rebecca managed to catch up with me two-thirds of the way back. The incident must have unnerved her, because she immediately took me to the ice cream store and bought me a cone (pralines and cream, my favourite) with some of her babysitting money, warning me not to tell my parents about what had happened just in case it scared them, too.

Years later I still go over the entire event in my mind and wonder.

The rabbit footprint could easily have been created by Rebecca and her friend, as "proof" to me that the creature existed.

But what did I see in the forest that day?

Two Unusual Experiences

MARIANNE SISLER

Marianne Sisler, a resident of Duncan, B.C., saw my request for "extraordinary experiences" in a local newspaper. She wrote to me on September 3, 1990, asking me if I was still interested in receiving one such account from her. I wrote to her immediately and encouraged her to write it out and send it to me. On October 15, she mailed me these two typescripts, reproduced here with a minimum of editing. In her covering letter, Sisler included the address of her daughter who lives in Alberta, should I wish to confirm the story about the strange appearance of her deceased father.

◆◆◆

Experience No. 1

One Friday afternoon, early in the year 1975, I was working all alone, except for one other girl, in the office of the company for which I worked. Our reception area was in the front. Behind it was the office area, where the girl was working. The coffee room was in the rear. You could look from the front door straight through the office area to the back door, although it was quite a distance.

I began to walk to the back to get a cup of coffee. As I walked back with my coffee and was in the middle of the office area, I felt a terrible cold. I sensed its presence around the bottom of my legs. It was not the normal feeling of cold. I looked around but I could see no one near the front door. The girl was busy writing something in the office area. So I turned around to see if someone had entered through the back door. There was no one there. I took one step to one side and then back again. The cold was gone. I felt relieved that the girl had not seen what I was doing.

After work I went home and forgot about what had happened earlier that day. My husband, who had suffered a stroke some months earlier, was lying in bed, unable to move or walk very well. Now, the layout of our house is important. It was built in the 1940s and there was no centre hallway. The main floor was laid out like a square divided into four rooms. The den and the living-room were connected on one side, the kitchen and the bedroom on the other. The hallway and the bathroom were off the kitchen.

Late that evening I was standing at the kitchen counter preparing some food for the next day. All of a sudden the hair on the back of my head felt as if it was standing on end. I have read about this sensation in books. But now I realized the effect the authors were writing about. It felt as if someone was standing behind me. I knew my husband could not leave his bed without being heard. The front door and the back door were both locked. I turned around slowly and then I saw the form of a man. He was dressed in a dark grey suit and he was walking into the living room. Curiously, his head and his hands were not visible. Even so, I knew from the shape of the figure that the figure of the man was that of my father. My father had died in 1952 in Holland. The figure walked right across the living-room and entered the den, which was pitch black.

I was not afraid, but still I did not follow the figure into the den. I remained in the kitchen and continued to do what I was doing. A few minutes later, the hair on my head and neck stood up again. I turned around and saw the dark figure walk again into the living-room. Then it disappeared.

When I finished what I was doing in the kitchen, I went to bed. My husband was asleep in his bed. We each had our own bed since his stroke. I covered myself with the blankets, leaving only part of my head uncovered. Suddenly I felt that something was touching my hair. The touch was as light as a feather. I peeked out from under the blanket and in the darkness of the room I saw the dark form again. This time I did not move, but hid more snugly under the blankets.

The next morning was Saturday morning so I did not have to go to work. I thought about what I had experienced and told myself that I had imagined it all. At the time I was under a lot of stress so I blamed everything on that. My daughter Sandra, who lived on her own, arrived to go shopping with me. We talked in the kitchen about work, but I did not mention what had happened to me the previous day at the office or at home.

Sandra went into the bedroom to comb her hair. Our full-length mirror was fastened to the bedroom door. Sandra had closed the bedroom door to use the mirror. In our bedroom there was a staircase going up to another bedroom. A few minutes later she joined me in the kitchen and asked me if I believed in ghosts. I looked at her somewhat in surprise and told her that I did. Then I asked her why she had asked that question. At first she did not want to tell me anything. So I asked her, point-blank, "Did you see him?"

Now it was her turn to look surprised. "What do you mean?" she asked. She then told me she had seen this shadow walking across the landing into the upstairs bedroom. She told me that her hair stood on end and that a cold chill ran down her spine. I then told her that she had seen her grandfather.

During the week that followed, I could feel the presence of this shadow in the house. Sandra came over once or twice. Each time she said, "He is still here, Mom!"

The following Saturday, when I got up in the morning, I knew that the presence was gone. Sandra came over later that day. The first thing she said was, "Oh, he is gone now!"

When I went to visit my mother on the Sunday after Sandra and I had each seen the dark form, she handed me a photograph of my father. It was a black-and-white photo that I had not seen before. He was wearing the suit I had seen him in. My mother did not say why she had felt like giving me that photo. Then I told her what had happened to Sandra and me. She said nothing at all. Then we talked about another subject. I never did find out from her if she had the same experience we had, or why she felt she had to give me that photograph at that particular time.

Experience No. 2

It was October 1979. This particular Sunday, my daughter Susan and I visited my mother, who lived in a seniors' housing complex in Edmonton. But my mother, who had heart trouble, was not feeling well. She suffered a massive heart attack while we were there.

The evening of the funeral I was alone in the den of our house. My husband had already gone to bed. Suddenly the telephone rang. When I picked it up, there was the sound on the line that you hear when you call long distance.

I said, "Hello," and waited, thinking it might be a call from Holland, where my mother's sisters still live. No one answered. Again I said, "Hello."

All of a sudden my mother's voice called out, "Lottie, Lottie!"

So I answered back and said, "Mom, this is Marianne!"

The voice did not call out any more. I sat with the telephone in my hand for several minutes. The line remained open. Finally I hung up. When I picked up the phone again, the line was normal.

Lottie was my mother's best friend. She lived in the same seniors' complex. They were doing St. John's Ambulance work together.

My Hair Stood Up on the Back of My Neck

BRENDA BIGELOW

I receive numerous letters addressed to me care of my various publishers. The following letter arrived on my desk on July 30, 1992. It was handwritten on lined paper by Brenda Bigelow, and it was written with conviction. It tells about some poltergeist-like episodes that took place in a duplex in Calgary a decade and a half earlier. Here is the text of the letter, minimally copy edited. It speaks for itself, yet it does not speak alone; the letter that follows it, contributed by Lynn Chellew, the correspondent's sister, refers to the same incidents.

◆◆◆

Dear Mr. Colombo,

My name is Brenda Bigelow. I am writing to you about an experience I had when I was a teenager. My family and I moved into a duplex, 206 Allen Crescent S.E., Calgary, AB, in 1976. We lived there for four years. I never felt comfortable in that house. I always felt as if someone was constantly watching me and at times I felt a presence in a certain room. The worst place in the house was the basement, especially in the one corner where the washer and dryer were. The only room I really felt good in was my youngster sister Lynn's room. I never felt a presence in her room. No one liked to go down into the basement, not even our dogs. The dogs would stand on the top of the stairs, look down, and whine. Sometimes I could hear someone going down the stairs but no one was there. What I am about to tell you will sound so outrageous that I still find it hard to believe. I slept in the basement by myself for three years. I did not sleep well during those three years. Sometimes the washer and dryer would start up and no one was there to start them up. No laundry was ever put in them. My mom would blame me but I never did it. One Christmas Eve, I was sleeping downstairs with our dog Barfy. (I had to carry him downstairs with me.) At about 3:00 a.m., I woke up. Barfy was on my bed growling low and looking at the wall opposite the bed. I looked at the wall and between the only two windows in the whole basement appeared two narrow, oval shapes of light, the brightest light I have ever seen. I had never seen light so bright in my life before or after that. That light must have covered an area of the wall three feet long. It was there on the wall for no longer than a minute and before I realized it, it was gone. I ran over and looked under the stairs, but nothing was there to reflect the light. I was so terrified I ran all the way up the stairs, with Barfy following me, and I stayed upstairs till morning. I also recall one time when my mother was visiting a friend upstairs. I went downstairs for a nap. It was about 7:00 p.m. I was dozing off nicely when all of a sudden my hair stood up on the back of my neck and on my arms. I felt a strong presence behind me. I knew if I turned around I would see him. (I always thought of the presence as a man; so did my sister Lynn.) It continued to look at me and I remained lying on the bed for two or three minutes. Then I felt it slowly leave and go out of my room. I turned around and I saw a shadow on the floor, but no one was there to cast it! (I swear to God this is true.) I ran all the way upstairs. That night it took me a very long time to fall back asleep. I was very terrified. One day I went over to see the people who lived on the other side of us in the duplex and I asked them if they felt strange in their place. They looked at me as though I were nuts and said no. I asked my family, years after we had moved out of the duplex, what they thought of it. Both my mother and my father said they didn't like it, especially the basement. In fact, I remember my mother hated the basement so much she would always ask one of us to come downstairs with her whenever she had to do the laundry or get something from the freezer. My brother Gary hated the house, especially the basement and his bedroom closet. Gary said that whenever he opened up his closet door, he expected to see something frightening in it. He also told me about a time when he and his girlfriend were in his room listening to tapes. They were the only ones at home at the time. Anyway, they both heard some noises coming from the kitchen. It sounded like someone was rummaging through the silverware drawers. They both went out to see who was there. No one was in the kitchen, but the silverware drawer was wide open and some silverware was scattered on the floor and counters. They searched the house but no one else was home. My sister Lynn also did not feel comfortable in the house, especially the basement. In whatever house we lived in, before or after the duplex, Lynn always slept in her room with the door open. But in the duplex, Lynn said she felt better when the door was closed. Also, Lynn's room was the only one she or I felt "safer" in. All that I say in this letter is true. I never felt that the presence in the duplex was ever going to hurt me, but I still did not feel comfortable, especially when it felt like someone or something was always watching me! That's what I hated the most. I am 30 years old now but I still cannot forget how I felt in that duplex. Sometimes I still have dreams of that presence staring at me behind my back, and I wake up scared. I go to sleep every night with the hall light switched on and my door wide open. To this day I am terrified of basements. I will never, ever forget that duplex and all that happened there.

Sincerely,
Brenda Bigelow

The House Seemed to Be Watching Me

LYNN CHELLEW

L ynn Chellew lives in Calgary, Alta., and her letter arrived on August 10, 1992. I am reproducing it in its entirety, with minimal editing. The correspondent's account of what it was like to live in a duplex that might well have been haunted is intriguing in its own right; it is also intriguing in light of the fact that these details substantiate and corroborate the independently prepared account that had been earlier sent to me by Brenda Bigelow, the correspondent's sister. (See the previous letter.) What is interesting is to compare the accounts written by the two sisters. Indeed, I find myself wondering how many subsequent occupants of "that duplex" are aware of "the presence."

◆◆◆

Dear Mr. Colombo:

My sister, Brenda Bigelow, told me that you accept letters from people about "experiences" they have had. She wrote to you about the duplex we lived in, in Calgary, years ago. I would like to share with you my experience in the duplex on Alan Crescent.

Unlike my sister, I never actually saw anything, but I surely felt that we were not alone in that house. The house seemed to be watching me all the time, as if there was a presence there. The only time I felt at ease was when I was in my bedroom with the door closed.

I feel I should stress the point that, until we moved into that duplex, I always slept with my bedroom door open, and often I had the hall light on as well. But the whole time we lived in that duplex, I always felt the need to have the door closed, as if to keep "someone" out of my room. At first I thought the reason I no longer kept the door open was I had simply outgrown the need for it. But when we moved from that duplex, I again began to sleep with my door open, and I still do it to this day. Only while we lived there did I feel the need to keep my door shut.

As I said, the rest of the house felt as though it was watching me. This feeling was strongest in the basement. There was a second family phone down there. It was on my father's workbench, beside the staircase. Whenever I used this phone, I felt I was never alone. Often I would quickly look over my shoulder, only to see nothing... but the sense of presence was still very strong.

I never felt I would be harmed by the presence. Like my sister and mother, I thought of the presence as a man. But I was always nervously aware of it being there.

Also, many nights, while up late watching TV, I would hear noises. They would come from the stairs that led to the basement, but when I looked, there would be no one there! Our dogs would sometimes approach the top of the stairs, perk their ears, and whine. But they hardly ever went farther than the top of the stairs. If we wanted the dogs to go down the stairs, we had to coax them.

Brenda and I were not the only ones who felt ill at ease in the house. My brother Garry said there were many times he expected something to materialize in the closet in his room when he opened the door. My mother hated to go into the basement alone, and whenever she had reason to go down, she always took one of us with her.

One year we had out-of-town visitors, my aunt, uncle, and two cousins from Ontario. My brother Garry and I were moved from our upstairs bedrooms to the basement so our guests would be comfortable. I was upset at losing my room to my aunt and uncle, but I was more upset at having to sleep for a couple of nights in the basement where I was sure "the presence" spent most of its time.

Garry and I spent the night downstairs. The next morning my brother told me that I had screamed for him to come to me. When he got to my bedside, I was sitting upright with my eyes wide open, looking terrified. He asked me what was wrong and I said, "Nothing, it's okay now," and simply laid back down calmly and fell back to sleep. Even though at the time I appeared to be awake and terrified, I have no memory of this dream at all.

My uncle also had nightmares while staying in my room. One nightmare was so bad that it sent him running and screaming into the living-room. He later said he thought there was a huge spider on him. To me, it was almost as though "the presence" did not want my brother and me to be in "his" basement and so tried to scare our guests away.

Since leaving that duplex on Alan Crescent, I have never again had the feeling that a house was watching me, and for that I am thankful. But the memories do stir me sometimes, leaving me with a cold feeling. Even though it has been some time since it all happened, I guess I will never forget that duplex.

I often think of searching the city records to see if there is a history of the house. Perhaps I will some day. But until then, I will always remember that duplex on Alan Crescent. I will think of it not only as the house we lived in, but also as the house that lived around, and along, with us.

May you always value "sweet dreams."

Lynn Chellew

Blue Boy

NEAL LANDON

For some years I contributed a weekly column on ghostly and other lore to *Toronto's Midtown Voice*, a lively community newspaper. For some years, Barbara Neyedly, its editor, invited readers to contribute real-life ghost stories for the publication's October issue to mark the advent of Halloween. I selected the best stories and their authors received gift certificates donated by local restaurants. The liveliest—or the deadliest!—of the stories were published under the general heading of "Glimpses from...Behind the Veil." Reader Neal Landon won one of the certificates for this story published in the issue for October 1991.

◆◆◆

Whenever I hear people use the expression "looked as though he'd seen a ghost," it is usually to describe a look of blind terror, witlessness, and a wearer who seems capable of doing little more than retreating into shock. But having actually seen a ghost and compared my reactions, I conclude that the phrase is not particularly apt.

In the final years of my marriage my wife and I lived in Scarborough, interred by our financial situation in an ugly cinder block of a structure that provided every one of its sixteen floors with bugs, rodents, cold rusty water from every tap, and a basement generator as dependable as the postal system. I never brought up the fact there was a ghost in my dwelling at tenant meetings or mentioned it to my wife.

The ghost looked to me to be that of a small boy, perhaps six to eight years old. He had unruly, medium-length hair and there was always a quick and merry look in his eyes. He smiled whenever he was spied upon playing his hide-and-seek games. Then he would vanish. He had Caucasian features although his skin was blue. His clothes and, for that matter, everything about him was enveloped in a fluorescent turquoise aura. He never uttered a word or stayed more than a few seconds in one place.

I wrote off the first four visits as inventions of fatigue, a hallucination caused by a faulty bulb blinking or the passing headlights from a car outside. Those times he just raced past me, a blue blur on the periphery of my vision, vaguely identifiable, but nothing to lose sleep over.

One night the glow caught my eye for the fifth time. I turned suddenly and there he was, exactly as I have described him. Right before my eyes he ran away from me, growing smaller and smaller, like a figure receding into the horizon until he was gone. It was too small an apartment. His actions had been confined to the same spot where he had been standing. It reminded me of a television set being turned off. Was I scared? I was more relieved than anything. I finally had a clear picture of what had been disturbing me, I thought, as I remembered the earlier instances.

Now, it's hard to rationalize a ghost, but compared to other creatures of the night, or rats, or bugs, a ghost is not difficult to accept. Over the next half year, he showed himself to me a total of three more times. Those visits went along the same lines as the fifth, so there's not much point in going into them now. One thing: I'd crouch to his level.

One night I was in the bathroom with the door open, when I heard my wife in the kitchen say, in a sweetly admonishing voice, "What are you doing here?" I knew she wasn't talking to our son because from where I was I would have seen his bedroom door open. He had been asleep for an hour. Hearing a sudden rush of air into my wife's lungs gave me a better idea of whom she was addressing. I saw her go charging through the apartment wearing an expression Clint Eastwood would have been comfortable with.

We checked in on the kid's room and, satisfied that everything was safe, returned to the kitchen. I assured her I had seen no movement of any kind around that door. When I pressed her for details, she shut right up and viewed me with suspicion. I confessed to seeing weird sights but would give her no details of my own. Her interest aroused, we agreed to a trade. Without saying a word we would write down a description of our visions and read each other's.

As it turned out, that had been her fourth and final sighting of the ghost. We talked about seeing him, about what it meant, what could be causing it, and what we could do about it until, after ten minutes, we exhausted our capacity to converse without repeating what we already knew, which amounted to very little. We simply never mentioned it again.

It wasn't like we wanted to go out of our way looking for trouble. We had enough problems with the real world as it was.

A year later the wife and I broke up. It wasn't the fault of the ghost.

I never even saw him again and haven't thought much about the whole experience in the interim. Naw, what happened with me and the wife was, well, actually I'm rather hard-pressed to come up with a cut-and-dried explanation for you.

So what else is new, eh?

Starry, Scary Night

PAT CONNOR

P at Connor is a Torontonian and the winner of a gift certificate from *Toronto's Midtown Voice*. Her story was judged a good one by its editors. It was published in the October 1991 issue as part of the spread titled "Glimpses from . . . Behind the Veil."

◆◆◆

The sobering reality of it all captivated our minds with a jolt early that morning in August 1976. We were not going to be alone during our overnight adventure Up North. And there was nothing on this Earth that was going to change this fact.

I was on a twenty-four hour leave from waterfront duties. My friend, whom I'll call Salty, and I loaded up the Blue Bomber with provisions and maps and headed north from Stouffville, Ont. We made no exact plans as to where precisely we were going. The sun was setting as we drove off the camp road onto the main highway. Our minds were overflowing with excitement and anticipation as we drove into the Northern Horizon, constantly remarking to each other about the wisdom of such an unplanned adventure, but we drew no conclusions.

The short first leg of the trip ended in Uxbridge and dinner at a small country inn. It was about 10:00 p.m. when we hit the road again, with Salty acting as navigator, using the North Star to guide us. As we drove, our senses were continuously treated to the beauty of an unfolding carpet of the stars and the dark forests, still green to the eye, despite the night.

There's something inexplicable about driving through the night on unlit highways with starry clear skies reigning overhead, headlights barely blotting out the darkness. Before the second leg of the drive ended, we concluded that it was uncharacteristic of us to set out on such a bold and risky drive into unfamiliar territory. Undaunted, we kept driving, knowing only that we were headed North. And that, we explained, we seemed to feel compelled to keep going.

We arrived in Fenelon Falls around 11:00 p.m. and promptly sought out a local tavern called the Skipper's Den. The friendly waiter sat us at a table beside a wall decorated by an antique porthole. We ordered drinks and chatted with the waiter, who asked us where we were from and where we were headed. We explained that we were on twenty-four-hour leave from a waterfront in the Stouffville area. However, we couldn't tell him our destination. The three of us were humorously mystified by this.

We left the Skipper's Den, then headed back to the car. After driving around Fenelon for a brief period, we headed into the Northern Horizon once again. About five miles north of Fenelon, Salty requested that I stop so she could answer nature's call. As she returned to the car, she asked, "Do you see that?" She explained that, as when we stopped, she thought that she saw a light a few miles behind us. She saw it suddenly rising into the sky and hovering over a nearby treeline.

I slowed down and observed the light. It was moving slowly, and as we drove, the road curved to the east. It became parallel with the treeline and we lost track of whatever it was. I then noticed in the rearview mirror that there was what I thought was another car. I signalled for it to pass. Then, suddenly, the entire car became engulfed in a brightness that flooded the road with light in front of us as well as behind us. We increased our speed dramatically, but the object above us sped along with us.

Then it was gone in a flash. Or so we thought. It reappeared above the treeline and was still keeping pace with us. The Blue Bomber was still co-operating at over one hundred miles per hour. We concluded that the object showed intent and that our lives were in danger. Salty took notes. I can't say precisely how long this segment of the experience lasted, but it was at least ten minutes in length. We passed one other car during this period. We saw it enter the highway at high speed from a dirt road, leaving a cloud of dust in its wake.

The light disappeared momentarily at a bend in the road. But once we rounded the curve, it was sitting about two hundred feet above the road. Then it shot straight up. I stopped the car to catch my breath. It was at this point that we could hear farm animals and birds. Perhaps they too were sensing what had happened.

Salty suddenly began to demand that I start driving again. She pointed to a shadow-like distortion in the sky, close to where we were parked. She said that it was still with us. Then the elusive object reappeared, this time noticeably dimmer, then brighter, until orange rings of light appeared at its base. Then they too brightened, and together the two colours of light began to pulsate, slowly at first, then faster and faster like a strobe light, illuminating approximately an acre of the treeline and adjacent fields.

Salty's words finally got through to me, and I began to drive frantically while our visitor kept us company, moving with us, sometimes ahead of us, at times beside us above the trees, until it left us a few miles shy of Kinmount.

At Kinmount, we begged our way into a bake shop, where the female proprietor was preparing goods for the next day. She listened to our account and advised us to promptly inform the OPP [the Ontario Provincial Police] using her phone. Afterwards, she soothed us with cakes and coffee and words of how she had gotten accustomed to lending her phone to strangers on recent nights—and on other nights like these over the last years. As we left, Salty glanced at the wall clock and screamed, "Look at the time!"

It was nearly 3:00 a.m. It couldn't have taken us all that time to make the short drive from Fenelon to Kinmount. After all, we had only stopped twice, and each time momentarily. We were also driving excessively fast for much of the distance. We had left Fenelon about midnight. The distance between the two towns is less than forty miles. It should not already have been 3:00 a.m.!

Our watches had to be wrong. As we started to compare their time with the time on the shop clock, the baker told us not to bother, adding, in her kind and quiet way, "Your watches are working just fine."

The Hairy Man

CATHY CRAIG

For the following account of a ghostly man, I am indebted to Fred Habermehl of Niagara Falls, Ont. He mailed the account to me on May 28, 1996. It was actually written by his daughter Cathy Craig, who lives with her husband, Stuart, and their children in a duplex on Briarwood Avenue south of Thorold Stone Road and west of Dorchester Road, Niagara Falls. Do they share their duplex with the "hairy man"? It is true that children enjoy the company of "imaginary playmates." Is the "hairy man" an "imaginary playmate"? Or is it the ghost of some real person?

◆◆◆

In 1981, we moved into a duplex on Briarwood Avenue, next to Meadowvale Park, in Niagara Falls. Almost immediately, our eight-month-old daughter, Tabitha, started seeing something. I would pass it off as just my imagination, a glimpse of something passing down the hall, a presence in the room when you knew you were alone, or a baby laughing at someone behind you, when there was no one there.

When she was old enough to talk, Tabitha and I were in the north end of the basement when she began to have a conversation with something in the dark laundry room at the south end of the house. I asked her who she was talking to. She replied, "The man."

"What man?" I asked, to which she replied, "The big, hairy man."

I immediately dropped the conversation, picked her up, and went upstairs. I kept all the lights and the TV on. I always knew there was something there and that she sensed it too. Her blunt response, as if I should have been able to see him too, was too much. Since we were usually home alone and I tend to hear things that go bump in the night, I never told anyone. I didn't want them to think I was nuts. That was the most obvious and haunting incident with Tabitha, and eventually the hairy man faded away.

In 1984, Deidre was born and the hauntings returned. The "hairy man" frightened her one day in the upstairs hall, when I sat within eye-sight in the living-room reading the paper. Deidre was playing quietly in front of the hall mirror. I glanced at her just as she jumped up with a look of terror on her face. She ran right up over my paper and onto my lap, screaming that the man was scaring her and he was going to get her.

Deidre's other memorable encounter was in the laundry room. I was putting clothes in the washer as she stood beside my leg facing the opposite way. She was talking to someone and I asked, "Who are you talking to?"

She answered, "The big, hairy man."

I looked to where she was pointing and asked her what he looked like, but she just lowered her head and stopped talking. I kept asking questions, trying to be calm and chatty, but she didn't speak of him again. I knew he was always around and she was aware of him. As with my first child, he seemed to appear less and less often as she got older.

In 1988, Michael was born and the man returned. By the time he was two, he had verbalized his sightings to his father and we discussed openly what I had known for years. On one occasion, at about age three, he had gone downstairs to sleep in our bedroom next to the laundry room. He wasn't down there long before he came racing up the stairs, saying, "Daddy, the hairy man wants to talk to you." His father, refusing to play this silly game, told Michael to tell the man to come upstairs if he wanted to talk to him. Seriously, as if the man was truly downstairs, Michael learned over the rail and bellowed, "My father says to come up if you want to talk to him." That night, because his son's reaction was so convincing, his father became a believer.

Two years after Michael's birth, our neighbours in the adjoining house, Chris and Roger, had a baby, Alyssa. Within the year, they had seen enough to speak openly to me about this presence. They had stories of their own. Roger was vacuuming the recreation room one day when he felt someone enter behind him. He began chatting with his wife. When she didn't answer, he turned around to see that no one was there. He later questioned his wife, who said she had not even been downstairs.

On another occasion, Chris was in the shower when she sensed someone else in the room. She struck up a conversation with Roger. When he didn't answer, she pulled back the curtain and found she was alone. Later, he confirmed he had never entered the bathroom. As with me, they knew their baby could see someone else in the house. They also felt something moving about. As Alyssa got older, the man faded.

In 1992, Chris and Roger moved to the house on the other side of us. Since then they have had twins, but the man has never appeared to them in that house, even though there are only ten feet between the two houses. The hairy man seems to be only in the two homes of the duplex and only when there are young children present.

PART III
HAUNTED HOMES
AND HOUSES

People love a story about a haunted house. Indeed, the two words "haunted house" trip off the tongue so easily! In the days before television, when I was a youngster playing on Pandora Avenue in Kitchener, Ont., I quickly learned from the other kids on the block which houses were "haunted" and which were not. Not that we had any reason to believe that any of them were haunted. We heard no strange noises coming from them. We saw no Caspar-like shapes flit about them at dawn or dusk or midday for that matter. We may not even have known who lived in them. But we could imagine hearing a weird noise, and we could be certain it came from "the brown house" or "the house at the corner" or "the house down the road." Some houses *look* more haunted than others. We had a pretty good idea what a haunted house looked like, and what ghosts looked like. Most children do.

There are different schools of thought about hauntings. Researchers claim that it is people who are haunted, not places. Investigators maintain that it is places and their memories that haunt people. It is possible to reconcile these schools of thought to account for the prevalence and persistence of ghost stories. Perhaps some people are more "sensitive" or "intuitive"; perhaps some places make people feel "sensitive" or "intuitive." There are certainly people whom psychologists call "fantasy-prone"; there are certainly places that produce unusual sensitivities (like temples and churches, crypts and churchyards). Some houses affect people as "friendly," others as "unfriendly." There is no disputing tastes, but the practitioners of Feng Shui, the traditional Chinese art or craft of "reading" the flow of forces, who maintain their discipline is something of a science, measure these forces. I like to think that every region has its *genius loci*, its spirit of place.

Here are some stories of the private houses and public buildings that have reputations as "haunts" that are to be found in villages, towns, and cities across the country. The reader today would have to travel in time as well as in space to visit these dwellings or domiciles, for many if not most of them are long since gone, though a few of the sturdy ones are still standing and still regarded as the dwelling places of the spirits. I have often wondered what happens when a haunted house is razed. What happens to its ghost or spirit? Does it travel to another house?

The Court House Ghost

There is a tradition that a ghost haunts the Court House in Whitby, Ont. The domed, Greek-style building, now known as the Whitby Centennial Building, has served the community in many ways since 1854. "A Ghost in Whitby" appeared in the *Sarnia Observer*, August 15, 1873. Apparently the article was originally carried by the *Whitby Chronicle*.

◆◆◆

A Ghost in Whitby
The Apparition Seen and Described

For some days past the ghost, which, it is asserted, has been seen in the neighbourhood of the Court House, has been the talk of Whitby. The apparition, according to report, is seen under various forms—that of a black dog, which suddenly assumes the shape of a rather tall man, and from whose eyes burning red flames seem to issue, being the most familiar. Others assert that the ghost has been seen leaning with both hands on a staff standing on the Court House steps, or walking slowly between the steps and the entrance gate, at "the witching hour of night." Those who have had the temerity to approach the midnight intruder allege that on their approach it has all at once disappeared as in a flame of fire, sinking, as it were, into the ground. Others say that the most sorrowful moaning has been heard to proceed from where the ghost makes itself at first visible, and in fact all sorts of versions are given as to what has been seen and heard of what people persist in calling the "Court House Ghost." Last night a gathering assembled around the Court House railings, and remained there until nearly twelve o'clock to ascertain what could be seen, but at that hour hurried home to bed, cold and disappointed at the non-appearance of his ghostship. After the departure of the crowd, however, it is stated that the apparition was again seen by respectable and creditable people, that it was a tall figure walking heavily with a cane, and frequently stopping to look up at the sky, and groan while making its round wearily through the grounds in front of the Court House. There are, as may be expected, all sorts of surmises as to what the trouble is, and a determination avowed by many parties to find out all about it, and if it be a trick, to expose those who would impose this latest ghost hoax upon a community.—*Whitby Chronicle*.

Poltergeist at St. Hubert

Here is a fairly detailed account by a newspaperman of poltergeist-like activities that took place in a house in St. Hubert, outside Montreal. The account appeared under the heading "Strange Doings" in the *Montreal Star*, May 25, 1881. The reference to Esther Cox in the heading is an allusion to the Great Amherst Mystery, one of the classic cases of a poltergeist. Readers showed a real interest in the activities of the poltergeist at St. Hubert, so the newspaperman contributed follow-up stories. These are reproduced here too.

◆◆◆

Strange Doings
A Mystery of the Esther Cox Order
A House in St. Hubert Which Is Possessed of a Mischievous Spirit
What the Spirit Does

On Monday, at 3:15 p.m., word was received at the *Star* office that strange doings were going on at St. Hubert which were so inexplicable in character as to warrant investigation in the interests of the public. At once it was resolved to send a reporter and on the stroke of the half-hour, that individual leaped from his cab on the platform of the car just as the train was moving out of the station. A rush to the Point, a whirl through the cavern of the Bridge, a short stop at St. Lambert, and then a delicious bit of riding to St. Hubert, with whiffs of the upturned mould from the furrows, and glimpses of wood and meadow through the window frame.

St. Hubert is a quiet little village nestling about the station, with the parish church half a mile away, and the houses of wealthy farmers ranged around. On alighting, the writer was received by the agent of the Grand Trunk, Mr. Ferguson, who put himself at the former's disposition, and procured a trap to reach the scene of wonder wherewith. This was out on the Queen's highway between Longueuil and Chambly, some five miles off. During the journey, the driver gave the names of the parties where the wonders were wrought, certified to their good standing in the parish, related the wonder and awe of the whole countryside, and altogether prepared his companion for a series of surprises. He was cut short by the appearance of Mme. Perrault herself, the mistress of the haunted house, who was driving into the village to see the *curé* and get some news from her husband, who is absent. Upon learning the mission of the writer, she began a voluble tale there and then, but finally offered to turn her horse's head and go back to her own house.

This was soon reached—a good, substantial country house of the second class, alive with children within and chickens without. It was soon bruited about among the neighbours that a *journaliste* was there taking notes, and quite a gathering of gaping men and women was the consequence. Going about from room to room, and from kitchen to garret, the following facts were elicited:—

On Saturday before last, 14th instant, the following pranks were played: On a bureau in the small sitting room were twelve statuettes or religious figures in porcelain, set in two concentric horseshoes, six in each. These were all found lying on their faces. They were set up. A little later found lying on their backs. Set up again. The third time they were found on their sides. Set up once more. The fourth time the heads were all put together as in the centre of the circle, and the feet laid out symmetrically as so many spokes of a wheel.

"Did you see this done?"

"No. But it was done at regular intervals, while no one was in the room."

"Sure no one was in the room?"

"Sure."

Nothing more occurred for four days, when the tricks were renewed thus:—A small table in the bedroom, which stood at an oblique angle from the wall, was set at right angles, then tilted on two legs against the bed, and one pillow and the counterpane were drawn over it. Since then some queer things have happened every day, which, because of their sameness, may be grouped together. Two little winding sheets, which had been stowed away in a valise, were laid out on the bed, as if to answer their original purpose. A woman's shawl hanging upon the frame of a door was thrown upon the bed. A cupboard standing at the foot of the bed was set ajar, and a pile of napkins and towels placed on the foot of the bed without being unfolded. A prayer book was wafted from the sitting room to the foot of this same bed. A little toy stove on top of a bureau was toppled over and a photograph leaning against the wall was thrown forward.

Mme. Perrault is a young woman of thirty-five, very intelligent and quite ready to give every information. The same of her mother. The household seemed more dazed than frightened.

"Any noises ever?"

"Only once; in the sitting room was a wicker armchair covered with books; when it was thrown down there was quite a racket. No other noises since then."

The mother and grandmother with five children deserted the lower part of the house at nights and took refuge for sleep in a small garret. A visit up there was amusing. Dresses hung up on pegs along the walls were taken down and stretched on the floor. The same with under-clothing, drawers, etc. Mme. Perrault's best black Sunday dress received special attention in this way. A roll of lace on a small table was nicely unrolled on the bed. One of the two windows of the garret opened spontaneously. In the kitchen four willow chairs were placed back to back and a buffalo robe was spread over them. That same robe was unhung from the wall and spread over a cart. The reporter saw this as it had just happened before his arrival. He also saw where two pil-lows had been put together and a quilt which was lightly tucked under the bedding had been rolled over them, making the figure look like a corpse laid out.

A thorough examination having been made, the next thing was to inquire into the cause. The act of removal was not witnessed in any sin-gle case, only the rag carpet was tucked up in the middle of the floor, and then spread out again as soon as the backs of the people were turned. But even in this case, no agent was seen.

"*C'est un diable, un sort,*" was the general verdict—a devil, a spell.

"What do you think of it?" Mme. Perrault was asked.

"God only knows," with upturned eyes and open palms outstretched. "My husband is working on the Intercolonial at Rivière du Loup, and we thought at first that he was dead and that it was his spirit returning to us. But Mr. Benoît, our member, telegraphed him and received a reply that he was well."

That settles the ghost theory. The writer, having nothing further to offer, prepared to go, but on his way out noticed a little girl of about thirteen whose eyes were queer, and who had twitching of the arms and facial features. Without saying anything, he drove back intending to call on the *curé* of the parish, the Rev. Mr. Hurteau. He was well received by that gentleman, and while the two were exchanging views in the garden, a horseman rode up in haste, and informed his reverence that the young girl in question had, immediately on our departure, been taken with convulsions and that it took two men to hold her. His reverence then decided to make a thorough investigation into the circumstances connected with the mystery, particularly as to the little girl, and the reporter sat down to await developments, which will be reported tomorrow.

◆◆◆

The St. Hubert Manifestations
The Result of the Investigations
What the Habitants Think It

In the *Star* of yesterday the details given about the singular occurrences at the Perrault farm, St. Hubert, were simply a series of facts, narrated as they were noted down, without any attempt at sensational effect, and on the best available testimony. No new facts having been developed in the past thirty-six hours, there remains only to inquire into the causes of these strange proceedings. With that view a second thorough visit was made to the house itself, and conversations were held with several sensible parties, chiefly among them the Abbé Hurteau, *curé* of the parish.

The first point to ascertain was whether the girl Ernestine Perrault had anything to do with the manifestations. Ernestine was called out and interrogated. She was shy at first, and refused to come. She is full-grown for her age, a brunette with elongated face and bright eyes, and her form is as lithe as a willow.

She said she remembered nothing of what happened during her convulsions; how they came on, or how they went off. During them, it seems, her eyes rolled wildly, she clutches at her clothes, and about her, and a breast pin of her mother's and a pair of her father's gloves that were in the room, went of themselves on the floor. She thrust her hand through a large pane of glass, splintering it to atoms, without making the slightest scratch on the skin or drawing a globule of blood. She was heard to mutter something about seeing some black object or other. The fit lasted about an hour. It began near the close of the writer's first visit, and terminated on the entrance of the *curé* into the house. This is rather hard on the journalist and a compliment to his reverence. The latter had an interview with the child, since when she has been calm.

The mother was interrogated at this point:—

"Has Ernestine ever had convulsions before?"

"Never."

"Is she a nervous child?"

"No."

There is a doubt, however, whether the woman understood the full import of that question. The girl *does* look to be of a nervous temperament; quick in movement, outspoken and self-possessed withal.

"Was Ernestine ever away from the house when the manifestations took place?"

"Yes, once or twice."

Further inquiries *aliunde* make this point doubtful. A strict account was not kept of the dates and hours of each commotion, and it is hard to be certain that the girl was away at any of them.

"Are you positive there was no one in the room when things were moved about, &c.?"

"Oh, yes, sir. I couldn't be more certain of anything. With seven or eight persons in a house of only three small rooms, we could not be deceived on this point."

This answer complicated matters. It set aside physical agency, which would have made the whole affair a jolly "sell." The veracity of the people is unquestionable, their intelligence good, and there seems no reason to believe that they could have been imposed upon.

Now, what about these convulsions of the girl? At her age there is no physiological ground to suppose that they were hysterical. Nor had they all the regular epileptoid symptoms — spuming, curvature of the face, and the unearthly initial cry. The matter is well worthy of medical examination, and if the symptoms should return in any form, the writer would suggest that the girl be placed in the hands of experts. Without any attempt at exaggeration, or pandering to a morbid curiosity, such manifestations are worthy of scientific attention, and should be treated with becoming seriousness. This is decidedly the sentiment of the Rev. Mr. Hurteau, who reasoned with much elevation on the subject.

Of course, there is a comic side to everything, and the rustic must have his legend. It appears that it is an old hag wandering up and down the ranges, in quest of charity, who threw a spell upon the house and girl. The reason she gives, in the forges and barnyards where she tarries, is that her husband once worked for Perrault, and in settling accounts there was a balance of $4.00 due him, which has never been paid.

"So long as that money is not paid, let them look out," saith Meg Merrilies, pointing her bony finger up the road.

This version is believed all about now, and quite satisfies the peasants' philosophy. Nay more, the venerable tramp is credited with a stretch of mercy, because she said that she might have done worse and filled the Perrault house with rats. This the people are certain that she could accomplish.

A debt of gratitude is due Mr. Ferguson, the agent of the G.T. at St. Hubert Station, and his lady for many acts of hospitality and attention. Mr. Ferguson will be remembered among Montreal marksmen as one of the crack rifle shots of the country, both in the G.T.R. Co. and the M.R.A. He has three cups, including the massive Brydges Cup, won three times out of five, and nine gold and silver medals, clasps and crosses for feats at Wimbledon, conspicuous among them being the Kalopore medal.

"The St. Hubert Manifestations" appeared in the *Montreal Star*, May 26, 1881.

◆◆◆

The St. Hubert Mystery

Our correspondent writes from St. Hubert:—

When the *curé* went to the house of Madame Perrault on Monday evening he ordered everyone in the house outdoors to see for himself that there was no fraud, and he arranged the bedding and chairs and closed the room so that no one could get in, and sometime after when he returned into the room the bedding was tossed and the chairs moved from where he placed them. I am also informed that the girl (the supposed medium) on coming home from school noticed one of the attic windows open, which was not usual, and she asked her mother why the window was open and her mother said that the windows were not open, at the same time going upstairs to make sure, when to her surprise the window was open and the floor was covered with clothing, scattered about every way.

"The St. Hubert Mystery" appeared in the *Montreal Star*, May 27, 1881.

◆◆◆

The Spirits at St. Hubert

To the editor of the *Star*:

Sir,—In your issue of Wednesday you give an account of a visit paid by your reporter to St. Hubert, and the doings of some mischievous "spirits" there. You treat the subject somewhat lightly, but to people who have watched the doings of spiritualists there is nothing strange in the pranks of the "spirits" at St. Hubert, even if they turn out to be as true as reported.

Do we not read in the Bible of Saul going to the witch of Endor, before a battle, and do we not know that the witch made the spirit of Samuel to appear, and foretell that Saul would be killed the next day, and killed he was. Are there not abundant proofs in the Bible to show that the belief in spirits was a common one, or are we to discard as a fabrication the story of the evil spirits being cast out of the swine.

I am as confident as I exist that all spiritualist manifestations are the doings of evil spirits. I have watched spiritualism closely and I never knew a medium yet who did not come to a miserable end. The evil spirits master them and the rest is easy. People will laugh at this, but people laugh at everything supernatural. The orthodox devil may be a myth, but the world is full of evil spirits, and it is through spiritualism that they give manifest evidence of their existence. They delight in sending messages from the other world, but they are not the messages from the dead but from the evil spirits, who never lived and who are of hell, whatever hell may be.

There is no other way of accounting for the mysteries of spiritualism as made manifest in the evil doings which surrounded Esther Cox and hosts of similar cases. I have seen a man myself who at the instant I saw him was eight miles away, and yet I heard his footsteps and saw him just as plainly as I see the paper on which I write this letter. And yet I did not see him, but some of those evil spirits which delight in mischief. The truth is that they are forever at our elbow, inciting us to evil, and all this simply proves what the Bible teaches.

Christian.

"The Spirits at St. Hubert" appeared in the correspondence column of the *Montreal Star*, May 28, 1882.

Supernatural Visitations

This is a highly readable account of a farmhouse infected with a poltergeist. No ghost appeared, but poltergeist-like manifestations were recorded, including a swarm of red ants! The account appeared as "Uncanny Doings" in the *Daily Sun*, Saint John, N.B., October 4, 1894.

◆◆◆

Uncanny Doings
At the House of Joseph McDowell, Kent Co., Ontario
Mysterious Rappings, and Stones
Fired by Unseen Hands
The Bushes Full of Grinning Skeleton Faces—
A Terrible Beast Appears to a Little Girl
(Special Cor. Toronto Globe)

Chatham, Sept. 26:—Having heard rumours of mysterious and uncanny happenings at the home of Mr. Joseph McDowell, on the 15th concession of Raleigh, a reporter drove out yesterday morning to ascertain whether or not the reports had any foundation in fact, and, if so, to get all possible particulars, and, if possible, to solve the mystery which surrounds the place.

Arriving at Mr. McDowell's, the scene of operations, we found Mrs. McDowell alone in the house, with little 13-year-old Lettie, an adopted daughter, who has been with her upwards of six years. Mr. McDowell, who was ploughing, was sent for, and, while awaiting his arrival, his wife told the following:

"I was standing outside, near the door, Saturday morning, after we had milked and had breakfast, working my butter. Lettie was just behind me washing the dish-pans. The rain barrel was at the corner of the house, about ten or twelve feet away, and in plain sight of both of us, when a stone the size of a small goose egg fell upon a board which was over the top of the barrel; but, though I looked up, I paid no further attention to it and thought nothing more of it until afterwards. I continued to work my butter, when showers of gravel came from under the house, where there was an opening barely large enough to let a cat through, and, flying to a considerable height in the air, fell on our heads, quite a bit of it getting into the butter I was working. I then kept watch, to see where the gravel came from, when the same thing occurred a second and third time, in rapid succession, and, though we could plainly see it go, we could not see anything throwing it. I took my butter and went into the cook-house, and, even after I was in there, a lot more gravel flew in the open door at me, and more stones went into my butter. I could see Lettie as she was standing at the door of the cook-house, and I know that she had no hand in it, and, besides, Lettie would not do such a thing. I told her to open the screen-door, so that I could take my butter in the kitchen. She tried to do so, but the door was swollen so that she could not. I set my butter down in the cook-house, and found the screen-door very hard to open. I then went back to get my butter, and just as I reached it a lot more stones came into it. I told Lettie to run down to the field and tell her father about it and tell him to come up to the house at once; which he did. In the kitchen I picked the stones out of the butter and put it in a crock, and started mixing bread. After I had been at that a little while large stones began to come through the window, breaking four panes of glass, and after them came nearly a bushel of gravel. When Lettie returned without Mr. McDowell, the stones were still coming in, and I myself went to fetch him, as the former run had made the girl feel sick. Cautioning Lettie to remain in the house, I left, and, during my absence, some animal, about three feet long, with a head like a cat and the same kind of whiskers as that animal, came to the screen-door and tore it with its claws. Lettie told it to go away, whereupon it growled at her, terrifying the poor child so that she dropped a stick of wood which she had picked up to defend herself, and ran, screaming, into the adjoining room. When I returned she was so upset with what she had seen that I could scarcely pacify her."

Mr. McDowell, who had left his ploughing to give what information he could, arrived at this juncture and took up the narrative:

"When Mrs. McDowell came running for me in the field and told me what had happened, I came up as soon as possible, and seeing the pile of gravel and stones which had come in the window, told her not to touch it until I came back. I then went out and brought in one of my neighbors, Ed Murdock, and we took out of the house over a bushel of the dirt, and sand and gravel were piled up on the window-casing, on the outside, to the height of the bottom of the glass. This I scraped off with my hand."

When asked as to previous occurrences, Mr. McDowell said: "Some months ago tobacco worms seemed to be gathering around the house from all quarters and made their way everywhere. One day my wife was washing in the cook-house when many of the disgusting things fell from the roof on her back and all over her. These worms, which came by hundreds, never touched anyone but my wife, and, after a visit of nearly a month, left as they had arrived, going in a body down the road.

"Soon afterwards myriads of red ants came up the concession, and, arriving at the house, came in and made an extended stay. These also would bite my wife most unmercifully, and not touch either myself or Lettie. I took her away for a while, and during the time she was away she was not bitten, but the moment she came home the ants met her at the gate. I then took her to a doctor, but he could make nothing of her case and could do nothing for her. After the ants had gone away up the concession in a body, crickets came in most unusual numbers, and they, like the others, appeared to have a special liking for my wife. A couple of weeks ago there were mysterious rappings all about the house, but we paid no attention to them; but on Friday night last the main trouble commenced and since then I have not slept a wink. I started to go to the station and had got to the railway, which passes about 40 rods in front of the house, when I heard something pounding. It sounded as though it was here, and I wondered what my wife was doing, but thought no more of it until on my return I learned that she and Lettie were sitting in the room when a great pounding and moaning were heard under the house, followed almost immediately by the same noise on the roof. Then came a rap like a man's knock on the front door, beside which Mrs. McDowell was seated. My wife says the knock was undoubtedly upon one of the panels of the door, and, as the wire fly-screen was shut and hooked, this startled her so that she would not open the door, but peeked out of the window, where, though it was a bright moonlight night, nothing was to be seen. Just after this an animal, similar to the one seen by Lettie on Saturday, was heard and seen by the latter sitting upon its haunches on the window sill, with its forepaws against the top of the second pane from the bottom, looking in. And every day since then, with the exception of yesterday and today, stones and gravel were thrown in and peculiar noises heard. On Sunday, my wife, with her sister, Mrs. Michael Broadbent, were in the cook-house, when stones were thrown in on them. Mrs. Broadbent went to the barn for her husband, who was there with quite a number of men, including myself. He went to the house with her, and he also saw the stones coming in.

"Nothing of this kind has occurred when I was present, and never yet when there is a crowd of folks around."

Upon being questioned as to what she saw, Lettie said: "The animal which came to the screen and tore it was the most terrible looking thing I ever saw. It was over two feet and a half long, with rough, shaggy, brown fur, a face somewhat like that of a man, but entirely covered with hair; it had long whiskers and ears like those of a cat. A short, bushy tail completed the picture. When mother went to get father I was reading aloud, when I heard the beast at the door, and when I looked up it had its head through a hole it had ripped in the screen.

"It growled at me, and I threw a stick of wood at it and ran into the other room. While there I thought I heard it in the room, but cannot be sure, as I kept the door shut until mother came back. Monday night, while Mr. McDowell was at the station, I saw the same animal sitting at the window, with its feet upon the pane. I also saw the stones coming into the house. The most of them came right up the side of the house from under the back doorstep, and when on a level with the window turned right off sharply and went in. After I had shut myself in the room on Saturday I looked out of the front window and saw the beast jump the fences and go away towards the bush. It did not run, but jumped, all the time taking over half the width of the road in a leap."

Daniel Broadbent, upon being questioned, said: "Night before last (Monday), between dusk and darkness, I went with my brother, Albert Broadbent, to Joseph McDowell's farm, to see for myself what there was, and whether or not there was any truth in the many incredible reports which were being circulated concerning the mystery surrounding the place. I took my double-barrelled shotgun with me. Upon arriving at the farm, I sat on a log a few feet away from the cook-house. Mr. McDowell asked me to come in and have tea with him; but, having had supper just before going, I thanked him, and said I would stay where I was. I had not been there fifteen minutes when a considerable quantity of gravel, amongst which were several stones about the size of a hen's egg, fell in a perfect shower on the top of the cook-house and upon us. It appeared to be coming straight down, and landed with great force. A few minutes later it fell again, whereupon I got up, went to the door and told Joe I had seen enough to satisfy me. I stayed until nearly 9 o'clock, but neither heard nor saw anything more. Before taking up my position on the log on which I was sitting, Albert and I thoroughly searched every nook and cranny which could possibly afford a place of concealment for any practical joker, and I know the missiles were not thrown by human hands, though where they came from is, and must remain, a mystery."

An old resident, who stands high in the estimation of all—his name will be withheld for the present—in reply to the reporter's question as to the cause of the supernatural visitations, said: "It is nearly half a century since I came to these parts, having come here when I was but a young man, and at that time there stood in the bush, just about where Joe McDowell's little house now stands, a small deserted and tumbledown log hut, which, even at that early date, no one would pass after night. A little bit after I came here—I was in my prime then and proud of my unusual strength—I heard tell of the 'haunted hut,' as folks called it, and openly made fun of those who refused to pass. I never thought of trying it myself until one day one of the young men remarked that they noticed, with all my brave talk, I myself never travelled that path. It was immediately arranged that I was to make the trip that same evening at dusk, leaving half the party at one end of the path and meeting the rest of them about half a mile past the hut. I started in the best of spirits and took with me a good pistol with which I was a first-rate shot. When I arrived near the hut the very atmosphere seemed stifling and peculiarly oppressive, and yet I was not afraid, but pushed on until I arrived just about where the present haunted house now stands. What happened then I never knew further than that I met a man dressed in plain, badly worn clothes going in the opposite direction. When I was nearly up to him I said: 'I thought I was the only one around here not afraid to pass the—ghost, but I see I am not,' and I put out my hand to shake hands with him and congratulate him on his pluck. He took my hand in his, when to my horror I discovered I held the hand of a skeleton, and then I saw that the head of the one whose hand I held was only a fleshless skull, the stare of whose empty sockets seemed to fairly freeze the very marrow in my bones. At the very moment I took its hand the bush on every side seemed full of grinning skeleton-faces, which glared at me from behind every tree, and filled the air with hideous, discordant laughter. Then fine gravel began to rain down upon me, after which came stones of increasing size, which bent me to the ground insensible. When I recovered consciousness I was lying on a lounge in my own house. They told me they had found me lying on the cow-path through the bush. I never told the story to anyone till today. Nor did I ever go near that spot again after nightfall."

These Unquiet Forms

T he following story is well told and comes from the Christmas issue of the *Victoria Daily Colonist*, December 25, 1897. It is easy to imagine the story or tale being read with gusto by the grandfather or the father to the rapt enjoyment of the rest of the large family gathered around the roaring fire. I wonder how many of them slept well that night, without nightmares.

◆◆◆

A Real Ghost Story
Two Strange Visitants Who at Night
Appeared to a Citizen of Victoria
White Figures Who Flitted into an Undertaker's
and Asked to Be Buried

Though in these days of prosaic commonplace, many of the old-time Christmas ways are falling into disuse, still there is a lingering charm even to the minds of the "grown ups," not to mention the little people, of a thrilling ghost story. Who of those who have come from the colder parts of the world does not remember some night before the lights were lit, and when the forks of flame cast strange shadows on the wall, the little circle gathered round the grate while the story-teller was relating some blood-curdling tale in which ghosts bore a leading part? One who has not known this pleasure has lost—well, it is only those who have experienced it who can remember the delicious thrill of creepiness crawling up the back when a snap of the burning log, or the sudden falling of a coal on the fender, came just at the climax of the tale. Such great writers as Dickens and Thackeray well understood this feeling and ghost stories figure prominently in their Christmas tales. But though one often hears of ghosts, and though some fellow knew another fellow who saw one, it is very very infrequently the case that it is granted to any favoured individual to see a real live ghost.

Just imagine what one would feel to see two ghostly figures flit into one's house and ask to be buried—two restless souls who begged to be laid at rest. Yet this is just what happened in this city of Victoria in these days of the commonplace.

On Thursday night, when the black clouds shrouded the moon and the far-off electric light on Douglas Street shone so as to hide the pit-falls in the sidewalk, a closed carriage suddenly pulled up in front of Hanna's undertaking rooms. The door of the vehicle was opened and from the coach there glided to the sidewalk two white figures, shrouded from head to foot in long flowing robes. At such a time of night no mortal man surely could have traversed six feet of sidewalk without becoming entangled in a nail or stubbing a toe on a projecting plank, but these ghostly figures flitted smoothly the boards and entered the undertaker's shop.

Evidently these unquiet forms were weary of this world, for they had no sooner entered the store than they asked to be buried. There hung around these visitants a strange aroma, and by its scent the young man in the establishment knew that he was in the presence of spirits (apparently rye). He declined to bury the spirits; but one of them, stretching himself at full length in a coffin, begged to be buried. At this juncture Mr. Hanna returned and naturally, as the spirituous visitants had neglected their burial certificates, he as a good citizen had to refuse their pleadings. They might be dead, but without a certificate the poor spirits must float around and curse the red tape that forbade them to be interred without dying in the regular way.

Mr. Hanna not only refused to bury the strangers, but turned them out and telephoned to the police. Ghost stories were all very well to read about, but he had no use for any spirits at his place as he is a temperance man.

The police sallied forth to hang the ghosts and later on captured one without his shroud, refreshing himself at a bar—and so it turned out that they were not ghosts after all, but a couple of young men who thought they were having a good time. The one captured was charged with being drunk, as he evidently was, and as he failed to show up in the police court yesterday morning his bail of $10 was forfeited. And so it turns out a very commonplace story after all; not nearly as interesting as if Mr. Hanna had taken the ghosts at their word and buried them.

To Put It Mildly, We Were Amazed

ROY T. REID

The editor of the *Edmonton Examiner* kindly ran my request for accounts of "extraordinary experiences." The request was answered more than six months later by Roy T. Reid, a reader of that weekly newspaper. Here is Mr. Reid's letter, dated Feb. 28, 1991.

◆◆◆

A clipping has been sitting on my desk for a number of months now; it originated in a local Edmonton-area newspaper, and it asked if anyone had a good ghost story.

I am not certain if this story qualifies as such, but it is something that a number of people experienced one evening. All the details were later recounted and found to be correct.

At the time we lived in Winnipeg, Man., at 261 Beacon Street. The year would have been somewhere around 1937, when I was twelve years old. (I am estimating this, as I am uncertain of the exact year, although 1937 is a close estimate.)

To set the stage, I will explain the circumstances at the time of our adventure. The house next to ours was occupied by a husband and wife—two of the biggest bootleggers in the city, very nice people and good neighbours nonetheless. It was a very cold winter night, with a temperature in the –30 degree Fahrenheit range. The house then had a large, full-width veranda and steps of wood-frame construction; it was roofed over; and it had a rail bannister. The inner hallway was approximately sixteen feet long, with a stairway leading to the upper floor of the house which a couple of my parents' friends had rented. The house was old, even in the 1930s. It is standing today, much as it stood then.

We—that is, my mother, the couple from upstairs, and I—sat in the kitchen, talking. The lady renter and I sat where we could look into the unlighted (and very dark) hallway, while Roland Young sat with his back against another wall and around the corner next to our kitchen table, where my mother sat on the opposite side, also unable to see down the hallway.

What happened next was agreed upon by all present. We all heard footsteps on the veranda steps crossing to the front-door area. We heard the storm door open, followed by the inner door; then we heard them closed. We all heard someone slowly mount the stairs to the upper floor and cross into the kitchen area. A board in the upper floor squeaked as it always did when anyone went into the kitchen. It sounded as if the person were elderly and tired as well as familiar with the location; we agreed the steps were those of a male because of the weight and gait. We also agreed that they seemed weary.

Our first thoughts were that someone had mistaken our home for the one next door. With this in mind, Roland took a butcher knife (in case it was required) up the stairs to eject any intruder, while the three of us remained at the foot of the stairs in the now-lighted hallway. After much searching under beds, and in closets, he came down to tell us there was no one there. There was also no way anyone could exit through a window short of smashing the glass pane, as all windows were secured by four "buttons" from the outside. To put it mildly, we were amazed. Yet we were in agreement that we had heard the same series of sounds.

Nothing before nor afterward occurred while we lived there. So it's anyone's guess as to what caused the event. I am providing a sketch of the lower floor as a possible assist. I don't believe anyone was alarmed by the event. Rather, we were puzzled as to the cause and as to why it had happened.

Ghostly Footsteps on the Stairs

GRANT MACRAE

Here is the story of a haunted house in Calgary, a story with an aftermath. (Not all reporters follow up their stories; Grant MacRae did.) The case was described by Jack Strickland in his "Purely Personal" column in the *Calgary Herald* on October 31, 1941. Strickland prefaced the column with the following explanation:

Somewhere in Sunnyside, in a house on a short street just under the hill, the ghost of one long dead may walk again this All Hallow's Eve.

On Wednesday, three men made an offer through this column—L.Z. Allen-Sidney, Silas F. Dent, and T.C. Silnkard, psychic research workers. They would investigate any and all Calgary ghosts brought to their attention, and allow their findings to be published in this column.

Today they met a man who lived in that house in Sunnyside when first he came West about twenty-two years ago. That man was Grant MacRae, now living at 804 9A Street Northwest, and this is what he told them....

He added a postscript to the column that went like this:

And, add our three research men, they will keep their bargain—
they will investigate immediately and report their findings
through this column.

The surprising conclusion of their investigation into the haunting of
the Calgary house appeared in the next "Purely Personal" column on 1
Nov. 1941.

◆◆◆

It struck me as strange at the time that such a well-finished home with
beautiful floors and a large garden at the rear should have remained
empty and the rent very low while houses were so scarce in the city. My
next-door neighbour was one of Calgary's old-timers and she it was
who proffered the first information.

After inquiring if I was not afraid to be so much alone in the house
after dark, I remarked that I could not understand the strange noises on
the stairs like a man walking in his stockinged feet. Then she blithely
informed me that the woman who had lived there prior to my coming
had been carried out in hysterics in the middle of the night because she
had met something on the stairs.

"And," continued she, "nobody can stay there more than a few
weeks—something gets on their nerves."

This treading of the ghostly footsteps on the stairs and in one room
upstairs kept up continuously day and night. So when a friend of mine
from Winnipeg wired that she would like a few days with me while
breaking a journey I was glad.

Nevertheless, I determined not to spoil her visit by telling her anything about this. Underneath I was myself a bit sceptical and when his
ghostly lordship haunted elsewhere, I'd say to myself, "It's just an animal of some kind, or perhaps the lay of the ground beside the hill,
causing the house to move."

After my friend's arrival she looked at me rather strangely and inquired, "Don't you sleep well at night? Being in a strange bed I woke up several times in the night only to hear you padding around in the hall." I rather guiltily passed it off with some lame excuse, but she left quite worried about my insomnia.

About a month later I had a letter from home again. An old Scotch lady about eighty years of age would like to spend a few days in Calgary on her way north. Scarcely knowing the old soul I again decided to keep quiet.

Well, I can assure you she kept the ghosts at bay and for one solid week I never heard a sound, and she, though her hearing was perfect, made no remark of a visitant. The only explanation I can give you is that she went to bed every night with her open Bible on the table beside her and a glass of whisky for consolation. Such a combination must have been too much for the other spirit.

I stayed there about four months and on giving notice to the trust company, one of their head men visited the house and offered to sell the place at a ridiculously low figure. When my answer was final he admitted they couldn't keep tenants there on account of this mystery and showed me the marks still showing where the company had torn down part of the partitions and opened up the chimney.

I related the whole thing to my brother in Winnipeg. About two years later he happened to be in Calgary, and coming in one evening to dinner remarked with a grin, "I've got news for you; call it coincidence or anything you like, but I've just met a man who is on talking terms with your ghostie."

Then he related that while sitting chatting in the office of a friend of his in one of our large mills, the latter remarked that he would like him to meet a very fine man who worked there, especially if he, Donald MacRae, cared for ghost stories. Lo and behold, this man began to relate much of what I have already told, only he must have had something the rest of us didn't for the ghost was quite pleased to talk to him every night and hold long conversations. I never found out if a ghostie really has a voice or if this man was clairaudient as well as clairvoyant. He admitted being a spiritualist.

Another yarn I heard about that house was that an old farmer and his boy lived in it while it was under construction, and he put everything he owned into it and went broke. Then, to make things really lurid, he is supposed to have gone insane and possibly murdered the boy, as he was never seen around the place again, and—whisper the owls and black cats—maybe his body is buried somewhere around the place.

I give you this in detail, and as far as I am concerned, it is true. I've never heard who lives there now or if there are still noises heard.

◆ ◆ ◆

The ghost of Sunnyside is seeking the light.

Today our psychic researchers talked with a man who lived with that ghost for nearly nine years, who not only heard him but saw and talked with him and finally convinced the ghost he must go back to the spirit world, never to return.

That man is Joseph Parken, retired now, but who today still lives in the house on that very street under the hill, at 564 9th Avenue Northwest. Joseph Parken had heard stories of strange doings when he moved into the ghost's habitation in 1919, and he hadn't been there long when he got firsthand information.

One morning, as he was shaving, there was a terrific crash, "as if every window in the house had broken into a thousand pieces," to use his own words. That was the first time he noticed anything strange about the house.

And then it happened, night after night—those slow, measured steps as of a person walking upstairs, then down, then up, then down, endlessly, all night long.

Joseph Parken had heard how that ghost had bothered those who lived in the house before he, himself, came to it. There was the young couple who came to that house to live on their wedding day.

In the dead of that first night, husband and wife ran screaming from the house in night attire, never to return. There had been others—the ghosts put an absolute limit of four months on any person's stay.

That ghost never bothered Joseph Parken—except for that endless night prowling: there was one heavy step, then one light one, as if the ghost had an injured foot.

Then one night he met the ghost, face to face on the stairs. He could not distinguish the features, but he knew it was his nocturnal visitor.

Clairaudient as well as clairvoyant, Joseph Parken questioned the ghostly figure. It told him the story of a terrible wrong, of a bitter resentment carried over the years by the ghost.

The ghost had lived in that house many years ago, it told him, when first it was built, Joseph Parken believes. Relatives envied it, schemed to get rid of it so that they might live there.

Finally they had been able to convince the authorities that the ghost was insane. He had been taken off to Ponoka, where he died some years later. Now he could cross over from the other side, he could once more occupy the house he felt was rightly his. That was why he drove others away.

Joseph Parken told the ghost he was doing the wrong thing, that he was only retarding his own advancement in the other world.

He told the ghost he should look for the light and seek to follow it. Why should he bother all these persons who had never done him any harm?

That was in 1928. "I never saw him again," said Joseph Parken, "except once, when he came back to thank me for my advice and to tell me that he was no longer troubled."

He added, "And so far as I know, no person who has lived in that house since has been troubled in any way."

Three Ghostly Experiences

JOAN E. SKIDMORE

One Thursday morning I was the guest of Steve Madely on his phone-in show on CFRA Radio in Ottawa. For a while we chatted about real-life ghost stories, then Steve opened the lines to hear from callers. Thirteen callers shared their experiences on air. A good many listeners wanted to tell their stories but had no opportunity to do so. They were encouraged to contact me directly. A number did.

That explains the genesis of this letter from Joan E. Skidmore of Gloucester, Ont. She has had a number of odd and ghostly experiences. She was born in Ottawa in 1941. "I am a third-generation Canadian," she wrote. "My ancestors were German and British. I am a homemaker and mother of five grown sons, and we have two grandchildren. My husband and I will be celebrating our thirty-fifth anniversary this coming October. I sew, knit, crochet, garden, read, write poetry, and love camping."

♦♦♦

February 18, 1994

Dear Mr. Colombo:

I am writing after hearing you on radio station CFRA this morning. The topic was ghost stories.

Here are three of my ghostly experiences.

The first experience occurred in 1955, when our family was living at 20 Chamberlain Avenue in Ottawa.

My Aunt Annie, my maternal grandmother's sister, had lived with us the previous year. Her health was not good but when it improved she moved to Pembroke, Ont. Then she took ill again, and my grandmother travelled to Pembroke to stay with her.

My mother, my sister, and I were in the kitchen washing the dinner dishes when we heard footsteps on the back porch. The steps sounded as if someone was entering the room beyond the kitchen. We searched high and low but there was no one there.

A short while later my grandmother phoned us from Pembroke to say that Aunt Annie had passed away. Aunt Annie had always sat on the back porch.

In 1976 my husband was transferred to Kitchener, Ont. We bought an old brick house at 100 Moore Avenue. The house was situated quite close to a cemetery.

Shortly after moving in we realized that we were not the only occupants of the house. We apparently had the company of several ghosts. The ghosts were seen or heard by all the members of our family. We had five sons who at the time ranged in ages from six to sixteen years. It was a fascinating experience.

The original owners of the house, the Beerwagon family, had spent their entire married lives in the house. The land had been given to Mr. Beerwagon by his father. Mr. Beerwagon was a stone mason and he built the house in 1911. He brought his bride to their new home. They raised seven children and departed the house in death. We were told that they had the services of a live-in housekeeper named Mary.

My first ghostly encounter in the house was with an older woman in the upstairs hallway. She seemed to float past me. I was sure she was carrying laundry over her arm. I saw her several times, but for some reason I did not mention her appearance to the other members of the family. One day my eldest son came and told me about a woman he had seen in the upstairs hall. He described the same women whom I had seen, and he said that she appeared to be carrying something.

Our next visitor was an older gentleman. My oldest son told me that this gentleman had sat on the edge of his bed. He also said that he had gotten into the car with him. My husband suffered a serious injury, so we set up a bed in our living-room. A leather chair stood near his bed. My husband told me about an older gentleman sitting in the chair. He said he thought the gentleman was smoking. My son had also mentioned that the gentleman smoked.

My husband had renovated our attic, turning it into a large bedroom. We were startled to hear someone pacing back and forth in this room. The floor was carpeted yet we could hear the sound of footsteps on bare wood. One day, when I was the only one in the house, I was sitting in the room on the second floor near the stairway. I could hear footsteps come down the stairs. My hair felt as if it was standing on end.

Once the footsteps on the stairs started up, they were heard again and again by our family. Often the steps would be heard descending the stairs from the second to the first-floor landing. These stairs were carpeted; the stairs from the attic were not. However, all the footsteps sounded as if they were on bare boards.

Our third son slept in the attic bedroom. Every so often he complained that I was calling out his name to wake him. But I had not called him.

At times the window at the back of the attic room would open by itself. My husband had installed a new Pearson window that slid sideways and was difficult to open or shut. One day I closed the window and then sat down, only to watch the window open all by itself. There were no high winds and the room was electrically heated.

Our house was often filled with the delicious aroma of baking, usually chocolate. This occurred when I had not been baking. There were no baking odours coming in from outside. When my sister came from Ottawa to visit us, she also mentioned the smell of baking. While talking to the next-door neighbour one day, she began telling me about Mrs. Beerwagon's love of baking. After her children had grown up, she used to bake cupcakes full of nuts, which she placed outside for the squirrels.

We had a bathroom off the dining-room. Originally the dining-room was the kitchen, and the bathroom was the summer kitchen. The bathroom door kept opening to the point that we had to install a chain lock on the door for privacy.

One evening my husband and sons were downstairs watching television. I was upstairs in bed reading, when a woman started sneezing. I searched the bedroom and the entire upstairs but found no one there. I was the only one upstairs.

We had decided to take out the dining-room windows and install patio doors and build a deck. We called for estimates. Three contractors came separately. The house seemed to come alive, especially upon the arrival of the third contractor. Lamps shook. There was banging in the basement. The house seemed so unsettled. This was the one time we felt nervous about our ghost. As a result, we decided against undertaking the renovation.

Once in a while we would hear things being moved about in the basement. When we checked, everything was always in place. I later learned that Mr. Beerwagon had placed a cot in the basement and he took naps behind the furnace. He also puttered around down there.

Our second son's girlfriend, who is now our daughter-in-law, maintained that our house made her feel nervous.

Before we bought 100 Moore Avenue, it had been rented to students. It was then purchased by a family of four and they undertook extensive renovations. After we sold the house, it apparently changed hands several times.

In all, we spent five years with ghosts from the past wandering through our rooms. This was the first home that I was glad to leave. On moving day, we never looked back, and never shed a tear.

Throughout all these ghostly experiences, for some reason or other, we never spoke about what was happening to anyone other than my sister and her husband.

My third ghostly experience came about in 1984. We were again living in Ottawa. Around 3:00 a.m., I was awakened by the sound of my Great Aunt Myrtle calling out my name. At the time Aunt Myrtle was in the hospital in Pembroke. She was very close to us. She was ill with cancer. Later that day we learned that she had passed away. Upon talking to my sister that day, she told me that she too had heard Myrtle call out her name, around eight o'clock that morning.

My maternal Grandmother had very strong intuition. She would always know when something was wrong. She would call me to say she had not slept all night because something was wrong at our house. She was usually right.

This gift was passed down to me. Sometimes it almost frightens me.

Possibly these stories will be of interest to you. It feels good to tell someone about them.

Sincerely,
Joan E. Skidmore

The Beautiful Lady in White

Mrs. M. Kirkpatrick is a resident of north Woodstock, Ont. She was born in Chelsea, England. She read my request for true-life "ghost stories" in the Woodstock weekly newspaper *Sentinel Review* and sent me her own account of the appearance of the Beautiful Lady in White in 1965 or 1966. I received her handwritten letter on May 25, 1990.

The account is interesting in two ways. Although the ghost was not seen by Mrs. Kirkpatrick, it was observed by both her young son and her adult house guest. She later learned that there was a local tradition about a wandering spirit which inhabits small stone houses or cottages, as well as the story of a suicide in her own house.

It seems that local lore is supportive of local experience. Or is it the other way round?

◆◆◆

I once rented a stone house on a farm at R.R. 7, Woodstock. The house was later burnt down, but its remains are still to be seen.

I lived there with my two boys, then ten years old and twelve years old. They slept in separate bedrooms upstairs. We were in the house several years.

It was getting towards Christmas. One night, my younger son told me the next morning that a beautiful lady in white came into his room and smiled at him. This happened for a few nights in a row.

Once I had some friends stay overnight. I put one of them in my younger son's room. Nobody had mentioned his story about the beautiful lady in white, especially not me, as nobody else had seen this lady.

Anyway, the next morning, our guest came down. He asked me if I had gone into his room. I said no, because I had no reason at all to go upstairs or into his room. Anyway, as he described it, this beautiful woman in white came into the room, looked at him, smiled, and then went away.

By this time I was getting "the willies." I decided to move back into town. I figured the house must be haunted and the ghost must be a beautiful lady.

By this time it was very near Xmas of the following year. I was about to have another child.

One day I picked up the *Sentinel Review* and read about a ghost. There was this story of "The Lady in White." Evidently she was about to marry and her future husband had built a little stone house for her. He got killed in a crash on the eve of their wedding. So she went around to all the stone houses looking for her husband. She was harmless, according to the article.

I never saw her, but my son, who is now forty-two years old, will swear to this day that he saw the Lady in White. My guest saw her, too, but unfortunately he is now deceased.

I found out afterwards that a man's wife left him and he hanged himself in the little stone house in which we lived.

I believe in ghosts, as I saw two myself in England. I saw the famous ghost of Dr. Phene, well known on King's Road in Chelsea, and I saw the spirit of a nun when I was a young girl. So I now believe in ghosts.

I only wish I had seen the Lady in White. I may have been able to console her. She only goes to stone houses, and whenever I see a stone house I always think of the Lady in White.

This is a true story.

The Ghost of Joseph Gillespie

DAVID JEFFERY ESSERY

Often the days leading up to Halloween are busy ones for me, as I am sometimes asked to appear on radio and television shows to talk about ghosts and spirits. I usually agree to do so for two reasons: I might have a new book on the supernatural or the paranormal to promote; I enjoy chatting on open-line programs with callers who have strange experiences to share with listeners...accounts that might go into my files.

On October 29, 1999, I was the studio guest of host Maureen Taylor on TVO's *More to Life*. We enjoyed hearing a series of viewers' stories about hauntings. The last story we heard was from a male with a deep, rich voice who identified himself as Jeff. Jeff told the story of the ghost of Joseph Gillespie, a kind of guardian spirit. Maureen and I were quite charmed with the story and the storyteller. On air I asked Jeff to leave his phone number with the studio operator and I would contact him thereafter for further particulars.

Later that day I phoned Jeff and it turned out that his full name is

David Jeffery Essery and that he is a graphic designer who had worked for the Canadian Broadcasting Corporation (on the *Wayne & Shuster Show* and *Mr. Dressup*). I interviewed him and then wrote up this account of living with a guardian ghost. He kindly read it and revised it. The revised version was completed on 15 Nov. 1999.

So here it is. Meet Joe.

◆◆◆

The name Essery is Welsh. I was told it was once spelled with a d-apostrophe: D'Essery. The family of thirteen brothers dispersed from Devon, so that any Essery you find nowadays is a direct relation. I myself was born in Toronto on October 11, 1942.

I believe I am psychic. At least I am open to the idea of spirits. They don't frighten me in the slightest, but I didn't expect to cohabit with them in the flat over a bakery shop.

The bakery was Rood's Bakery Shop at 2618 Yonge St., Toronto, across from Sheldrake Boulevard. I moved into the flat about 1974. You entered through a door on Yonge Street and climbed a flight of stairs to a hallway. At the rear was a porch and a bedroom. The kitchen and the bathroom were near the entrance and the dining-room and living-room, divided by an arch, were at the front overlooking Yonge Street. There was not a straight wall in the whole place.

Within minutes of moving in, I saw something. Standing near the front windows, where he could peer out and yet watch me, was an old man. He was transparent and yet he had colour. He was wearing a brown suit and it was shiny. It was the kind of cheap suit that grows shiny with wear until it falls apart. He usually wore a brown suit but sometimes he wore a blue one. It too was shiny with age. He was of average height, slightly stopped, in his eighties, I would guess, and balding. He seemed very curious.

At the time, I didn't think much of the sight of the old man. I acknowledged his presence and went on with my unpacking. That seemed to be enough. I didn't think much about him. There was an old gentleman who ran the Sheldrake Barber Shop a few doors south. He was the barber and being well into his eighties himself, he knew everything and everybody and I did need a haircut.

Now, when you're psychic, you get a sense of whom you can talk to about such matters. "So who's the old gentleman in the brown suit that I keep seeing? He certainly seems very interested in everything."

"That's Joseph Gillespie," said the barber without any hesitation. "He used to own the building, the one with the store and the flat. He used to live around the corner on Craighurst Avenue. He lived alone and he was absolutely paranoid about theft. He liked to own and acquire property but he wouldn't own objects because they could be stolen from him. He wore a suit until it fell off and he lived quite simply, one overstuffed chair, ate out of cans and the like. I don't think he ever bought a newspaper; he always read mine in the store."

I believe that the spirit of Joseph Gillespie was attracted to me because I had a tremendous collection of masks, sea shells, prints, and puppets which lined the walls of the apartment. My Christmas tree had over three thousand ornaments on it. It was an artificial tree that sparkled with miniature objects that I had picked up on my various travels all over the world. Ghosts, as you know, are attracted to shiny things and the tree lights would reflect on these tiny detailed objects. He could enjoy looking at them for hours and, best of all, he didn't have to take responsibility for them. He could enjoy all my stuff. His "unfinished business" was, in fact, to learn to enjoy things for sheer pleasure; something he had never allowed himself in life. I came to feel that Joseph was a kind of guardian of my apartment.

He was a generally friendly spirit and the guardian of my things, but he was not always pleasant to have around. One Christmas, when I had put the artificial tree up, I allowed the branches to settle. While they settled, I lounged on some cushions on the floor listening to music. Suddenly I was sharply beaned on the forehead!

There was not a spare space on any of the walls, as things were hung everywhere. One of the masks, high on the wall, was from Mexico. It was a devil's head surmounted with a wooden carved blue bird. On its own, the wooden bird's head was torn off its neck, thrown past the Christmas tree about twenty feet and hit me square on the forehead! It didn't hurt much but it did register Joseph's complaint at the delay in erecting the tree. The rest of the mask still hung in place on the wall.

It was the only physical contact I had with Joseph, but he did move a lot of my stuff around. He loved to hide keys, those symbols of security. He would swipe them from the middle of an empty table where I would have placed them in plain sight. He loved to do this when I was in a hurry to leave. After just missing countless buses, I soon learned that if I swore directly at Joseph, he would put them back again. The funny thing was that when he returned them, the keys were always freshly cleaned and highly polished.

Once, he took the stopper from the kitchen sink, which was actually a deep laundry tub. When I couldn't find the stopper anywhere and couldn't do the dishes, I pounded my fist on the edge of the tub and yelled at him, "Joseph!" and called him a few things angrily. Suddenly, the large stopper appeared out of nowhere, hovering above my head! Then it fell into the sink. There were no shelves or ledges overhead so it couldn't have fallen off anything. I thanked him, placed the stopper over the drain, and did the dishes.

When I left the flat, I would turn off the lights and leave through the front door, making a big thing of locking up for Joseph's sake. Many times, on returning later that evening, the front door would be ajar to Yonge Street and all the lights would be on. I would make a lot of noise climbing the stairs just in case. Nothing was ever disturbed. It was Joseph showing off. His authority inside the flat apparently extended to three steps up from street level. To make things easier for him, I hung a brass policeman's button from a string just inside the front door. Any visitor only had to touch that symbol of security on entering and Joseph would know you were not a thief.

Aside from being beaned with the bird's head, he never hurt me. He didn't want to take the chance of my banishing him from the premises. No one else ever saw him but they sure felt his presence. He would suddenly change the temperature in the room on entering. Sometimes he would sit down between two people and they would both shiver. You could then take a thermometer and record the sudden drop in temperature. Sometimes, when friends came to visit and were sitting around, he would freeze just the tips of their noses.

All that was about ten years ago. During that time, I lived alone. Guests would stay there once but no one would stay there alone. They were afraid.

A person did stay in the apartment for three weeks once during October when I was in Europe. He agreed to stay but Joseph didn't like the idea and at the first opportunity hid his keys. The friend decided to keep the front door locked for security and enter by the back door off the rear sun porch. Bad idea. He had to use a fire escape, the way a thief enters. Joseph was apoplectic. One night, when the friend was sleeping, he was awakened by a tremendous crash from the front room which shook the entire building. He raced there and saw that a fifteen-pound piece of slag glass, which usually sat on a corner cabinet over three feet high, was sitting on the floor. It had not fallen because it was not chipped or broken and the floor was not at all scuffed. One of the many masks on the wall had been lifted up off its nail from above and been placed carefully face down on top of a series of specimen sea shells which covered the rest of the surface of the cabinet. Not one of the shells was in any way harmed. The nail that had held the mask was still secure in the wall. Every picture in the entire apartment was tilted. The floor was freezing. It was so cold that you could see your breath. When you think of it, this was very strange because there was a bakery with ovens in use directly below the flat.

Yes, Joseph Gillespie was a hilarious old Scotsman with a wicked sense of humour. He had owned the building and when I moved in, he was reluctant to leave it. Everything in it was stuff for him to enjoy. He was certainly not ready to go yet. He had felt that time had been stolen from him even though he had lived to a ripe old age. I considered him a roommate and he was welcome to protect the flat and its contents. I like to think that we both learned something during our years together and we wish each other well.

I moved away when the owners sold the property. The bakery moved up to Thornhill, I think, and the barber is long gone. I now live in a condo in downtown Toronto. I consider myself psychic. I have heard voices, or part of me has. I psychically shop. People tell me that I should write a book about the things that have happened to me here and all over the world. I have collected many things, from Bali, Asia, the Far East. There, they live alongside their gods. There is a constant balancing between good and evil. I am totally at home with that. Some of the masks still have energy. There are some I would never wear.

One of the many incidents happened to me in that flat but it did not involve Joseph. During the Second World War, my father rescued an entire orphanage full of children in Sicily. He had an audience with the Pope because of it. At the time, the priest in Sicily gave my father a rosary that he believed contained a sliver of True Cross. I had it and one day absent-mindedly hung it over the knob on the end of a hot-water radiator in the front room. Later that evening, I was watching television in the room and the rosary began to swing back and forth of its own accord, but I left it there and went to bed. Later that night, I awoke freezing with cold. The temperature in the bedroom had dropped. It really dropped, thirty degrees. Even my eyes were cold. I sat up. There were moving pinpoints of orange light tracing lines in the dark air at the end of the bed. The heavy smell of incense filled the room. I was seeing the lights from a censer. I could not see the censer itself, just the lights from it. I could smell the charcoal as it continued swinging. I got up in the dark and went down the hall toward the bathroom for a glass of water. The cold floor crunched beneath my bare feet. I ran the tap and glanced in the mirror. Instead of me was the image of a hooded monk!

Next day, I retrieved the swinging rosary off the radiator. I carefully fastened it to a brass hook in the bedroom wall. It did not move there.

I never saw the monk again.

I Never Felt Comfortable Alone There

GLORIA DOVE KAVANAGH

Gloria Dove is the professional name of Gloria Dove Kavanagh, a musician and singer of Country, Western, Bluegrass, and Gospel songs. She lives in the picturesque town of Elora, Ont. I sent her a letter of inquiry when I learned from the photographer Jack Kohane, who was photographing haunted houses in nearby Fergus for my book *Mysteries of Ontario*, that Gloria was known to have had some strange experiences in her house in Elora. She replied on September 14, 1998. I wrote back and encouraged her to write an account of her experiences, and this she did on September 29, 1998. I keyboarded this and wrote to her again and she replied on November 20, 1998. Here, finally, is her account of her experiences in different houses in Fergus and Elora.

Gloria Dove's latest CD is called *Traveller of the Night*.

◆◆◆

In July, 1980, my husband, Bill, and I purchased the house at 195 Barker Street in Fergus, Ont. It was built around 1826. At the time our two children were young, eight years old and six years old.

The large stone house was old and we started to renovate it that August. We ran into difficulty renovating the upstairs and ended up tearing most of the downstairs apart, as the joist had to be replaced to straighten the floors so we could do work on the upstairs.

In January of 1981, I was wakened up by coughing in the attic. I thought I was dreaming and went back to sleep. In the morning I got up and went downstairs, and the sound of coughing never crossed my mind, until my daughter came down and said, "Did anyone hear the coughing in the attic last night?" I didn't want to believe what I was hearing, but I told her that I had heard it. She wanted to know who was causing it. I just told her I didn't know.

Bill suggested we move the beds downstairs so we would not hear the coughing sound again. We did that and raised a curtain between our bed and the children's. A few nights later, I was awakened by the sound of boots walking in the house and the sense that someone was standing by the curtain staring at us. I was so frightened I could not move to wake Bill. Finally he stirred and I managed to tell him someone was in the house. We got up and looked around but no one was there. We went back to sleep.

The next morning, when Bill and I talked about what had happened that night, my daughter told us of her experience. She said that when she saw the man, he was already inside the house. He was standing in the back room and staring into the main part of the house. He was pointing a rifle ahead of him and not aiming it at her. She could see his hat on his head sideways. She said that he had come there every night since we had moved downstairs.

We started to tell some neighbours what was happening but they thought we were completely ridiculous. So we quit telling them and kept our experiences to ourselves.

We moved the children's beds back upstairs but kept ours downstairs near the back entrance to the house. Again we raised a curtain but this time along one side of the bed. That night I heard the sound of boots walking on the floor. They sounded to me like big army boots and I had no idea where the sound came from. The fan on our wood stove stopped of its own accord. A chair began rocking.

This time I woke up Bill and we got out of bed. The fan on the stove came on again, the chair quit rocking, and we heard the sound of some-one running in army boots, fleeing the house. All this happened at the same time.

The next morning I got up and checked all the doors. The fan seemed to be in working order. We didn't have a rocking chair and none of our chairs had uneven legs. There was a chair near the stove but it was not a rocking chair.

It was time to find someone to help us. I called a lady in Fergus who had lived a few doors away back in the 1970s. Her name was Pat Mestern and I knew she had something in her house sometimes, and I asked her if she could tell me what to do as we were really upset. We told her everything that had happened. Everything had taken place over the last two weeks. She said to leave it to her for a few days and she would get back to us. She said I should talk to "it" with my mind and ask it what it wanted.

The next thing I knew, a night or two later, it was in the house again, shutting the stove fan off, rocking in a chair, and walking around the house in boots. So I asked it what it wanted. All that I could hear faintly was "you." I poked my husband to get up, "It's in the house again!" and I hollered at it to get out now because it was in my house. Everything happened the same as before. The fan came on, the chair quit rocking, and the boots whooshed by. My husband went to the door and opened it and our cat raced out meowing as if it was following someone. We could actually feel its presence at times.

I phoned Pat again and told her what had happened. She said that we could have someone like a psychic come to our house, but she added that she had found out something very interesting and said that we really didn't need to be afraid of it. She had contacted the previous owners of our house and learned that the grandfather had served in the Boer War. He had come home from South Africa in the wintertime, and he liked to sit by the stove and rock in his rocking chair. He had died in the house. She believed that he didn't like the house being disturbed with renovations. She believed that when we completed our renovations, the disturbances would stop.

The presence played tricks on us. Quite a few times we had to get up in the night and turn the television off because it would turn the set on full blast. One particular night Bill called to me to tell me to turn the hall light off, so I did. Partway down the stairs Bill said, "I thought I asked you to turn the light off in the hall." I told him that I had, but if it was still on, I would turn it off again. Before I got down the stairs, the light was on again. I hollered at my son to turn the light off. He did so and before my eyes it jumped right back on again. So I finally said, "You want the light on, we'll leave it on." The next morning Bill switched it off and it stayed off. We checked the switch and the socket but there was nothing wrong with them.

Sometimes Bill and our daughter would hear people eating and laughing in the old part of the house. He would holler at them to knock it off and it would be quiet. This happened many times with him and a few times with my daughter.

The years 1987, '88, and '89 were quiet ones. The house had been renovated by now and there wasn't much in the way of "the presence." In all, we owned the house from 1980 to 1989. I never felt comfortable alone there. Bill and I separated in January 1989 and I left the house for good.

Bill passed away in January 1997.

Dan, my common-law husband, and I moved into this very old home at 16 McNab Street in Elora on October 1, 1997. Within a few days of moving in, I sensed something was odd. I was upstairs at the time and thought someone was watching me from the back part of the house. I looked but nothing was amiss. I let it go at that and went about my business. But every now and again it felt like something was there.

One morning at the end of November, I was awakened by a very gentle knocking on the bedroom door. I thought I was dreaming and dismissed it. The next morning, I was awakened by the knocking again. This time I wasn't dreaming. The third time it happened, I knew I had a problem. About four days passed and I was in the bathroom in the early evening when I heard what sounded like a pile of books falling over. I ran into the back room but there was nothing there. There were no books there to fall over.

Four or five days passed and Dan went away on a trip. I decided to vacuum the upstairs, starting with the bedroom. I took the vacuum cleaner upstairs and set it up in the bedroom. Then I decided I would vacuum the room the next day, after I had sprinkled the rug with carpet cleaner. I had a package of Cow Brand baking soda on a shelf behind the door. I had used it on the carpet a few times because the cat that belonged to the previous owners had left its smell in the room. I decided I would use the baking soda the next day to deodorize the room and then vacuum it.

The first night alone in the house I was too nervous to sleep upstairs, so I slept on the couch downstairs. The next morning I got up and went upstairs to get dressed. I opened the bedroom door and there was the Cow Brand baking soda sprinkled all over the carpet. The box was sitting on the bed, not on the shelf behind the door. I was so shocked I couldn't even use the phone in the house. I went across the road to use the neighbour's telephone. I called Pat Mestern, the lady in Fergus, the one I had called years before. I told her what had happened. I thought perhaps the presence from the other house had followed me after all these years.

Pat asked, "Does it feel the same?" I said that it didn't.

She asked me what I sensed it was. I said that it seemed to me it's a child.

She said to go home and just say that you don't have time to vacuum but you'll clean it up this time. You're not to ask it its name.

Pat thought perhaps it was a child playing mischievous tricks. I feel that this is so because I have since learned that the original owners, when they lived in the house, had two young boys. The family was not sure what has happened to them. A relative is checking this out for me.

Also, when I talked to Pat, she asked me things about the house. She wanted to know the location of the room where the disturbance was coming from. Had it been ripped apart by the previous occupants? Pat figured if we got the room back together again, the disturbance might stop.

When Dan returned home from his trip, I told him what had happened. He said nothing. He just listened. Well, one night I was away and came home and he was sitting in the living-room with his arms crossed. On the table was a small rack from a planter that I had set up at the top of the stairs. I asked him what it was doing on the table, but he didn't answer me. I had to go to the bathroom rather quickly, so I ran upstairs. At the top of the stairs there was a clump of dirt from the flower-pot on the floor. I went to the bathroom and came back downstairs and asked why the dirt was up there on the floor. He didn't answer me. I asked him what was wrong. He said that the "thing" in the house had thrown the rack at him when he was coming down the stairs.

I believe that it wanted him to know for sure that it was there.

My daughter came back from Alberta early in the summer of 1998. She helped me put the bedroom back together. Since then we have had no more problems in our house.

I Felt a Certain Peace

DONALD L. COMBE

It has been said that the most haunted communities in Canada are Fergus and Niagara-on-the-Lake. There are no statistical accounts of ghostly reports arranged by locale, and any such estimates must be on a per-capita basis. Perhaps what draws the ghosts and spirits to the picturesque community of Niagara-on-the-Lake on the shores of Lake Ontario are its many graceful residences, dwelling places erected by the United Empire Loyalists and maintained by their descendants to this day. Many of these buildings have long histories as haunts.

Niagara-on-the-Lake is also renowned as the home of the Shaw Festival. In fact, it is the only theatre in the world dedicated to the works of the playwright George Bernard Shaw. Now, Shaw was a rationalist who dismissed all belief in ghosts or spirits. Yet his innate curiosity was such that he read then-current books about psychical research; he even reviewed a number of them for the London press. In one review he made an amusing comment on the classic English ghost story. With his customary wit he wrote about "the classic—that is, untrue—ghost story." Shaw noted that it was a human characteristic to tell ghost stories, if only to account for the many strange and unusual things that have happen to people through the ages.

Donald L. Combe is a descendant of the U.E.L. who lives in an old house in Niagara-on-the-Lake. Knowing my interest in the supernatural and the paranormal, he kindly faxed me the following account of a peculiar disturbance. I have reproduced it as I received it.

◆◆◆

Thursday, May 9, 1996

Dear Mr. Colombo:

I live in an 1838 house in the old town of Niagara-on-the-Lake. Shortly after I moved here, I noted some strange behaviour by my Scottie, Andrew. This normally rational and pacific animal, who never had ill will toward anyone or anything, and who certainly never growled, took to sitting in the corner by the front door where he stared intently into a blank wall and carried on a low and rather disturbing growl. This behaviour of Andrew's went on from time to time and made no sense at all, but I felt certain he knew something that I didn't, but which he probably thought I should.

One night I was in the cellar immediately below the spot where the dog was used to growling, and I heard a dripping sound on the floor above my head. I concluded that I had overwatered some large pot plants that stood nearby, so I ran up with a rag expecting to find pools of water. To my amazement there was nothing on the floor. I looked about and decided I had imagined the event and returned to the cellar. In a few minutes the sound began again. Now I was certain that a water pipe had burst, so I dashed back up the stairs. Again I found no water, and look as hard as I might, there was no explanation of the dripping. I returned to the cellar and the dripping continued, but as I had no explanation, I ignored it.

There were no further episodes of the dropping sound, nor were there any further episodes by the dog with his mysterious growling.

Some time later I discovered that there had been a murder in this house and that the location of the growling and the dripping sound was where the hapless soul had died. He had been bludgeoned, and a trail of his dripping blood led to the front door as he tried to escape from the house.

The man who had been killed in December 1971 was a simple soul who had been murdered in hope of a few dollars. He was greatly liked by the townspeople and sadly missed. The date that I experienced the dripping sound was the anniversary of this poor man's death.

There was a relief for me in hearing the story, as it explained the phenomena the dog and I had experienced. He never visited either the house or the dog and me again. I felt a certain peace that a troubled spirit had departed from the scene of its trauma, and I certainly experienced neither fear nor apprehension.

Faithfully yours,
Donald L. Combe

The House at 430 Elgin St. E.

ROBIN LYCETTE

Here is a detailed and dramatic account of a series of effects that took place in the 1980s in a house in Oshawa, Ont. The effects resemble those attributed to poltergeists, but with a difference.

The account was written and sent to me by Robin Lycette on April 19, 1997. In the original letter and in subsequent correspondence, I learned at the time that Robin (one of those genderless names) was a male student in his late twenties who was completing a bachelor's degree in education at the University of Regina.

"One of my projects last year involved the writing of a narrative about an event which impacted my life significantly," he explained.

"The story enclosed is the result of that writing. From my memory, it is all entirely true, although the current owners of 430 Elgin St. E. think me to be somewhat of a nut. (I sent them a copy.)

"This does not surprise me, as the strange occurrences still take place this day—but not in that house. The 'thing' described in the story seems to be in some way connected to me, not so much the house—but I'm not sure what to make of it or what to believe any more."

So maybe the house is not haunted by a poltergeist. Maybe Robin has his own familiar spirit....

In subsequent correspondence, Robin elaborated on the current situation: "There have been some recent experiences in my downtown apartment. My landlord, who lives one floor above me, has asked me several times to make it stop. The same things started happening again last January and are periodically witnessed by my occasional visitors. Maybe I should explain it over the phone—it's tricky to explain."

I asked Robin specifically about his background, as I am aware that strange experiences are quite often reported by people of Gaelic background. "My ancestry? Interesting question. Well, as one might guess, the name Lycette is French. As far as I know, my great-grandfather, or perhaps his father, came from Northern France. Both grandparents on my mother's side are British." Who knows, there may be Celtic blood that flows through his veins. In any case, here is his story....

There is a reference in the story to "Attempted Possession," which is a ghostly account included by ghosthunter Eileen Sonin in her book *More Canadian Ghost Stories* (1974).

◆◆◆

In 1983, we moved into a house at 430 Elgin St. E. in Oshawa, Ontario. The previous occupant of the house was an elderly lady whose husband had passed away some time earlier.

It was a small house containing only two bedrooms and a very small kitchen. What used to be a garage was now a family room, yet there were only the three of us and it certainly looked very comfortable.

Shortly after moving in, my mother and stepfather made a few observations that were clearly out of the ordinary. When they read in bed in the evenings, they could hear me when I would come home from a girlfriend's house. One night, like normal, they heard me come in the door, close it behind me, walk through the hall, go around the corner, and enter my room. They called out to me; I did not answer. They thought that perhaps I was very tired or upset.

I can state, truthfully, the real reason I didn't respond to their greeting. The fact is that whoever or whatever came through the door and made its way to my bedroom was certainly not me. I didn't actually come home for another hour, when my confused parents again heard me enter the house. My mother deduced that I must have come home the first time, crawled out my bedroom window, and returned through the door again an hour later. After all, such behaviour is normal for a teenager. However, this explanation was no longer acceptable when the same thing happened the very next night when I was already home. This occurred up to five times a week.

The apparent visitor must have had some awareness of our bedtimes because "it" only "came home" and walked through the halls when we were in bed. When "it" came home, the door would be closed loudly enough to wake all of us up. Frightened after hearing the door open and close, I would sit up in bed waiting for it to make an entrance into my room as that was the place it always headed for when not occupied by myself. Before long I slept on the couch in the living-room.

In a few weeks, we began to have problems watching TV. In the middle of a program the set would shut off and could not be turned back on. Then we tried a light in the same electrical outlet, only to find that the outlet itself was dead. This led us downstairs to check the fuses. After opening and examining the fuse box, we discovered that the fuse responsible for operating the television and a few other electrical appliances had been unscrewed and neatly placed on the nearby table. Someone had taken the fuse out. Weird. We replaced it and all was back to normal, for a while at least.

Next "it" would pick on the stereo, unscrewing the appropriate fuse and taking out a few lights with it. Incidents of this kind started to occur daily. We soon found out that our friend especially hated it when anyone operated the vacuum. The first few attempts at vacuuming lasted only for a couple of minutes, then only seconds, and then not at all. The very second anyone removed the vacuum cleaner from the closet, lights would go off and you could be sure that no outlet in the house would provide electricity for the machine to operate. We thought this was funny. We even demonstrated the effect to friends. When company came over, we would just take out the vacuum, go around and plug it into about six different sockets in turn, and watch everything in the house shut down. Then we would go downstairs to observe every single fuse removed from the fuse box.

Many of the occurrences seemed to be a little spooky but they were still harmless. It was even entertaining, providing you were not in the house alone. When my parents were out of the house, I too made a point of not being home alone or of having someone visit with me. As long as I did not have to be there alone, I did not mind being there so much.

After we got used to the nightly front-door-hall routine and the electrical mystery, something else occurred. This time, it was not so cute. My mother was spending time working in the basement one evening. It had a section divided off which had been renovated in the 1960s and was now somewhat of a recreation room. As it was empty and stark, my mother was hanging pictures and curtains on the walls and windows. The only ornament or decoration left by the last owner was an old round mirror. It was a little smaller than a stop sign. It had grooved edges and was truly ugly. My mother made her way around the room hanging pictures in various places, trying to make the place look cheery. When she came to hammer a tack in one particular wall (the west wall) she found that the tack would not penetrate the panelling. This seemed odd since the wood panel wall could not be more than half a centimetre thick. She tried a slightly larger nail but it bent. A third nail was attempted in another location of the same wall but the effort was still futile. Confused and frustrated, she put the hammer down on the nearby bar and took a break to light a cigarette. On the counter behind the bar, she noticed a small piece of paper. She picked it up, noting that it was an old business card that named some accountant in Scotland. As she examined the card, the corner of her eye caught a quick flash of movement. Turning her head, it was almost too late to see anything more, but the hammer she had been using was gone. She described it as lifting itself off the bar, floating into mid-air, and then flying right into the mirror. There it vanished. The mirror remained intact, but my mother did not. She was at the top of the stairs in record time. My step-father looked at her and said, "You look like you've just seen a ghost."

She told us what had happened.

"You've had nothing to drink, have you?"

My mother was angry at our suggestion and could not have been more serious. She was visibly frightened. We went downstairs to investigate and found nothing out of the ordinary except for three bent nails that we had heard mother pounding on earlier. Without a hammer, we could not test the statement that this wall could not be pierced by nails. Somehow, neither of us wanted to attempt it anyway.

This "thing" possessed more power than we had originally thought. It seemed as though it was setting down certain rules in the house. First of all, there was to be no vacuuming whatsoever. Only some television and music was permitted. and there was to be absolutely no hammering on the west basement wall. What else could there be?

Although my brother Waryn did not live with us, he sometimes came by to visit. One night in the summer, he showed up with his girlfriend and two other friends. No one was home at the time but the house was unlocked so they walked in.

At the top of the staircase leading downstairs was a door opening into a hallway. The door remained closed at all times, as the open position prevented people from walking through the hall from the kitchen to the front foyer. The door was also equipped with a slide lock on the upstairs side, making it possible to lock someone downstairs if so desired. Most of the time the lock was secured in place. It felt safer that way for some reason. We only opened the door to go downstairs for a given reason.

This night, Waryn and his friends sat in the kitchen, when Waryn realized that he had to go out to his car to get something. When he came back into the house he made a strange discovery. His friends were crowded around the basement door, holding a fireplace poker, ready to attack whatever it was on the other side of the door trying to get out of the basement. As the door was locked, the knob twisted frantically and the door itself shook on the hinges, as if someone on the other side was desperately trying to get the hell out. They did not dare unlock the door to investigate, but rather made a quick exit and left our home.

Now, more than ever, we wanted an explanation for the things that were happening. We were afraid to go downstairs, as there seemed to be something very unfriendly about the basement. This led us to wonder about Mrs. Dewland, the former owner of the house, and whether she had experienced such things. At this time we had lived at 430 Elgin St. for two years, but we could still remember the process we went through when we bought the place, as well as the circumstances of the lady we had bought it from.

Before we actually purchased the house, we thought there was something strange about its owner. One curious thing about Mrs. Dewland was the reason she was moving out. She did not have one. The new house that she moved into was only two blocks away and was the very same size as her old house. It seemed rather strange that a woman, after living in one residence for more than thirty years, would pick up and move to a different residence in the same neighborhood for no particular reason. It was not as if Mrs. Dewland needed to be taken to a retirement home. At the time of the purchase we felt it was curious, but it was none of our business. We liked the house and asked no questions.

Before actually buying the house, we made a few extra visits to Mrs. Dewland in what would soon be our new home. She would greet us at the door, gladly let us in, and show us through each room. She never took us downstairs to see the basement. If we wanted to go downstairs, we had to go it alone. Perhaps her age may have prevented her from going up and down stairs, but there was something more to it. She made it quite clear that she preferred not to go down there.

There was nothing wrong with her legs, and age did not prevent her from visiting the basement.

When people live in the same house for a long time, the fact is obvious from the boxes, household items, and various sorts of junk collected in their basement. This basement did not fit such a description. There was not a single box. With the exception of dust, the place was empty. Somewhere in a corner there were a couple of laundry machines which were included in the price of purchase. Despite the machines, Mrs. Dewland preferred washing her clothes at a laundromat. One would think that it would be much easier and faster to bring laundry down a flight of stairs rather than carry it outside, put it in a car, and drive it across town. Again, we did not question this unusual practice. Even then, we concluded that there must have been something about going downstairs that did not agree with her. It is interesting to note at this point that the house she moved into did not have a basement.

Recently I read a story called "Attempted Possession" which documented a woman's experience with a supernatural being that attempted to control or influence her thoughts. Was her name Kitty Cockburn? When this person was home, she lived in fear. She sometimes had a vision of herself being murdered. She also feared that the water she drank was poisoned and that some kind of monster lurked behind the bedroom curtains when she slept. Not only her, but everyone living in the apartment flats of her small Toronto building had the exact same thoughts and visions while at home. Away from their home, they considered themselves to be well-adjusted, happy people. While they were home in their apartments, they felt as if they were living a nightmare. They concluded that some kind of evil presence existed in the building and that it exercised morbid mind control over them. Whatever it was, it had the ability to plant horrible thoughts into the minds of people near it.

I mention this story because today it helps me to understand something that once happened to me over the Christmas holidays at 430 Elgin St. I came home from a friend's house in the middle of the afternoon. I poured a cup of coffee in the kitchen and headed towards my bedroom. I walked by the living-room to find that our Christmas tree and the surrounding furniture were a blazing inferno and the room was filled with smoke. Terrified, I dropped the coffee on the floor and ran outside. I stood outside in the snow, contemplating my next action. Before going to use the neighbour's telephone, I peered through the living-room window only to see that our Christmas tree was in perfect condition and that the interior of the house appeared to be normal. There was no inferno. When I later told my mother what I had seen, she wondered if I was using drugs. "I swear to God, mother, I know what I saw. The house was on fire!" I exclaimed that I wanted to move away. Our "thing" was getting carried away, and we were now afraid for our safety.

After Christmas, my stepfather announced that his office was being moved to Albany, New York, and that the three of us were going to accompany him to the United States. Our house sold quickly and, like Mrs. Dewland, we made no mention of the supernatural incidents to the incoming owners. We left and moved into a brand new house in Ballston Spa, New York. While unpacking an old box of junk in our new home, my mother found the hammer.

A Ghost Called Matthew

JIM YOUNG

I was the guest of Bill Carroll on the radio show *Toronto Talks* on February 8, 1994. The show is heard on AM 640 and Q107 and has a wide listenership. Bill and I talked on air with seven callers. We could have talked with seventeen listeners, as the switchboard had lit up like a Christmas tree with incoming calls!

About a week later I received the following letter from Jim Young of Barrie, Ont. At the time of the incidents described in this account, Jim was working as a data processing operations manager and Shirley was a lab secretary in Barrie. Then they moved to Eganville and then back to Barrie. The account speaks for itself. And it speaks volumes!

◆◆◆

February 10, 1994

Dear Mr. Colombo:

Yesterday I tuned into the Bill Carroll show and was disappointed to discover I had missed the first part of the show featuring you as the guest. The topic, as you know, was ghosts and poltergeists. This is the reason why I am writing to you.

I am submitting our "ghost experiences" to you for your evaluation and possible inclusion in your new book about ghosts in Ontario.

It started here in Barrie in 1990, shortly after my wife, Shirley, and I purchased a home on Wilson Court. In the beginning, of course, we were unprepared. We didn't make any connection between what was occurring and we didn't anticipate future incidents. So we didn't make careful notes as to the dates or the order of the events. They are described here the way they happened, though not necessarily in this chronological order.

At our house on Wilson Court, when we were in the master bedroom or the main bathroom, we would often hear music. It was usually a little louder in the bathroom, which was in the middle of the house. It did not have an outside wall. The music wasn't clearly distinguishable, but sounded like the faint signal of a modern radio station or stereo without any commentary. On a couple of occasions we tried to trace the source of the music by going outside or opening windows to see if a neighbour was playing music loudly nearby, but we could hear nothing, even though we could hear the music inside these rooms before and after checking outside.

We used the middle bedroom in our house as a small study in which I had my computer set up. One evening the lights and power went out in that room. After checking the panel box, we discovered no switches had been tripped. Even more peculiar was the fact that the TV in our bedroom, which was on the same circuit as the computer, would still work. I mentioned this to my brother-in-law, who is an electrician, and he suggested there might be a short somewhere that should be checked out. We didn't follow up on his recommendation. After a couple of weeks the power mysteriously returned to the room, and we had no further problems with the power for the rest of our stay in that house.

The "spookiest" event, however, happened one night when I was not home. I was working on a special project at work that required me to stay there all night. In the middle of the night, Shirley was awakened when she felt someone leaning on her pillow and pulling her hair. At first she thought I had come home early, but when she turned to look, there was no one there. Shirley immediately called me at work to tell me what had happened, as it had given her quite a scare. When she spoke to me, Shirley told me that she had a creepy feeling that someone or something was there.

In 1992 we moved to a small home near Eganville where most of our "ghostly" experiences have happened. Shirley had a ceramic doll in the shape of a little girl who was lying on her side praying. Its mate had been broken by her abusive common-law husband in her previous relationship. On two different days, we returned home to find the doll on the shelf turned 180 degrees and facing the wall. The first time this happened I assumed she had turned the doll, perhaps while dusting it, and Shirley had assumed that I had done it for some reason or other. When we talked to each other about it, however, we both confessed that we had not touched the doll. The only explanation we could come up with was that it had been done by the ferrets. During one of their runs out of their cage they might have disturbed the doll. We couldn't really comprehend this happening, as there were several other figurines on the same shelf, none of which had been moved. Anyone who has ferrets would quickly realize that, clumsy in their investigations, some of the other figurines would certainly have been moved if not knocked off this narrow shelf.

The second time this happened, however, we noticed the dust on the glass shelf on which it sat had not been disturbed and the outline of its proper position was clearly visible. We were now certain it was not the ferrets, as we had checked the shelf frequently, particularly after their last run, so they could not have moved the doll without disturbing the dust.

Shortly after we had moved into this house, we painted the back doors and door jamb. As it was summer, we left the inside door open at all times, except at night. On the way out one day, I noticed deep scratch marks on the inside of the jamb that had recently been painted. The scratches were inside the two doors and therefore could not have been caused by an animal from outside. At that time we had not only the two pet ferrets but also a cocker spaniel puppy. It would have been impossible for any of them to have caused these scratches, as they were far too deep for even the puppy to have caused it. He just simply didn't have the weight or strength to dig that deeply into the wood. Furthermore, the scratches were probably too high for even the puppy to have reached. In fact, there are scratch marks on the door that our puppy *did* make, which are hardly visible on the paint. There is absolutely no comparison of these two scratch marks. We have not repaired the door jamb, and the scratch marks remain there to this day.

Around this time, one of our two canaries died, for no apartment reason. I buried him in a shallow grave in the backyard. A couple of weeks later, his mate also died, and I decided it would be appropriate to bury them together. I returned to the spot where I had buried the first canary to discover he was lying on top of his grave, although there was no evidence the ground had been dug up or disturbed since I had dug his grave there. Although it was starting to decay, the bird did not appear to be mutilated, as it would have been had a wild animal or neighbour's cat or dog dug it up. It would have eaten the dead bird or carried it off.

I have a bad habit of often being excessively neat and organized, to the point where I will face the canned goods in our cupboards or the beer in our refrigerator. One morning I noticed the loose change that I had left on our dresser a couple of days earlier, neatly lined up in rows of pennies, dimes, and nickels. It was something that would not be out of character for me. However, I had not done this. In fact, if I *had* lined them up, I would have placed them in neat piles, as opposed to laying them out side by side as they were. When I asked Shirley why *she* lined the coins up, she told me she had noticed them but thought I had done it.

On the top shelf in our bedroom clothes closet, we keep a box of massage oils that I use to give Shirley back rubs. Upon noticing one of the bottles sitting on Shirley's dresser, I assumed she was hinting that it had been a while since I had given her a back rub. However, when I confronted Shirley about this, again she had assumed it was *I* who had got the oil out.

By now we realized that we had a presence in our house. We affectionately named our ghost "Matthew" for no particular reason other than that it was a name that just popped into my head.

As I slept in one morning, I woke to hear my name whispered very clearly in my ear. I had been awake earlier and knew Shirley was already up, but I had fallen back to sleep. I assumed Shirley had come back into the room but I rolled over to find myself alone. I immediately got up and went to the far end of the house where Shirley was and discovered she had not been even close to that end of the house since she had risen some time earlier.

I began on occasion to see Matthew as small "wisps" of white light floating across the rooms. Most often, these sightings were made from the corner of my eye and disappeared as I snapped my head around for a better look. One night, however, as I lay awake in bed, I clearly saw Matthew float past the clothes closet. Our house was isolated in the country, where it is very dark at night. No cars were travelling down the road at the time and there was no light source that I could find that would have caused a reflection. Matthew did not appear to look like I would have imagined a "ghost" should look like, based on what I had read up to that time. However, a short while ago, I saw a television program about some people who had captured some ghosts on video. Their ghosts were very similar to Matthew, with the exception that theirs moved very quickly. There were a number of them and they were slightly larger than Matthew.

Our cocker spaniel, during this time, would often walk around the house with his nose in the air, as if following some aroma around the room.

In the bathroom, I once heard scratching coming from some spot nearby. The ferrets' cage was right beside the bathroom, so I first thought they were awake and making the noise. When I left the bathroom, however, I discovered both ferrets sound asleep. Yet the scratching continued. I didn't mention this to Shirley at the time because I was afraid we might have unwanted rodents in the crawl space, although before that time and any time since I have never found any trace of anything other than insects in the crawl space, a space that is well sealed with a concrete foundation and close-fitting doors.

Shirley has often felt a tugging on the covers at the bottom corner of the bed on her side of the house and occasionally still does. (Although we have since moved to Barrie, we continue to visit the house in Eganville whenever we can.)

In July of 1993, we moved back to Barrie to a basement apartment, where we are presently living. This Christmas past, we had a few candy canes hanging from various places, including a cardboard box which is temporarily serving as a filing cabinet for me. Shirley got up one morning to discover a candy cane, the only one different from all the others, lying in the middle of the floor. We no longer have our dog and the ferrets are locked in their cage and only allowed out for supervised periods during the day.

About a month following this incident, I got up one morning and found one of Shirley's negligees, which usually hangs on a hook in the bedroom, lying in the middle of the living-room floor, not far from where Shirley had found the candy cane.

I discussed this with a friend once, who told me that ghosts didn't normally follow people from house to house. Another friend, however, asked, "Who makes up the rules for ghosts? Can't they do just about anything they want?"

I am not suggesting that there is not a logical explanation for some of these occurrences. Furthermore, they may or may not be related to each other. I have merely made a note of them for interest's sake.

If you have any questions about these incidents, please don't hesitate to contact me at any time. Should you wish to include them in your new book, please feel free to do so.

Sincerely,
Jim Young

There Was a Story Behind It

CATHERINE P.

I have the following story from Catherine P., a resident of Hamilton, Ont., courtesy of the journalist John Mentek. He published this account in a feature titled "Ghost Stories" which appeared in the *Hamilton Spectator* on July 29, 1995. It is an interesting account because it shows how a vision that occupies but a few seconds of time may change the rest of a person's life. At the author's request I have given only the initial of her last name.

◆◆◆

I work for the Board of Education. About five years ago, I was a custodian. One summer day I was on the third floor of a school, cleaning the girls' washroom. No one else was there at the time but the caretaker and myself.

I came around the corner and saw a woman washing her hands at the sink. I thought, "The water's not running. Why is she washing her hands when the water's not running?"

I remember exactly what she was like. She had a white blouse, her hair was in a bun, she had a long skirt on. She was bent over and she had both hands underneath the faucet.

It happened in seconds, and then she was gone.

My hands, my forehead, everything just started to sweat. I walked out of the washroom, went downstairs, and said, "I'm not feeling well. I'm going home."

Later, I went and saw somebody about it, because I wasn't sure if I'd seen somebody or not. She said that I actually did see something, because even though it had only lasted for a few seconds, I have remembered what she looked to this day.

Her face was in profile. She was young, about thirty. The dress seemed old-fashioned, like the early 1920s. Her hair was brown.

When I realized that she wasn't really there, and then she was gone, I was startled, but I wasn't scared of her. It was like I wasn't really there at all, like I was looking at a scene far away from me.

There was a story behind it. She was supposed to be somebody who worked in the school and killed herself or died in an unusual way. The story is that she loved working there, and that this was her life, so she stayed.

I couldn't talk to anyone about it for three years. But when I started telling other people, they started talking about things they'd seen or heard too, and I found out that other people had seen her.

Security people say they won't go into some schools late a night. There's one where they hear children laughing in a classroom, doors slamming, and children running in the gym late at night. One man said he'd never tell anybody because they wouldn't believe him.

It Circled Behind Me

HELEN HEALY

H ere is a mood piece that by focusing on the writer's reactions requires the reader to imagine the worst. "It Circled Behind Me" was awarded first prize in *Toronto Midtown Voice*'s annual Halloween true-ghost-story contest. It was published in the October 1995 issue. Its author, Helen Healy, won a dinner for two at a downtown restaurant... compensation, but not enough perhaps, to offset the horror and fright she experienced that night in the early spring of 1990.

◆◆◆

It was early spring of 1990 when I walked out the door of that house for the last time. I sensed the dark force that had tormented me was watching me from the blackened windows, smirking, self-satisfied in its success to drive me away. I hurried on, believed that I would never return.

I first saw the house a month earlier in daylight when I jumped off the streetcar still holding the address of my new job in my hand. The old two-storey rowhouse looked ordinary enough, though a little out of place in this dreary, desolate industrial area of King Street East. It had been renovated and converted to offices, flanked on one side by an overpass and on the other by buildings inhabited only by day.

The main floor was office space for another company. The office I was shown to was on the second floor at the top of a steep staircase, off the middle of a long, narrow hallway. The door to the attic, and a room with a kitchen and bathroom, was at the back end overlooking the parking lot. An empty room, looking over the street, was at the front. The attic, I was told, was rented by a woman living in Barrie who was going to use it when in town on business.

Within minutes the day shift left and I was alone. A strange feeling of uneasiness came over me that I shrugged off as being the unfamiliar surroundings. I had begun processing the paperwork when I heard movement in the hallway right outside the door. I got up from my desk and looked up and down the hall, seeing nothing. I checked the other two rooms. My stomach was tightening as the first queasiness of fear rose in me. It had gotten dark suddenly so I switched on lights, moving faster and faster to reach every light I could find.

The shadows took on elusive forms that I couldn't quite identify. My scalp was warm and prickly as the hairs rose on the back of my neck. I knew I wasn't alone. Every step I took felt like something was right behind me, breathing, staring, gliding malevolently with hands groping for me but just out of reach.

Evil images popped rapidly into my mind like subliminal messages. I was panicking with my imagination, I told myself, and needed to get back to the safety of the office to calm down. My heart was hot and thumping wildly by the time I reached my desk. The sounds continued as I forced myself to work. I didn't dare to go to the bathroom down the hall. When my shift was over I ran from the house to the relative safety of the deserted, dark street to wait for the streetcar, not daring to look back at the house.

I needed the job so I went back every night, but each time with increasing dread. It was always the same unexpected thumps and bumps and sliding, slithering sounds along the wall, each night gaining intensity—until the last night. It was the worst.

It began with sounds of footsteps and furniture being moved and objects dropped in the attic apartment above me. Thank God, she's here, I thought, relieved that the woman from Barrie had finally moved in. I was comforted knowing another human being was near by.

Until I felt the unknown evil force coming closer and closer up the hallway. I clutched the desk as I sat frozen, facing the open doorway. I never closed the door, out of fear of seeing the horrible thing lunging at me when I opened it. My fingernails gouged into the wood. I talked out loud and sang distractedly. My entire body was tingling and buzzing like I'd stuck my finger in a light socket. My desk began vibrating and shifting. Even if I'd wanted to jump up and run, I couldn't. I was pinned in my chair by a powerful force. At the doorway I could see energy forming, whirling molecules coming together. A figure, barely perceptible, glided towards me. My eyes froze wide and I was close to passing out. I couldn't yell for help. I was paralyzed.

It circled behind me, swarming over me, and I felt fingers of electricity combing through my hair. I went blank. The next thing I remember was lunging through the door onto the street right into the woman from Barrie, who was just arriving.

I never went back. I don't know how long the woman stayed, but I know that the company moved out shortly after. Someone had discovered, concealed in a boarded-up hole in the wall in the basement, a painted pentagram and a wilted rose.

Elevator Ride

LIV M. PRAVATO

Liv is short for Livia. Livia M. Pravato lives in Weston, Ont., and submitted this true story to the Halloween issue of *Toronto's Midtown Voice*, October 1994. The scary piece was a prize-winner.

◆◆◆

It was three o'clock in the afternoon and a Monday. I was feeling fatigued and hadn't had a full break all day.

The garment company where I worked was undergoing some renovations. These were on the second floor where the main showroom and offices were located. The age of the five-storey building was evident from the chipped paint on the ceilings and walls from the old factory windows that didn't open and had been greased by companies past. The floors and stairs creaked with every step; old wood and the smell of mould surrounded you as you walked in. The elevator had a single grey door that jerked open to a view of brown panelled walls made to look like real wood. The square-shaped buttons on the control panel showed signs of use. There was a clinging brown film which encompassed clean white spots where thousands of fingers must have poked the keys to get to each floor. And as with other things that have aged, this elevator took its time and you could almost sense its "I'll get there when I'm ready" attitude.

The third and fifth floors were vacant. We were using the fourth floor as a storage area for some of our merchandise until the renovations were finished. I was the sucker who had the grand job of fetching whatever was needed from the fourth floor. It was usually quicker for me to walk up and down the stairs rather than wait for the elevator. I was so tired by the hundredth trip I couldn't help but take the elevator down. I pressed the outside key and a green light illuminated the downward arrow. I could hear the wheels and cords of the elevator slowly working to get to the fourth floor where I waited. The grey door jerked open to show the small cubicle of brown panelled walls. I stepped in and lazily leaned against the side that faced the control panel. The number two button glowed a pale yellow as I pressed it. The doors closed and I awaited my descent. I thought to myself that if this elevator broke down right now it would be a great excuse to have a break and maybe take forty winks.

The door clumsily slid open. I had started to step out when I noticed that I was still on the same floor. I jumped back in and thought to press the button again, on the off chance that I hadn't pressed it hard enough the first time. The door closed. Nothing happened. The door opened. I repeated my actions and the door closed again, then opened, then closed. It wouldn't stop! I was so confused I started pressing all the buttons for all the floors. The door wouldn't stop opening and closing.

"I was just kidding!" I yelled. "I didn't really mean for you to break down!" Finally I came to my senses and pressed the "Door Open" button. The elevator door opened and stayed that way to give me just enough time to get out. I was breathless, as I watched the elevator door quietly close and the square lights above light up, one after the other, as the elevator slowly made its way down to the basement.

I ran down the stairs, thinking that now I would surely be fired because I took so long. I planned to answer questions of why I was yelling and who I was yelling at upstairs. I walked into the showroom. A couple of customers were browsing. The manager looked up as I walked in. She said nothing.

Quickly I said, "Sorry it took me so long."

"What do you mean?" she asked curiously. "You were only up there for a few minutes."

"I was?" I said with a surprised look on my face. It had seemed like an eternity.

Nobody even heard me yelling. It was as if I had been the only person in the building at the time. I had such a strange feeling. I couldn't help but think of why the elevator would do that, right at the moment when I thought of it breaking down. Was it my imagination? Or did it really happen? Anyway, I wasn't going to take any more chances.

At five o'clock, I saw people getting on the elevator. It was working normally now. I took the stairs. There was no way I was going to go back into that elevator. Especially since I came to the conclusion that it probably knew... what I was thinking.

The Possession

KATHRYN NEWMAN

Every year, thousands of people visit the Stephen Leacock Memorial Home on Old Brewery Bay outside Orillia, Ont. The site is one of the country's leading "literary shrines," perhaps second only in attendance to L.M. Montgomery's Green Gables in Cavendish, P.E.I.

At Old Brewery Bay, the knowledgeable tour guide leads visitors through the fine old house, drawing attention to its peculiarities as well as to the foibles of its one-time owner and occupant, Stephen Leacock, who was, in his day, the country's leading humorist. Even today, half a century after his death, there are more of his books in print than those of any other Canadian author.

Leacock was a professor of economics at McGill University in Montreal, so he was able to spend only the summer months on Old Brewery Bay. Here he completed many of his articles and essays, as well as his classic collection of linked stories *Sunshine Sketches of a Little Town*. As far as I know, Leacock held no views on the subject of the afterlife, though in a number of sketches he spoofed the pretensions of spiritualists. In one comic sketch he asked the rhetorical question, "What lies 'back of beyond'?"

On a number of occasions I have joined the visitors to the site on a guided tour of the Memorial Home, and each time I learned something new about the man and about human nature. On each visit I sensed the presence of Leacock's spirit, the good spirit of bonhomie and mischief, but never that of a malicious sprite.

Could it be that the malicious sprite is the legacy of the humorist's sole child, young Stephen Lushington Leacock?

"The Possession" was written by Kathryn Newman, a Toronto journalist, for the Halloween issue of *Toronto's Midtown Voice*, October 1994. It was declared one of the winning entries.

◆◆◆

Stephen Leacock's home in Orillia is a fine sprawling old mansion stocked with memorabilia from Leacock's life.

In the spring a group of writers met to learn more about Leacock, the humorist, and to bask in the literary inspiration that oozes from the grand old house.

I had no idea that the house was haunted. However, when I first appeared on that fateful morning, I had a strange sense something was awry.

I stood outside the house and peered up at the bedroom windows. I felt I was being watched.

The moment I stepped across the threshold, I knew my instincts were right on. This house was haunted, and whoever, or whatever, was interested in me.

I was led through to the rear of the house, where the kitchen is situated.

Luckily for me, I was standing next to a writer who just happened to be psychic.

I began to feel dizzy, and the whole room began swirling. The floor was moving right under my feet. "You have to protect yourself. Build an imaginary wall of mirrors," she said.

I was aware of someone, or something, intensely evil watching me.

Something touched me. It was cold, unhuman, and the hairs on the back of my neck stood up straight. I wanted to run from the house, but I am a writer, and I just had to find out what this thing was.

I was determined to get to the bottom of this ghostly mystery.

The main hall felt cold, and I felt those unseen eyes on me once again.

I walked into Stephen Leacock Jr.'s bedroom, and I froze. A fine mist hovered over the bed. Staff had reported footsteps on the stairs ... doors opening, and closing, and many other unusual happenings. But I had never heard anything about mists.

It seems that Stephen Leacock Jr. was a person of small stature. He was known to have a rather nasty disposition, and stories tell of how he took pleasure in butchering goats on the pool table and the kitchen table.

I felt that the spirit was that of Stephen Jr., and he was angry, and haunting the bedrooms and halls of the house.

I should have left well enough alone. I should have made my very quick exit and left while I still had time.

The moment I crossed the threshold I felt a grey mass envelop me. I could not breathe. I was paralyzed. It seemed the ghost was waiting for me.

I don't remember coming down the stairs. But I was told later that I was leaping down three steps at a time. I ran out of the house and pointed an accusatory finger at my psychic companion.

"Hey you, look at me," I screeched. I was definitely not myself.

I returned to another building on the grounds where the seminar was underway. The psychic sat next to me. She was watching me all the time.

"All right," she whispered under her breath. She grabbed hold of my hand very tightly. Then she began to drive the spirit out of me.

It was a most unusual experience.

I felt the mass of evil being pushed down through my body, and a light coming in through my head.

At one point I remember an intense light entering into my body and driving the spirit out through the ground.

The psychic was mentally chasing the spirit back into the house. He was intensely angry, cursing up a storm. I felt much better after my experience. However, I was still very shaken.

I returned to the house once more that day to use the washroom before I left for the journey back to Toronto. The floor and walls began to move and to ooze a greenish substance. I ran from the house vowing never to step into Stephen Leacock's house again unless an exorcism was performed.

I was so unnerved by my experience that I slept with the light on in my room for a week.

Until recently I could not bring myself to talk or write about this incident. I felt that the ghost of Stephen Leacock Jr. might still be listening in to my thoughts and listening in on my conversation. Is he?

PART IV
EERIE, SCARY PLACES

Accounts of hauntings that have taken place on the high seas and in cities appear in earlier sections of this book. This section features hauntings that take place in unlikely places.

There are ghosts and spirits in the old castles and ancestral homes of England, Scotland, Ireland, and Wales. There are not so many castles and ancestral homes in Canada, but the few that we have boast their own supernatural inhabitants. Indeed, practically every public building that is at least a century old has its ghostly resident. Enterprising journalists, anxious to write "something scary" for Halloween, often invite psychics, mediums, and channellers to visit these buildings, walk through their halls, linger in their drawing rooms and private quarters, and then describe what they "see" or "feel." This usually produces good copy, and often surprisingly scary stories. There is a bit of this spirit in this section, which features stories about public buildings and odd and even non-existent places.

When He Came to
Life Again

PETER JONES

Much cultural lore and many of the spiritual traditions of the Ojibwa people, which would otherwise have been lost in time, were preserved in written form by Peter Jones. One of his books that is particularly valuable for the light it sheds on the native belief system is titled *History of the Ojibway Indians with Especial Reference to their Conversion to Christianity... With a Brief Memoir of the Writer and Introductory Notice by the Rev. G. Osborn, D.D., Secr. of the Wesleyan Methodist Missionary Society* (1861, 1970).

Jones was a Mississauga Indian learned in his people's traditions who became a convert to Christianity. He was converted by Methodist missionaries and, ordained a minister, he preached the social gospel among his own people. He found more comfort in the monotheism of Christianity than in the pantheism and polytheism of his native religion. "In all my fastings I never had any vision or dream," he confessed, "and, consequently, obtained no familiar god, nor a spirit of the rank of a pow-wow. What a mercy it is to know that neither our happiness nor success depends upon the supposed possession of these imaginary gods, but that there is *one* only true and living God, whose assistance none ever did, or even can, seek in vain!"

Here is a passage from Jones's book which documents or dramatizes the native notion of the afterlife, what the white man calls "the happy hunting grounds."

◆◆◆

The following story, which was communicated to me by an Indian named Netahgawineneh, will serve to illustrate the source whence they derive their absurd ideas of a future state:—

In the Indian country far west an Indian once fell into a trance, and when he came to life again, he gave the following account of his journey to the world of spirits.

"I started," said he, "my soul or spirit in company with a number of Indians who were travelling to the same spirit land. We directed our footsteps towards the sun-setting. On our journey we passed through a beautiful country, and on each side of our trail saw strawberries as large as a man's head. We ate some of them, and found them very sweet; but one of our party, who kept loitering behind, came up to us and demanded, Why were we eating a ball of fire? We tried to persuade him to the contrary, but the foolish fellow would not listen to our words, and so went on his way hungry. We travelled on until we came to a dark, swollen, and rapid river, over which was laid a log vibrating in a constant wavering motion. On this log we ventured to cross, and having arrived at the further end of it, we found that it did not reach the shore; this obliged us to spring with all our might to the land. As soon as we had done this, we perceived that the supposed log on which we had crossed was a large serpent, waving and playing with his huge body over the river. The foolish man behind was tossed about until he fell off, but he at length succeeded in swimming to shore. No sooner was he on land than a fierce and famished pack of wolves fell on him and began to tear him to pieces, and we saw him no more. We journeyed on, and by and by came within sight of the town of spirits. As soon as we made our appearance there was a great shout heard, and all our relatives ran to meet us and to welcome us to their happy country. My mother made a feast for me, and prepared everything that was pleasant to eat and to look upon; here we saw all our forefathers; and game and corn in abundance; all were happy and contented.

"After staying a short time, the Great Spirit of the place told me that I must go back to the country I had left, as the time had not yet arrived for me to dwell there. I accordingly made ready to return; and as I was leaving, my mother reproached me by all manner of foolish names for wishing to leave so lovely and beautiful a place. I took my departure, and soon found myself in the body and in the world I had left."

Unnatural Visions

Here is a quaint news report about the appearance of some strange creature or "unnatural object" at a hotel in Parkhill, Ont. It was titled "Fearful Sight," *London Daily Advertiser*, July 8, 1870. The suggestion of the newspaper writer is that not everything is as it seemed.

◆◆◆

Fearful Sight
The Devil Looking in at Parkhill
through the Bar Room Window
[From a Correspondent]

Allow me a little space in the columns of your valuable paper to describe one of the most fearful sights that ever was seen in this village, as witnessed by six or seven persons.

On the night of Thursday, June 30th, at about eleven o'clock at night, the inmates of a certain hotel in Parkhill were apparently enjoying themselves carousing, singing sacred songs, and having a regular jollification, when suddenly appeared at the bar room window a most fearful-looking object taking a look at them through the window, and more particularly at Mr. Hastings, who generally is styled "The Deacon." The size of this unnatural object was about two feet in length, and not quite as broad, covering nearly two large panes of glass; its body was smooth, having four arms or legs extended with long, slender claws, and a fifth leg emanating from its body, upon which it turned backwards and forwards on the window. Its head was rather small, but therein were placed two fiery eyes, which stared like fiery globes at the inmates of the bar room. One would think that the age of such unnatural visions had long ago passed away. The consternation and awe of the beholders of this object cannot adequately be described, particularly that of Hastings. To his horror he beheld two flaming eyes looking at him through the window. What to do in such a crisis he did not know, imagining that he was the object of pursuit, and feeling himself unprepared to accompany the old gentleman he took to his heels, and bound for the hall door, leading to the stairway; summoning all his strength and courage, the deacon with one or two such strides as he never before in his life had made, found himself at the top of a flight of stairs twenty feet long. But unfortunately for the deacon, he nearly lost his coat tail in his flight, it having come in contact with the railing. A dint of about an inch deep is said to have been left in the post.

The incident is all the talk in Parkhill; though there are those who profess to know that the object purposely placed at the window was much less formidable than the excited imagination of Hastings pictured it.

Haunted Prison

Is it surprising that prisons and jails (or gaols, as they used to be called) are believed to be haunted? After all, most places of incarceration are old buildings, and over the decades and centuries old buildings gather old stories. A well-built prison is probably the community's second oldest structure, after the church or the council hall. As well, the prison-yard around the jail often served secondary purposes: as the site of an execution on a hastily erected gallows; as the burial site for the executed prisoner. Such was the case with the gaol in Hamilton, Ont. "Haunted Cells" comes from the *Kingston Weekly*, January 14, 1884.

◆◆◆

Haunted Cells
Ghost of McConnell, Murderer,
Said to Walk in the Corridors of Hamilton Gaol

Eight years ago Michael McConnell, a Hamilton butcher, murdered Mr. Nelson Mills, a gentleman living in the West End of the ambitious city. McConnell was hanged for the crime on March 14th, 1876, and the *Hamilton Spectator* states the gaol is now believed to be haunted by the spectre of the murderer. Says the *Spectator*: With McConnell's death it might reasonably be supposed that the affair would end, but it seems that his perturbed spirit will not rest quietly beneath the cold, cold ground and stubbornly persists in haunting the east yard, and what is known as the east basement corridor. On the western side of the corridor the "black holes" or punishment cells are situated. These are small apartments provided with nothing. Prisoners are put there for six, twelve or twenty-four hours, according to the nature of the offence. Now a man might naturally be presumed to have a horror of staying in a dark and comfortless cell, but prisoners dread to go, not only for that reason, but because they declare they are haunted by the ghost of the man who was hanged on that wild March morning so many years ago. At night they say the ghost flits from room to room and tramps up and down the long corridor with a ceaseless stride. On the night of March 14th they claim that the awful scene on the scaffold is all gone over again, and a ghostly figure, with a black cap on top, falls through a trap door and dances for a minute in mid air. Then all is still. The figure straightens out, and death claims its own. The turnkey of the jail said to a *Spectator* reporter that the bravest and best prisoner in the place would cry like a child and consent to undergo any punishment sooner than be put into one of the black holes with McConnell's ghost to keep him company. But men who had never been accused of cowardice will shrink and shiver and pray not to be consigned there. Governor Henry was spoken to. He laughed at the idea and said he had never heard of it before. But, all the same, any man who had spent any part of a night in one of the black holes will tell you that McConnell's ghost keeps him company, and they all stand in mortal fear of being sent in with it.

Fire Spook

Winter fires were quite common in isolated farmhouses. So were reports of "fire spooks" and other poltergeist-like outbreaks involving combustions and conflagrations. Maybe there is too much energy in the air! "Fire Spook at Millville" appeared in the *Saint John Daily Sun*, June 7, 1888.

◆◆◆

Fire Spook at Millville
Forty-seven Fires in Forty-eight Hours
Mysterious Fires Break Up a Quiet Country Home
(Fredericton Gleaner)

The fire spook is again at large. This time it is carrying on its work of devastation in a hitherto quiet home at Holwand Ridge near Millville.

On Friday and Saturday of last week it was currently reported about town that mysterious fires, similar to the Woodstock fire mystery, had broken out in the house of Duncan Good near Millville, and was destroying his property and peace and happiness. The report, however, was not credited at the time, but has since been confirmed by eye witnesses of the mystery. The report is true enough—too true for Mr. Good's liking. It is the talk of the whole country round about and hundreds have gone to visit the scene of desolation. Mr. Estey, merchant at Millville, was among those who visited Good's place at the time the fire spook was doing its work.

He states that while he was there and examining the different places where the fire had broken out, an almanac hanging from a peg on the side of the wall suddenly caught fire, and in an instant the almanac was enveloped in flames. He stood aghast. He was informed that that was the 47th fire that had thus mysteriously occurred during the 48 hours previous to his visit. Curtains, bed clothing, cushions, carpets, books, articles of clothing, had alike been visited by the fire spook. The fires, however, occurred only in the daytime, and when they were least expected. Nor were the mysterious fires confined to the house, but the barns and outbuildings were also haunted by the strange visitant, one of the barns being totally consumed by the fire spook.

Mr. Pinder, of Nackawick, was also an eyewitness of one of the unaccountable fires and has many remarkable stories to tell about its work. During Wednesday of last week the fire fiend proved the most destructive, fire breaking out in nearly every hour of the day; first in the house, then in the barns or some of the outbuildings.

Our Millville correspondent writes under the date of June 1st:

At last we have a thorough sensation, all our own, which looks as if it might have the effect of giving us a world-wide celebrity. On Howland or Beckwith Ridge, some two miles east of this village, live a family named Good, who have for years been working and living along the same as the rest of us poor mortals, with nothing pointing to the great celebrity they are now enjoying. This sylvan quietness was broken suddenly last Monday by the appearance of fire in their dwelling, which was easily extinguished, but this forerunner was followed on the following day by the breaking out of fires, very mysteriously, in different parts of their dwelling, consuming clothing, bedding, papers, etc., in fact of whatever appeared to be of an inflammatory nature. This continued all through Tuesday and Wednesday, until the family were compelled to remove from the dwelling. One of the odd phases of the affair is that the fire does not catch at night, or while anyone is looking for it.

On Thursday, about one o'clock, their barn caught and was consumed, with some farming implements and about six tons of hay.

Mr. Good, in describing the fire in the barn to your correspondent, said it appeared to flame up instantly, and in an inconceivably short time the flames burst from every quarter. The fire resembles very much the burning which caused so much excitement in Woodstock about a year ago.

The inhabitants, for miles around, have visited the scene, and it is rather amusing to listen to the different causes assigned for this. It may well be styled mysterious fire, witchcraft, visitants from the world of spirits, judgements for sins, &c. It appears to have brought to the surface all the latent superstition natural to the natural man. The most sensible reason, according to my mind, and I have minutely examined the premises, is put forth by Mr. Earle, railway agent here, who claims it is caused by the escape of natural gases only inflammable when coming in contact with certain gases contained in the atmosphere we breathe. Let the cause be what it may, it is certainly to us mysterious.

Your correspondent would very much like to see the matter thoroughly investigated by scientists, and a preventive found.

Mr. Good's loss will be quite a serious one to him, and take years of patient toil and frugality to replace.

A Subterranean Story

CHARLES HOWARD SINN

"**A** Subterranean Story" appeared in the columns of the *Manitoba Daily Free Press*, Winnipeg, April 22, 1890. It was written by one Charles Howard Sinn and was reprinted from the *Washington Critic*. It is a lost-race story with a Canadian locale. The style is such as to convey a semblance of verisimilitude. No doubt it delighted Manitoba readers at the time of its publication.

This tale bears some resemblances to a novel of fantastic adventure published in *Harper's* in 1888. I am thinking of James De Mille's *A Strange Manuscript Found in a Copper Cylinder*, which was composed about the same time that Sinn was writing this narrative. But Sinn's tale will never rival De Mille's for drama or imagination. But then De Mille's tale is fiction, and Sinn's is fact... or is it?

Here there are possible references to the Columbia River and to Mount Assiniboine, the highest mountain in the Rocky Mountain chain, which is situated on the Continental Divide between the present-day Trans-Canada Highway and the U.S. border.

◆◆◆

Last summer the schooner *William Haley*, of Galveston, trading among the West Indies, was becalmed near the Gulf Stream. The second day the captain's curiosity was aroused by a strange floating mass, and he ordered the mate to take a boat and examine it. The mate returned towing a log, from which the men had cut away the marine growth which had made it seem at a distance like a sea monster. The captain ordered it to be hoisted to the deck, declaring that in forty years spent at sea he had never found anything like it.

When laid on the deck it was seen to be about twenty feet long and two feet in diameter. It was of some very hard, dark-coloured wood, like palm, charred in places, and worn and broken, cut and torn, as if it had been whirled through torrents and maelstroms for hundreds of years. The ends were pointed, and five bands of dark metal, like bronze, were sunk in the wood, and the whole bore evidence of having passed through intense heat. On closer examination the log was seen to consist of two parts, and these bands were to bind it together. The captain had the bands cut, and in the exact center, fitted into a cavity, was a round stone eighteen inches in diameter. The rest of the wood was solid.

The captain, more disappointed at this result than he cared to confess, picked up the stone wand and was greatly astonished at its lightness. Examining it more closely, he remembered that when a boy on the old New Hampshire farm he used to find hollow stones with crystals in them—geodes, as he afterwards heard them called. This was probably a geode, placed in this strange receptacle for some unknown purpose. He carried it to his cabin and put it into his chest.

Two months later the old captain returned to his cottage on Galveston Bay and placed among his curiosities the geode he had so strangely found in the Gulf Stream. One day he studied it again, and the sunlight chanced to fall upon a narrow, irregular line.

"I declare," said the old man, "it looks like as if this stone had been patched together!"

He struck it with a hammer and it fell apart and proved to be filled with small pieces of yellowish brown wood. The shell of the stone was about an inch thick, studded over inside with thousands of garnet crystals. It had been broken into three parts and fastened together again with some sort of cement which showed plainly on the inside.

The old captain poured the pieces of wood on the table. They were perfectly dry and hard. They seemed like strips of bamboo and were numbered and covered with writing, made by pricking marks with some sharp instrument like an awl. He found the first piece of wood and began to read, for it was in English. The work of deciphering the tiny dents on the bits of wood soon became the captain's chief occupation. He copied each sentence off in his old log book as fast as it was made out. Five or six sentences were about all his eyes would stand without a rest, so that it was a long time before the narrative was at all complete. The narrative runs as follows:

Heart of the Rockies,
About Sept. 17, 1886

I am an American, Timothy Parsons, of Machias, Me. I have no living relatives. I write this in a vast vaulted chamber, hewn from the solid granite by some prehistoric race. I have been for months a wanderer in these subterranean spaces, and now I have contrived a way to send my message out to the world that I shall probably never see again. If some miner, tunneling in the Rockies, comes upon a vaulted chamber, with heaps of ancient weapons of bronze, bars of gold and precious stones that no man may number, let him give Christian burial to the poor human bones that lie in this horrible treasure house. He will find all that is left of my mortal frame near the great ever-burning lamp, under the dome of the central hall. That lamp is fed from some reservoir of natural gas. It was lighted when I came, months ago. For all I know otherwise, it has burned there for thousands of years.

The entrance to this sub-montane river is in the Assinaboine mountains, north of the United States lines. I was a prospector there for several years, and I heard stories among the older Indians that a river greater than the Columbus had once flown where the Rocky mountains now are; that the Great Spirit had piled the mountains over it and buried it deep underground. At last a medicine man, whose life I had once saved, told me that he knew how to get to the river, and he took me into a cavern in a deep gorge. Here we lived for a week, exploring by means of pine torches, and at last found a passage which ran steadily downward. This, the Indian told me, was the path by which his ancestors, who once lived in the middle of the earth, had found their way to the light of day.

I think we were about 3,000 feet below the entrance of the cave, when we began to hear the sound of roaring waters. The sound increased until we stood by an underground river, of whose width and depth we could form no ideas. The light of our torches did not even reveal the height of the roof overhead. My guide told me that this was the mother of all the rivers of the world. No other person except himself knew of its existence. It flowed from the end of the north to the extreme south. It grew ever warmer and warmer. There was a time when the people lived along its channel, and there were houses and cities of the dead there and many strange things. It was full of fish without eyes and they were good to eat. If I could help him build a raft he would float with me down this river. The old, old stories said that no one could go upon it for many miles. It ran down a hollow under the mountains.

We built and equipped our raft and launched it on the most foolhardy adventure, I do believe, that ever occupied the attention of men. We lit torches and set them in sockets on the raft, and we were well armed. For two weeks we moved down the high archway at a steady rate of only about three miles an hour. The average width of the stream was about 500 feet, but at times it widened out to almost twice that. It swarmed with many kinds of fish, and they were very easy to secure. The rock walls and roof seemed to be of solid granite. We were below the latter formations.

As nearly as I can calculate we were about 1,000 miles from where our voyage began, and nothing had yet happened to disturb its monotony, when we began to find traces of ancient work and workers. An angle in the wall was hewn into a Titanic figure; at another point there seemed to be regular windows, and a dwelling was perched far up in the granite dome.

The Indian told me more of the traditions of his race as we drifted past these things. "They were very great people who lived here. They had many things; they knew more than the white men. They are all dead now." And I gathered from his chance remarks that he thought they had left secrets in their cave dwellings which would make him the biggest Indian on the continent if he could discover them.

Suddenly we found that the river was flowing much faster, and we failed to check our raft. We went over a waterfall, perhaps 70 feet high, and were thrown on a shelf of rock at the side of the river below. I was unhurt, but my companion was so badly injured that he died in a few hours. I repaired the raft after a fashion and continued the voyage, finding it impossible to contrive any way to scale the sides of the waterfall and attempt a return. All our torches were lost, and the attempt to proceed further seemed but the last act of despair. A few hours later I saw a light gleam over the river in a very remarkable way, shining clear across, as if from the headlight of a locomotive high up on the wall. This aroused me somewhat from my stupor and misery. I sat up on the raft and steered it close to the edge of the river to see what wonderful thing had happened.

As I came nearer I saw that an irregular hole was in the wall 1,000 feet above the water, and the light shone out through it. It was a cheerful thing to look at, and I hung to the granite and shouted, but to no effect. Then I saw a broken place in the wall a little further down, and let the raft drift along to the base of a broad though much worn and broken flight of steps winding up the cliff. That brought me at last to the place of the light, a domed hall overlooking the river, hewn out of the rock and having in its centre a metal basin with a jet of natural gas. I have had to cut off a part of this metal basin since, but I have not harmed the inscriptions. There are many gas jets, but in the other chambers I have had to light them.

I have lived here for months, and I have explored all the chambers of the place. There is no escape, so far as I can see. The river, 20 miles below, plunges down vaster descents, and the water gets so hot that I should be boiled alive if I tried the voyage. I have discovered a log of tropic wood like palm and a geode in which I can send a message to the world of sunlight. Perhaps this will get through the fires and float to the surface somewhere. I am convinced that the river which brought me here flows on into the Gulf of Mexico, and that sooner or later my log will be picked up. Perhaps this river is really the source of the Gulf Stream.

I will not write down my discoveries, not in their order, but as a whole. My story must be brief, or this scant means of record will fail me.

This place seems to have been approached only by the river. It consists of six large, domed halls, connected with a seventh, in which the light burns. There are swords of bronze, spearheads and other weapons stored in one chamber. There have been costly fabrics also, but they have perished, and only a few fragments are left. In another hall are many treasures accumulated.

One hall is especially the hall of pictures and of writing. I spend many hours there. I see the history of this race—their wars, their heroes, their mythology.

The most wonderful chamber of all is the hall to the north. That is the chamber of death and silence. When first I entered this hall I lighted all the gas jets. Around the walls were high cases of drawers and on the front of each was a portrait. I examined them for hours before I felt any desire to do more. Among them I observed a very beautiful face—that of a young girl just entering womanhood. This wonderful race possessed the highest artistic skill and delicacy of expression. The face of this girl, except that the colors had faded, might have been the admired master-piece of the Paris Salon. I felt a sudden interest in the face and caught the drawer handles and pulled it out. In the wide, deep space into which I looked lay, robed in white, her hands folded, the form of the girl whose picture was outside. How beautiful she was. She lay as if only asleep. Then slowly, as I looked, the whole figure melted down and faded away to a pile of dust. I closed the shrine and touched no more of them, but I often go and look at the faded painting and think how lovely the girl was.

The paintings on the walls of this mural chamber show that the people had two systems of disposing of their dead. The great mass were consigned to the river, but the bodies of all those who were famous for beauty, wisdom or any good quality were preserved by a process of embalming, which they evidently thought would make them endure for ages. There are probably 12,000 separate bodies here, and they represent more than 20 successive generations, if I rightly understand the system of family grouping. If people lived as long as they do now, there was an average of about 15 additions each year to this great Westminster Abbey of the past. From a sort of map painted on one of the walls I obtain the idea of many and thickly populated communities which used this place as the sepulcher of their chosen few.

Evidently that was before volcanic outbursts made the channel of the river like a cauldron boiling over endless fires. All along the course are towns marked, groups of rock-hewn rooms on the cliffs, populated lands on the river, promontories from whose sides fountains of light seemed to spring. Did thousands of people once live and find happiness in these vast vaults of death? Things must have been very different then from now. They must have had many reservoirs of natural gas. The animal life in the river must have been much more varied. Indeed, there are pictures in the Hall of War, as I have named it, that show two things plainly—that there were thousands of caverns extending over hundreds of miles, and peopled by animals with which the heroes fought, and that the river was swarming with existence.

Moreover, I find everywhere, chief of the symbols of life, in the most sacred places, a food root like a water nut, from which grew white leaves and seeds. There must have been some electric principle evolved here, by the vast warm lakes of the river, lit with soft light everywhere at certain seasons. For now I come to the strangest fact of all that I gather from the records of the race; these people had two kinds of light: one they found and lit—that they knew as the lesser God of Life; the other, coming from north to south, twice each year, filled for many weeks the whole channel of the river, from depth to dome, making the very water translucent. The water root and its grain ripened and were harvested in the last days of the light. Two crops a year they gathered, and held their days of the feasts of the great God of Life.

I have tried to put together all I can of their picture writings and their paintings, so as to understand what sort of men and women they were. I confess that I have learned to admire them greatly. They were a strong, brave, loving and beautiful people. I am sorry they are all gone. I never cared half as much about the dead Etruscans or Carthaginians. The earliest chapter in their history, so far as I discover, is a picture of a line of men and women descending into a cave and a dragon pursuing them. This seems to point to a former residence on the face of the earth, and to some disaster—war, flood, pestilence or some fierce monster—which drove the survivors into the depths of the earth for shelter.

But all these thoughts are vain and foolish. I have explored the cliffs of the river and the walls of the mighty halls which shelter me. I have attempted to cut a tunnel upward past the waterfall, using the ancient weapons which lie in such numbers on the floor. The bronze wears out fast, but if I live long enough something may be done. I will close my record and launch it down the river. Then I may try to cut my way out to the sunlight.

Here the story closed. Some day, perhaps, an old man, white-haired and pale as one from the lowest dungeon of a bastille, will climb slowly out of some canyon of the Rockies to tell the world more about his discovery of a lost race.—Charles Howard Sinn, in *Washington Critic*.

A True Ghost Story

These days people enjoy reading long, scary novels by writers of horror fiction like Stephen King. A century ago people found they enjoyed devoting an hour or so of an evening to reading told-as-true reports of ghostly visitations. These appeared in the columns of their daily and weekly newspapers.

Here is one such ghost story. It was written more than a hundred years ago in the leisured style of the period. It tells a fulfilling tale of a death followed by a form of rebirth which in turn is followed by a redemption of sorts. It is strangely comforting.

It was titled "A True Ghost Story" on its initial appearance in the *Moose Jaw Times*, October 4, 1895.

◆◆◆

Not many years ago, people used to sneer at ghosts and ghost stories much more than they do now, and one would constantly hear people whisper to one another (while some individual was relating his or her experience): "Ah! it is very odd that these ghost stories should always be related at second or third hand. Now, I want to see a person who personally has seen the ghost, and then I will believe!"

Yes! People are more accustomed to hearing about ghosts now; and yet, even now, should it be a wife, daughter, or sister who ventures to narrate some supernatural experience, she is pooh-poohed, or laughed at, or told to "take a pill."

Now, I have seen a ghost—and am prepared to attest most solemnly to the fact, as well as to the truth of every word here set down. I have, of course, avoided names, but nothing else; so, without further preamble, I will state my case.

Some years ago I became the object of the infatuated adoration of a person of my own age and sex; and I use the word "infatuated" advisedly, because I feel now, as I did at the time, that neither I nor any mortal that ever lived could possibly be worthy of the overwhelming affection which my poor friend lavished upon me. I, on the other side, was not ungrateful towards her, for I loved her in return very dearly; but when I explain that I was a wife and the mother of young children, and that she was unmarried, it will easily be understood that our devotion to each other must of necessity be rather one-sided; and this fact caused some dispeace between us at times.

For many years my friend held a post at Court, which she resigned soon after she began to know me; and although her Royal Mistress, in her gracious kindness, assigned two houses to her, she gave them both up, to be free to live near me in B———; indeed, she gave up relatives, old servants and comforts in order that she might come and live (and die, alas!) in lodgings, over a shop, near me. But she was not happy. She "gloomed" over the inevitable fact that, in consequence of the difference in her home-circumstances and mine, I could not be with her every day, and all day long. I think she was naturally of an unhappy disposition, being deeply, passionately, and unjustifiably jealous, and also painfully incapable of taking things and people as they were. All this gave me often much annoyance; but we were, all the same, sometimes very cheerful and happy together, and sometimes—the reverse.

Later on, she, poor soul, was taken ill, and during months of fluctuating health I nursed her—sometimes in hope, sometimes without—and at moments during her illness she found strange comfort in foretelling to me, after the most "uncanny" fashion, things which she declared would happen to me after her death. They were mostly trivialities—little episodes concerning people and things over whom and which we had talked and laughed together, for she was gifted with a keen sense of the ridiculous.

Amongst other things, she said to me one afternoon:—

"This bazaar for which we are working," (she had been helping me for weeks for a charity bazaar, and I can now see her dainty little hands, as she manipulated the delicate muslin and lace. Poor, poor L——!) "I shall be dead before it takes place, and I shall see you at your stall, and on one of the days of the bazaar, an old lady will come up to you and say: 'Have you any of poor Miss L——'s work?' (mentioning me). And you will answer, 'Yes! here is some!' and you will show her this which I am working, and she'll say, 'Have you any more?' and you'll say 'Yes' again; and she'll carry it all off, and say she buys it for 'poor Miss L——'s sake.' And I shall know and see it all!"

I remember repeating, wonderingly, "What lady?"

She answered dreamily, "Oh! I don't know—but—some old lady! You'll see!"

And I am bound to say, this is exactly what occurred at the bazaar, months after her death; an old lady, with whom I was not acquainted, did buy all her work, having asked for it, and carrying it away "for her sake!" An old lady, too, whom I had never seen.

One other curious circumstance which attended her death was that, after looking forward with more than usual pleasure to my coming birthday (which she said would be "a more than commonly happy anniversary"), that was the very day on which she died!

I think that one of the sharpest regrets which I ever experienced in my life consisted in the fact that I was not with my dearest friend at the moment that she passed away. She had made me promise that I would be with her at the time, and, God knows, I had the fullest intention of fulfilling her wish, but on that very evening, of all others, I was called away, and she died in my absence. I had been sitting by her bed-side all the afternoon, and all that evening I had held her dear hand, and had kept whispering comforting words in her ear; but latterly she had made no response, and was, seemingly, unconscious.

Suddenly a messenger came from my house (not a hundred yards, it was, away), saying my husband wanted me at once, as one of my children was ill. I looked at the nurse, who assured me there was "nothing immediate" impending; so, stooping over my poor friend, I whispered—at the same time pressing a kiss on her forehead—that "half an hour should see me at her side again." But she took no notice, and much against my will I hastily, and noiselessly, left the room.

Throwing a shawl over my head I hurried across the square, and as I passed the church the clock struck twelve, and I suddenly remembered that—today was my birthday!

I got back in less than half an hour, and on my return heard, to my everlasting sorrow, that I had not been gone ten minutes before my dear L—— became restless and uneasy, then suddenly starting up in her bed, she looked hastily around the room, gave a cry, then there came a rush of blood to her mouth, and after a few painful struggles, she sank back, gasped once or twice, and never moved again.

Of course, I thought then, and do to this day, that she was looking round the room for me, and that she had died feeling I had broken my faith with her. A bitter, never-failing regret!

I have given this slight sketch of the feelings which existed between me and my poor friend (before narrating the circumstances of her supernatural visit to me), just to emphasize the facts of the alluring fascination, the intense affection, which existed between us during her life-time, and which, I firmly believe, have lasted beyond her grave.

Quite a year and a half after her death, my poor L——, with what motive I know not (unless it may have been, as I sometimes fondly hope, to assure me that she understood and sympathized with my sorrow at my having failed her at the moment of her extremity), appeared to me the same once—but never again. It occurred thus:—

I had been suffering all day from brow ague, and had gone early to bed—but not to sleep. All the evening I had been kept painfully awake by that same church clock which I have mentioned above. It seemed to strike oftener, louder, and more slowly than any clock I had ever had the misfortune to come across. Of course, my ailment of the moment caused the clock's vagaries to appear peculiarly painful, and I bore the annoyance very restlessly, with my face turned pettishly to the wall; but when the midnight hour began to chime, I felt as though I could bear it no longer. Muttering an impatient exclamation, I turned in my bed, so as to face the room, and looking across it, I saw my poor L——, standing close to a screen between me and the door, looking at me.

She was in her usual dress, wearing (what was then called) a "cross-over," which was tied behind; while her bonnet (which she was always in the habit of taking off as she came upstairs) was, as usual, hanging by the ribbon, on her arm. She had a smile on her face, and I distinctly noticed her lovely little white ears, which were always my admiration, and which were only half covered by her soft brown hair.

She stood—a minute it seemed—looking at me, then she glided towards me, and I, half-apprehensive that she was about to throw herself on my bed, exclaimed, jumping up in a sitting posture:—

"Dearest! what brings you here so late?"

With deep reverence be it spoken; but as soon as these words were out of my mouth I was irresistibly reminded of those spoken (Holy Writ tell us) by Saint Peter at the awful moment of the Transfiguration! Awed and dazed at the sight of the spiritual visitants, we are told he uttered words "not knowing what he said." These words of mine also seemed to leap to my lips, but with little meaning in them—if any.

As soon, however, as my voice had ceased, the apparition disappeared, and I remained some moments motionless.

One of the most curious features of the case is that, although I was very especially restless and awake at the moment of the appearance, I recognised my friend so completely, that I forgot also to recognise the fact that she had died; or, rather, it happened too quickly for me to bring that fact to mind. Indeed, it all took place in such a flash—in such a moment of time—so much quicker than I can tell it—and she looked so exactly like her well-known self, and that till she had disappeared, I really believed I was seeing her in the flesh! Of course, as soon as I had time to reflect, I remembered, and realized what it was I had seen!

I was not frightened, but I felt colder than I had ever felt in my life, and I have never felt so cold since, but the moisture seemed to pour off my body. I called no one to my assistance; all I realized was that God had permitted me to see her once more, and that perhaps He might send her to me again. But He has not done so, and, probably, now, He never will.

I lay awake all night afterwards, hoping for—and, I think, almost expecting—her again, and after the day had dawned I fell asleep.

Before telling my story to anyone, and dreading unspeakably all the doubting and sarcastic speeches which such a narration would inevitably call forth, I sent for my doctor, an old and trusted friend, and after making him talk rationally to me for some time, I asked him whether he considered me in an exalted state, or whether I had ever betrayed any hysterical tendencies. He reassured me heartily on these points, and then asked my reasons for such questionings. I thereupon opened my heart to him, and he neither ridiculed nor disbelieved, but, on the contrary, told me another case of the same kind which had lately happened to a friend of his; but he strongly advised me to keep my own council at present (which I did for some time), and kindly added that he did not look upon me as a lunatic, but simply as a woman for whom one corner of the curtain which guarded the unseen had been lifted.

In conclusion, I repeat I am ready to vouch for the truth of every word here set down, and also, should it be required, to give names—in private—to satisfy those who doubt.

The Train Was Late

Here is an account of a premonition of an impending disaster with a railway train, one that took the form of a mirage. "A Northern Mirage" appeared in the *Calgary Herald*, May 28, 1898. Apparently a longer version was published in the *Daily News*, London, England.

◆◆◆

A Northern Mirage
The Strange Experience of a Traveller in Winnipeg

There was a railway collision in England recently, after which the signalman who was brought to book for it asserted that he was sure the train had passed what afterward came up and caused the damage. Apropos of which statement, a correspondent sends the London *Daily News* this extract from a letter he had received from his son in Winnipeg:

> Arrived at Shanawan, my companion kindly offered to stay with me till the train came, but I set him off and took my stand on the track with nothing more substantial than a telegraph pole to shelter me from the icy blast. When I was left alone—sky overcast, curious kinds of mist in the air, the two farmhouses mentioned above out of sight, the wind howling around me, and the loose snow that the wind raised from the prairie driving past me in sheets, I thought it about as desolate a picture as I have ever set eyes on. As luck would have it, the train was late, and I had fifty minutes in which to enjoy myself alone. I was never so abjectly cold as when the train eventually came. I was rewarded by seeing a curious atmospheric phenomenon that I used to read of as

tantalizing weary travellers in the Sahara, and that, I am told, is common here under certain conditions, viz., the mirage. At least fifteen minutes before the train arrived I saw it suddenly leap into sight in a way that made me pick up my bag and hop off the track in double-quick time. Then I waved my handkerchief for it to stop, and suddenly I noticed that it had stopped about fifty yards off. I began to charge up the track so as to get on board, when it mysteriously and suddenly disappeared. A few minutes later I saw it again, only this time off the track, and running along the prairies. It gave me quite an eerie feeling, and I began to think that the cold had got into my head, and I cast superstitious glances around me to see if there were any more trains frolicking about in the snow, and suddenly I bethought me of what I had heard about the mirage. When I saw distinctly that the train had stopped, it must have been at Lasam, [the] nearest station, about nine or ten miles up the line.

This Ill-fated Engine

This is the story of a haunted locomotive engine. It seems an unlikely subject, but in my files there are stories about haunted engines, haunted railway cars, haunted stretches of track, haunted railway tunnels, and even a haunted roundhouse. This news story appeared as "A Haunted Locomotive on the Intercolonial," *St. John's Daily News*, St. John's, Nfld., December 9, 1904.

◆◆◆

A Haunted Locomotive on the Intercolonial
Engine 239—The Man Killer—
Said to Be Infested with a Ghostly Visitor—
Several Engineers Have Been Killed on Her—
Has Unenviable Record

Has the I.C.R. a haunted engine?

This question is agitating the minds of the public generally, and particularly the knights of the throttle and their assistants in the cab who are employed on the government railway.

Is 239 haunted?

Is this ill-fated engine hooded?

The general opinion of I.C.R. men is that she is, and this particular locomotive is now looked upon with fear and trembling.

Superstition has its devotees in every calling of life. At the cradle the anxious mother will be heard saying, "The goblins will catch you if you don't watch out." Time goes on and as one enters the state of manhood he has his misgiving, his forebodings, governed by his superstitious make-up; the sailors at sea, the soldier in the battlefield, the ordinary individual in everyday life—each has his problems in this respect.

Probably no calling has more cause for superstition than that of the man in front, or in other words, the man who handles the throttle and lever, and to whose exactness, wisdom and foresight is entrusted the lives of the travelling public.

Coming back to the direct basis of these few preliminary remarks, no doubt the past history of engine No. 392 will be read with interest.

It is said, and on good authority, that since the construction of this locomotive for the I.C.R. several fatalities are recorded. Trainmen, and the public generally, remember the disaster at Belmont when Sam Trider, who for 30-odd years ran an engine between Moncton and Truro, met his death. The train on this occasion was running by Belmont station. Suddenly there was a smash and a general mix-up. No. 239 had left the rails. From what cause is as yet a mystery. She swayed to and fro and suddenly lunged to the right, toppling over.

Fireman Harry Campbell was thrown through the cab window and landed in a pile of snow dazed but uninjured, while Sam Trider, the engineer, met death at his post.

Again, 239 was in the wreck at Windsor Jct. In this, Driver Wall, an old and trusted I.C.R. man, lost his life. It was late in the evening and a C.P.R. train driven by Wall, and the freight from Halifax with Driver Mel Copeland, were to cross at the junction. Copeland passed the semaphore and danger signals, and the crash came. Four persons including Driver Wall were killed and several more or less injured. Upwards of 70 cars were derailed, many being dashed over the embankment and smashed into kindling wood.

On another occasion, No. 239 jumped the rail at Humphrey's mills and the driver and firemen miraculously escaped death or at least serious injury. Again, north of Moncton, she met with a serious mishap.

After each accident she was sent to the Moncton shops and repaired, and the query was frequently voiced by I.C.R. men, "Who will be her next victim?"

At all events, even the I.C.R. roundhouse cleaners at Moncton have a great aversion to working on 239. A story of a somewhat ghostly character is told.

It is reported that not long ago a cleaner, while doing some work around a locomotive, casually glanced into the cab, says that he saw a man standing at the throttle. Not having seen anyone enter the cab he hailed the supposed driver, and receiving no reply, again looked in, but the man had vanished. He made immediate enquiries, but nearby workmen had not seen anyone entering or leaving the cab.

The cleaner in question is positive that he saw a man there, and no argument can alter his opinion.

At all events the general opinion among the men is that 239 should now be consigned to the scrap heap.

Repairs and renovations to this locomotive during her career on the I.C.R. have gone to prove her a veritable white elephant.

The engine has been in the service of the I.C.R. for some two years and her record is an unenviable one.

The North Pole

Are the world's polar regions occupied by members of lost races or tribes? The wastes of the Arctic and the Antarctic are often depicted as safe havens, oasis-like regions that have supported colonies of civilized peoples otherwise unknown to history. These polar worlds are well known in the "lost race" novels familiar to readers of fantastic literature. They are frequently called travellers' tales.

Here is one such traveller's tale—in part a survivor's tale—of a journey made to an inaccessible place where there are incredible wonders to behold. "Saw North Pole" appeared in the *St. John Daily Sun*, Saint John, N.B., March 28, 1900. The name of the French Canadian adventurer is spelled "Le Joie" in the subheading and "La Joie" in the newspaper story itself. The story originally appeared in the *New York Herald*, a newspaper noted for publishing bizarre or highly imaginative tales that were said to be true. At the time of its publication, there was unprecedented interest in the competing claims of those adventurers who boasted that they—and not Peary or Cook—were the first explorers to "attain" the North Pole.

◆◆◆

Saw North Pole
Strange Story of a Trapper—
Joseph Z. Le Joie, a French Canadian,
Excites Interest of Scientists by Claim
That He Visited "Farthest North" and Found New Race

New York, March 18:—Joseph Zotique La Joie says that he discovered the north pole and a new race of people. He is a French-Canadian hunter and trapper, who has spent many years in the Arctic regions. His story is a marvellous one. By the request of the *New York Herald*, and accompanied by one of the *New York Herald*'s reporters, he went on Wednesday last to Washington. He courted scientific investigation of his stories, and they are now being scientifically investigated.

At the Hotel Raleigh in Washington on Wednesday last Mr. La Joie met General A.W. Greely, chief of the signal service and an Arctic explorer of great fame; Admiral George W. Melville of the United States navy (retired), of whom Melville Island is named and who is recognized as one of the greatest living authorities on Arctic matters; Professor J.W. McGee of the Smithsonian Institution, of world wide celebrity as an ethnologist, and other great scientists. Not one of these scientists is willing to unqualifiedly endorse the statements made by M. La Joie. All have found in his explanations some apparent inconsistencies, but all have also found in them much accuracy concerning matters with which they are well acquainted.

On the whole, it seems that there is probably considerable truth in the strange stories told by M. La Joie. That the man penetrated far into the Arctic is certain. He claims to be able to substantiate all of his amazing statements by producing relics of the new race of people which he found in the "farthest north," and even by showing the bodies of two natives of this strange tribe, which he says are cached within comparatively easy access.

In December, 1886, according to his narrative, La Joie and his father started from Montreal for Battleford, Northwest Territory. After three years' hunting through British Columbia and Alaska he arrived at Great Bear Lake in the fall of 1889. Game having grown scarce, he determined to push further north with a partner, a man named George White. Toward the spring of 1892 they found themselves near Cape Brianard. Hunting in this vicinity, they learned from the natives of an iron post left by some explorer. On this they found the following marks: "82 degrees latitude north, 83 degrees longitude west."

To the north of this a few miles they made their camp in May, 1892. This camp was established at the junction of two immense icebergs, and White proposed that they separate and each take a ten days' journey on three diverging points of ice to find the best hunting ground. La

Joie, while returning, felt on the seventh day a tremendous shock like an earthquake. It meant that the ice had parted and that he was adrift. Admiral Melville, the other day in Washington, agreed that La Joie's description of the phenomenon was accurate. The berg drifted to the north. For three days he lived on fish, hoping against hope that a wind that had sprung up from the south would drive him back to the mainland. For a period of thirty-six days he was adrift, he says, amid terrible storms of snow, hail and sleet. Land was sighted on several occasions, but he was unable to get ashore. On the morning of the thirty-seventh day, having eaten six of his dogs and suffered many torments, La Joie found that the berg on which he had drifted had touched land. He got ashore with his remaining dogs. He says that the farther north the berg drifted the milder became the climate.

That night La Joie was awakened by the barking of his dogs. He jumped to his feet and found that he was surrounded by a tribe of copper-colored natives, who were shooting at him with bows and arrows. La Joie was armed only with a knife and a club, but his double suit of skin protected him from the arrows. The next day they were willing to treat for peace.

He describes the men whom he joined as belonging to a strange race, speaking a tongue entirely unlike that of the other natives whom he had met in his travels. Their complexion, he states, was of a reddish-brown hue, and their eyes and hair were either black or brown. The men were very large, averaging more than six feet in height. Their clothes were made of skins and shaped after a strange fashion. He remained in the camp five months. The party, having concluded the hunt in which they were engaged, took La Joie with them to their principal settlement, a five days' journey across a rocky country. They came finally to the entrance to a great cave. The sub-chief in charge of the party summoned to the mouth of the cave the great chief of all the tribes which inhabit that country. The leader scrutinized the stranger for a period of five minutes, and then said something to his people in their native language. The stranger, thinking that they were about to kill him, turned and ran until out of the range of arrows, then, stopping, he took from his pocket a flint and a steel. With these he struck fire. La Joie gathered some twigs and built a fire. For a few minutes the natives watched him, and then approached, threw down their bows and arrows, and indicated that they wished to be friends. They had known nothing of fire previously.

La Joie states that he soon came to live with the natives on terms of the most friendly intercourse. Owing to the reverence in which he was held, they made him, he says, the chief and ruler of the tribe, a position he held for two years. Since his arrival on the island La Joie's attention had been repeatedly attracted by a strange and apparently volcanic light. This shone forth steadily at all times, casting an effulgent glowing over the surrounding country. La Joie determined to investigate. He finally set forth with a party of natives and came within full view of the great mountain from which the light seemed to come. Here he discovered what he firmly believes to be the north pole.

A Fable Turned Fact

TOM HYLAND

When I was researching the book that was eventually published as *Haunted Toronto*, I realized the text should be illustrated with photographs of the interior and exterior of the Church of St. Mary Magdalene. I had none, and this was a shame. The church, which is located near Harbord and Bathurst Streets in Toronto, has a notable musical tradition as well as a notable spirit, and both of these involve one man: Healey Willan. I wanted to do it proud.

Members of the congregation cherish the memory of Dr. Willan, who was for much of his professional life their resident organist and choral conductor. Lovers of serious music across Canada respect his legacy as a leading composer and musician. It is no secret that Dr. Willan said that on a number of occasions he was astonished to behold "the grey lady" in the church when he knew no one was there!

My need for photographs led me to Tom Hyland, a long-time member of the gallery choir of the church and a close friend of Dr. Willan's. Tom was a character in his own right. Until his retirement he was employed in the photography department at Eaton's downtown store. A skilled photographer, he showed me his sensitive black-and-white portraits of Dr. Willan and also a number of fine atmospheric shots of the church's interior. He allowed me to reproduce a group of these in the entries on the church and its organist in my book. We established a rapport and Tom eventually shared with me the belief that he too had seen the ghost. At my request he prepared a narrative account of his experiences and sent it to me on November 13, 1997. I am very happy to be able to include that account here.

Tom Hyland died before his account appeared in print. Thank you, Tom, wherever you are.

◆◆◆

At this time of writing, I've lived almost seven years beyond my allotted three score and ten. My rather mature age, combined with the problem that I write of an incident close to fifty years old, makes this narrative exercise a most taxing effort. But yet it affords me the nostalgic pleasure of reliving some precious moments of the past.

There seems to be an indignant consensus among young people—especially hard-rock enthusiasts, aspiring computer analysts, and other adolescent ignoramuses—that older persons lose their memories. Or, as they playfully put it, "marbles." This, of course, is completely false! After all, we've lived longer, have a great deal more to remember and, if we didn't discard the trivia, we'd burst our memory banks! Therefore we are inclined to remember the importance of the personal; treat the impersonal as excess; embrace the fact, but dismiss the inexplicable as coincidence. Thus, in order to put to rest any concern as to my mental stability, and to bolster your belief in the validity of this tale, I must meander through some of my personal history that has a direct bearing on your assessment of myself and my sanity.

I began singing, as a boy soprano, in the Anglican choir of Christ Church, Belleville, before my eleventh birthday. I soon became lead boy and soprano soloist. Then, with the onset of manhood, successively graduated through the choral ranks of alto, tenor, to bass. Also, for several years, I served as choir librarian for that parish choir. (You might say—with all that training and responsibility—I knew every piece of music from the top to the bottom and the correct alphabetical sequence of our complete repertoire!) The duties of that post gave me free access to the church, day and night. Quite often, I laid out Sunday morning's music in the choir stalls the Saturday night before, and became accustomed to being mortally alone in the building. The loneliness of those occasions gave birth to my lifelong addiction to test the acoustics of the empty church by the sound of my own voice.

In September, 1945 (my wife and I having moved to Toronto from our native Belleville in the summer of '44), I had the extremely good fortune to be accepted as a bass member in the gallery choir of the Church of St. Mary Magdalene by its eminent director and precentor, the late Dr. Healey Willan. The gallery choir consisted of sixteen voices in those golden days of liturgical music, and Willan left no stone unturned to achieve choral perfection. Time seemed to be expendable. Within ten days, preceding and including Easter Sunday, we sang two full-length rehearsals, several short rehearsals, attended and sang eight services! *Nothing* was left to chance—not even the simplest of hymns—and, from our busy schedule of rehearsals, services, recitals, it was easily imagined the average choir becoming so totally exhausted they'd "throw-in-the-towel" and *quit!*

At the beginning of my lengthy tenure of service in the choir, I was a fledgling photographer. When I became familiar with Anglo-Catholic rites, the fluent beauty of properly sung plainsong, and the precision with which all rites, rituals, masses, motets, processions, etc., were performed, I fell madly in love with the music and the uniqueness of the church: the austere solemnity of its architecture; the inviting refuge of its colourful appointments.

There was a mystical aura about the place that defies adequate description. I can only suppose it was generated by the dramatic differences in its contrasts. The entire interior of the nave was bare and grey—walls; pillars; arches... cold as death! Whereas the chancel and side chapels were *alive* with warmth. In the Chapel of St. Joseph, a children's altar: pink in motif; portrait of child in field of wildflowers, butterflies, and birds. In the Chapel of Our Lady: heavenly serenity; blue, vaulted ceiling; Virgin Mother and Child looking down lovingly, forgivingly on all who came and all who passed by. In the chancel, sanctuary: aptly named high altar; massive canopy, seasonal trappings; candles; ever-present Host, and magnificent gold cross—resplendent—infinite—commanding reverence in the brilliance of its shining. And the huge rood suspended high above the entrance from the main, broad arch with its Christ seemingly saying, "This is the House of God." "Here is the Gate of Heaven." The all gave one a strange sense of feeling a part of antiquity, without being old, and a part of the present, without being blatantly modern.

Here, indeed, was ample opportunity for me to pursue the art, capture the mood, and make memorable photographs with permanent appeal. There were *so* many things and atmospheres in that building crying out to be recorded on film that I started toting my camera along with me.

Eventually, by trial and error, by investment in equipment and the sacrifice of persistence, my skill became quite effectual. The results of my painstaking efforts were soon rewarded by the friendship and confidence of the clergy, and I found myself in the enviable position of coming and going as I pleased at any reasonable hour of the day or night to photograph whatever I wished. Thereafter, I spent innumerable hours by daylight or incandescent light (and, sometimes, the near lack of either!) to satisfy my desire that the church, in its varied aspects of sanctity, should be visually preserved as a special environment for Christian worship. And I'm forever grateful that some of those prints have found their places in books, on record jackets and music covers, and in the homes of many individuals whose love of that church and its music was equal to mine.

The gallery choir never donned the conventional choir robes. To some, that may seem sacrilegious. But, if anything, it was the opposite, as well as unnecessary. Being seated high above the back of the nave, we were out of sight and hidden from the view of the congregation. The absence of those robes had three distinct advantages. First, it was economical, saving us the expense of upkeep and the wasted time of dressing and undressing before and after each service. Second, it was convenient, should we have to silently slip down the gallery stairs during the sermon and rush, via an exterior route, to the basement lavatory. Third—and perhaps *most* important—it saved us the emotional distress of feeling "holier than thou" along with the damnations of women's mortarboards and makeup!

Healey was kind and considerate to all people of good intent—especially the members of his choirs (there were two). But that did not deter his stern demand for their sincere devotion to *both* the music *and* the words. I can still hear his most oft-uttered critical precaution: *"Any* fool can sing *notes!"*

Our weekly rehearsals were held Friday nights between the hours of eight and ten, *precisely*, with a ten-minute "smoke and gossip" break approximately halfway through. The ritual choir (the other choir and an exceptionally capable group of men and cantor who sang [traditionally robed] in the chancel and responsible for all plainchant) held their rehearsal the same night, prior to ours, from seven to eight, and *again*, precisely. When we arrived, the two choirs joined forces to practise all music in which we had mutual or overlapping parts (hymns, responses, canticles, etc.) that was required for the following Sunday's services. They then departed and we continued with our rehearsal.

The rehearsal room was in the basement of the church, directly below the chancel and sanctuary. It was adequately large but had the advantage of "flat" acoustics which prevented echoes from masking errors. The outside entrance to that room and the basement was through a street-level doorway on the southeast side of the church and a landing for stairs that went up to the vestry, chancel, and nave, and down to our rehearsal room. When the members of the ritual choir made their exit, the last one out tripped the latch on that door, and any gallery member who dared to arrive later—without Healey's permission—would have to knock; be let in; come down those stairs and… face the music!

There were two petty annoyances that plagued the choirs, clergy, and congregation in those days, even though they were confined to frigid temperatures. That door to the basement, when opened, ushered in an arctic blast of air that came rushing down the stairs, flooding our rehearsal room with chilly discomfort. The other annoyance was caused by the heating system in the church. There were radiators spaced along the perimeter walls at floor level that made their presence known by their noisy expansions and contractions. One of those convenience eyesores, in particular, had the habit of infusing its off-key harmony right smack in the middle of our motet, or punctuating a solemn, sermon sentence with a loud "ssss" and a "bang"! Also, the supply pipes for those radiators ran beneath the floorboards of the chancel and chapels, leaving those boards *so* dry they "squeaked" at the least of foot pressures. In short, we were *all* thankful for warmer weather!

But I remember it *was* in the cold of winter when this disturbing incident occurred, for there were overcoats, hats, and parkas hanging along the walls on hooks and hangers—one of the few necessities in our rehearsal room. The others being a piano, a music cupboard, an assortment of wooden chairs, a washbasin, one-seater toilet, and a table on which Healey placed his music; sat upon with one leg up and one leg down to conduct, or lecture us for our (thankfully few!) faux pas and occasionally emphasize, by illustration, the proper pronunciation of ecclesiastical Latin…usually followed by a relevant witticism quoted from one source or another.

One Friday night, during our break, Healey called me aside: "Tommy, old man, be a good chap; run up to the gallery and fetch me my copy of…. You'll find it…." (I honestly can't remember the title of the organ score, nor where I should find it.) Giving me his key for the gallery door, he explained his need of it the following day and expressed his frustration for not having had time to go get it himself. So off I went.

There were two flights of stairs from the basement to the main body of the church. The one on the south side, which I've already described, and another on the north with a passageway at its top, running parallel with the chancel to a doorway for entry to the nave. I opted to take those stairs for they were nearer to the gallery stairway in the north-west corner of the church. In the passageway, there was a single light bulb in a pull-chain socket hanging from the ceiling. This I pulled on, opened the door, propped it open, and made my way to the opposite end of the church.

Healey and I had become close friends. So much so that I welcomed the opportunity, and pleasure, to stay behind after mass or evensong, lock up the gallery, and accompany him down to the basement, where a large pot of hot tea was waiting to lubricate the vocal chords of choir members… courtesy of a very kindly lady and parishioner, Mrs. Bailey. (I do hope I've spelled "Bailey" correctly. She justly deserves proper recognition.) On those journeys he might ask, "What did you think of the Kyrie this morning, old man?" or discuss a problem with the tempo in a certain hymn. (And you have *no* idea how vainly proud *I* felt at being asked for *my* personal opinion—sometimes advice!—from such a renowned musician as Healey.)

The path we travelled on those intimate occasions was the same as I followed in this instance, and so familiar I probably could have tra-versed it fully with my eyes closed, as in the unconscious sight of sleep. But the dim light from the open doorway partially lifted the eerie shroud of darkness from the unlit aisle and prevented me from bump-ing into a pew or two.

There was a high, spacious vestibule the full length of the west wall of the church for coats and hats and more silent and draft-free entry to the nave. It had three sets of double doors with the gallery stairway in the north corner. I opened one of the nearest set, switched on the vestibule light, and mounted the gallery stairs. At the top, I switched on the two lights in the gallery, unlocked the door, and went in. Unfortunately, the empty church proved too tempting for me to resist my youthful addiction, and I started humming, quite loudly, with a few bass "booms" thrown in to more enjoy the echo. Having found the requested score, I was about to leave the gallery when I noticed the effect of those gallery lights fading into the darkness of the sanctuary.

Always on the lookout for a different angle, different highlight, different shadow, I paused to analyze the photographic possibilities. I was standing near the back wall, and from that position could barely see the front row of pews in the nave as the gallery railing was table-top high and heavily draped to block the view of any obnoxious gawker from below. So I moved closer until I could scan the entire nave. Still humming, I looked down and caught sight of something so *totally* unexpected that I nearly fell over the railing in cardiac arrest!

There, below me, kneeling in a pew partway up the south side of the nave, was a woman on whom I'd never laid eyes before! I was *so* startled that my lungs forgot to breathe—my vocal chords ceased to function—and my eyes became fixed like a lifeless statue's! Her faded, grey apparel appeared to be more suitable for warm weather than for the frigid temperature outside, and, oddly enough, no protective outerwear was anywhere visible. I was so *petrified* by surprise and so mortified with embarrassment, my wits became *so* befuddled that I *could* not *think* straight, and could *not* determine whether to attempt a pleading apology for intruding on the privacy of prayer, or to vacate the premises as quickly and quietly as possible. But as she was an absolute stranger to me, and I, probably, to her, I thought I'd better *leave* it that way and chose the latter option.

As I locked the door, switched off the gallery lights, descended the stairs, switched off the vestibule light, and retraced my steps to the passageway door, I kept thinking it also *very* odd that my considerable vocalizing seemed not to have disturbed her! I did not look back. There was little point to staring at the blackness of the nave. But as I closed that door, pulled off the light, and descended the stairs to our rehearsal room, I felt an immense sense of relief at leaving her and the church to the darkness in which I'd found them.

When I entered the room, Healey was poised to conduct the second half of our practice. So I took my seat, after laying the copy on his table, and my common sense suggested that I shouldn't report the unbelievable lest I be deemed a loony—if not *called* one! But through the remainder of that rehearsal, I kept one ear cocked for the sound of a squeaky board overhead, and one foot firmly on the floor for the feel of a cold draft... but I neither heard nor felt either.

(There was a *third* oddity about that woman's appearance—a haunting enigma that's eluded my comprehension ever since that night. But now, in the poignant remembering of so *many* personal and related truths of the past, I've finally solved the mystery of her presence. *And* the motivation that's prompted my telling of this tale.)

I write this on the 10th day of November, 1997. Comes the 27th day of this month, my wife and I will celebrate our fifty-fourth wedding anniversary—God willing. On that Saturday date, 1943, we came to Toronto for our honeymoon. The following day, Sunday, the 28th, we attended High Mass at St. Mary Magdalene. The music of the Mass and motet that morning was exquisitely beautiful, and sung so clearly and devoutly by the gallery choir that I actually wept. (That, I think, is the greatest compliment that can be paid for a sterling, sincere performance.)

Shortly after I'd joined the choir, I learned of a particular area in the nave where the gallery choir could best be heard. A place almost in isolation with angels. It so happened, on that glorious Sunday morning of our honeymoon, my wife and I—by accident and because of its availability—sat, knelt, and prayed in that same area—perhaps in the very same pew where this grey-clad lady knelt!

The vivid recollection of that most precious time; that special place—that *separate* beatitude of beauty—had finally solved the riddle of the third oddity: It was her location!... As if in anticipation, she occupied the exact spot, chosen by many an astute listener as the ideal ambience to fully experience the ecstasy of sound floating from that loft in an a cappella halo of faultless harmony—veritably enveloping *all* within our resonant House of God in a polyphonous paradise of immaculate adoration!

Healey used to tell of a ghost, dubbed "the grey lady," who interrupted his private organ practice in the church by her visual presence. Frankly, I never knew whether to doubt his sober sincerity or marvel at his clairvoyant sensitivity... whether we had a female phantom in our midst, or a figure evolved in a spasm of indigestion! But, after putting all the facts of two and two (or twenty and twenty) together: the dark, unlit church; the late hour; the long-locked doors; the squeaky boards; the frigid temperature; the cold draft; her lack of outer clothing; her undisturbed composure, and the pew she occupied, I'm thoroughly convinced there really *was* a "grey lady," and I—most *surely*—had seen her!

Now this anecdote would still be a latent episode, locked for life in my own mind—straddling the fence of indecision with its facts, doubts, and possibilities—had it not been for a request from our local author, John Colombo, to supply prints of the church and Healey. These were gladly given and faithfully reproduced in two articles of his excellent book, *Haunted Toronto*, published last year (1996) by Dundurn Press. Obviously, I've read those entries *and* the book itself, and would urge all those interested in the subject of "ghosts"—however remotely—to do also.

Colombo's request and that reading had revived my lazy memory, and my ostentatious ego suggested *I* could write of "ghosts" as well as *he*! And since I had witnessed a bona fide visit of an apparition, I've given it a shot. And there it is... faults and all... and *that's that!*

Tom Hyland
The [yet] City of Scarborough
November 10, 1997

See the Dancing Indians

JACK SCOTT

"**T**he Night I Began to Believe in Ghosts" is the title of an article written by Jack Scott about his dream or vision of... well... "dancing Indians." The interesting article was published in the *Vancouver Sun* on August 28, 1971. Apparently it had appeared earlier in the *Victoria Times*. Jack Scott was a respected newspaperman whose columns were a delight to generations of West Coast newspaper readers. *Great Scott! A Collection of the Best Newspaper Columns* appeared in 1985.

◆◆◆

The Night I Began to Believe in Ghosts

Last weekend marked the tenth anniversary of my belief in ghosts, after a lifetime of scoffing at the supernatural and pshawing at the psychic, and it was fitting or coincidental or something that once more we were camped on the Valdez spit.

Let us now do a fast dissolve to that summer's day a decade ago when we packed our little sloop with a week's provisions and set off to meander down the water corridors of the Gulf Islands.

We had just the one commitment, a rendezvous with Gordon Graham, a longtime friend of mine who was then the entire RCMP detachment at Ganges on Saltspring Island, and his attractive wife, Lou. The plan was to meet us at the inside entrance to Porlier Pass, which separates Galiano and Valdez islands and where the fishing at this time of year is superb.

"We may not get there until around sunset," Gordon had said, "so it might be a good idea to set up camp before we arrive. There are some spots north of the spit on Valdez Island with a good shelter for the boats and close enough to the pass so that we can get fishing at first light. We'll look for you there next Friday night. Leave a couple of coho for us."

My wife and I had a sinfully pleasant week cruising through the islands, timing it so that we arrived at Porlier on the Friday. We took our limit of blueback along the kelp line outside the full boil of the pass and then went through at slack water and along the eastern shoreline of Valdez until I find the anchorage Gordon had mentioned.

It was a pleasant campsite. There is a sharply sloping beach of clam shell sun-bleached so white that it gleams like marble in the moonlight. We'd rigged a heavy tarpaulin as a tent on a grassy ledge behind the line of driftwood. At our back the cliff rose steeply into heavy timbers.

When the Grahams arrived at dusk in their little speedboat we pan-fried two of the blueback, watching the sun set over Vancouver Island and wondering what the poor people might be doing.

We sat a long time by the fire that night, watching the moon rising over Galiano and throwing its light on the still, dark water of Trincamali Channel and it was around midnight when we built up the fire with heavy slabs of bark, said goodnight and crawled into our sleeping bags.

It must have been around two or three in the morning when I was awakened by the sound of tom-toms. I lay in the bedroll, looking up at the reflection of the dying fire on the canvas overhead and wondering why I felt no alarm.

"It must be a dream," I thought, but then I knew it was not and I raised myself on one elbow and turned my eyes to the fire.

Beyond the glowing embers I could see a great crowd of Indians dancing in the moonlight. They appeared to be in full ceremonial dress. There was no sound from them, only the steady, muffled rhythm of the drums as they moved gracefully and sinuously in and out of the perimeter of the beach fire.

It was a beautiful sight to see, so much so that I felt no apprehension whatever, merely a delight.

I watched them for several minutes and then I leaned over to my wife to awaken her. "Come and see the dancing Indians," I was going to say.

At that moment Graham rolled over in his bedroll, got up noisily and threw several great pieces of bark on the fire. The tom-toms stopped. The Indians faded away. There was only the slope of the clam-shell beach, white in the moonbeams.

I lay back in the sleeping bag, marvelling at what I'd heard and seen and the next thing I knew it was dawn.

I did not mention the experience the next morning, perhaps because my wife is subject to extravagant dreams and I am generally so ill-tempered at her recounting them in great detail that I felt it wiser to keep this experience to myself.

I say experience rather than dream because the reality of it was so vivid that I walked along the beach looking for moccasin prints. There was, of course, nothing. No more than fifteen minutes later I had hooked into a thirty-two-pound spring salmon and that had the further effect of pushing the incident from my mind.

A week later Graham phoned me and suggested I drop down to the RCMP office to see something interesting.

On his desk was the mummified body of a young person and two sun-bleached skulls, also children's. They had been found on Valdez Island earlier in the week by two exploring boys.

"I've just been talking to a man in Victoria who's an expert on these things," Graham said. "He tells me they're from the burying grounds of the Haida Indians.

"And you know where they were found? Right where we had our camp that night! Seems there's a thousand or more Haidas buried all along the beach there, many of them victims of a plague or smallpox. Boy, I'll bet you'd have had a restless night if you'd known you were sleeping on top of these things."

I had then told Graham the story, just as I've told it above, as it happened, and Gordon, owning that he, himself, had felt some strange presence that night, suggested that one day we must return and hold a vigil, a suggestion he made only half in just.

That was exactly ten years ago and it wasn't until this last weekend that I found myself able to return to the island.

On Friday night and on Saturday night we were camped in exactly the same place on the Valdez spit with two other friends. None of us heard tom-toms. None of us saw a single dancing figure in the glow of the beach fire. Indeed, it was all so ordinary that I couldn't resist phoning my old friend, who is now up the Island.

"I guess it was a dream after all," I said.

"Now, just a minute," Gordon said. "What was the weather like Friday and Saturday night?"

"Pouring," I said. "We were drenched both nights."

"Well, I forgot to tell you what that expert told me in Victoria," Graham said. "The Indian ghosts only dance in the moonlight."

We Heard Odd Noises

FLAVIO BELLI

F lavio Belli is the curator of the Joseph D. Carrier Art Gallery at Columbus Centre in the North York district of Toronto. He combines the temperament of the artist with the talent of the curator.

In 1972, when Flavio was twenty-one years old and an arts student at Sheraton College, he shared quarters with a friend named John, a student of photography at Ryerson Polytechnical Institute. They lived in the basement of an old house at 56 Huron Street, Toronto. They may well have shared their quarters with a poltergeist.

Here is what happened when they moved in, as Flavio recalled for me at Columbus Centre's Café Cinquecento the afternoon of January 17, 1998.

◆◆◆

In 1972, I was an arts student at Sheraton College. For about six months, I shared quarters in the basement of an old house at 56 Huron Street (below College) with my friend John, a student of photography at Ryerson. Both of us were twenty-one years old at the time.

As soon as we moved in, we heard odd noises. The house was old, but it was new to us, so we felt the noises were explicable. But we soon realized the noises were not explicable, and they were soon followed by disturbances. There were knocks at the back door. We would open the door within ten seconds of hearing knocks, but there was never anyone there. If we shut the door, the knocks would persist. The knocks were not caused by the kids in the neighbourhood because at the time of the knocks they were nowhere in the vicinity.

The superintendent and his wife occupied the flat on the top floor and felt that any noises or disturbances were caused by the tenants of the house. The flat on the main floor was occupied by two female violinists who admitted to us that they were hearing odd noises now and then. But they made noises of their own—violin sounds! They moved out and were replaced by some people who wore odd scarfs and explained that they were members of a commune in the Yukon. The cultists had no prior knowledge of any poltergeist in the house or of any explanation for its activities. Some time later, employing a Ouija board, they claimed to be in contact with the spirit, and even gave it a name.

Then a truly bizarre incident occurred while we were entertaining some friends. John and I were laying out a table of food, including cookies and half a watermelon. Without any cause or warning, the watermelon-half on the table began to eject its seeds, wildly shooting them into the air! Seeds were zipping across the room and landing everywhere!

Everyone was astonished. John got up to leave the room and a number of seeds shot through the air in his direction. Peter, a friend from the main floor, on impulse, yelled out, "Stop it! You're going to hurt someone." Abruptly the seeds stopped shooting out. Some of the seeds that were on the floor rose up and down of their own accord, taking a few seconds to settle down. It was an odd experience.

Some incidents occurred during the summer weather. In the evening, using masking tape, John and I would tape the lever of the thermostat on off. In the middle of the night, the lever would be turned to high, causing the furnace to go on. Yet the lever was still tightly taped. No one else had access to the room but John and me, and neither of us had readjusted the lever. There was no mechanism for the thermostat to turn itself up.

One night we returned from a concert. It was about two in the morning and the house shook. We feared for our lives. We were standing in the hallway before going into our rooms, when we heard an immense explosion! Our immediate thought was that an airplane had crash-landed in the front yard of the house and that the house would catch fire. We raced out the door we had entered but outside the house we found everything to be quiet. We re-entered the house to find that nothing at all had been disturbed.

On another occasion, at night, I saw a globe of light glowing in the darkness of the room. I started to wake up John to point it out to him, but as he was waking up, the globe was slowly shrinking in size. By the time John was awake, the light was extinguished.

On yet another occasion, I was entertaining a Lithuanian nun in the living-room. On a window-sill sat a small piece of tile, about the size of a toonie, that had been used to burn incense. No windows were open. No wind was blowing, no curtain was flapping, but on its own accord, the tile simply flew across the room in the direction of the nun, narrowly missing her, but crashing into the print of Caravaggio's *Mother and Child* on the far wall. The print was hit but unharmed. The tile dropped to the floor behind a bookshelf. We were astonished. Later I fished it out and placed it back on the window-sill, where it regularly resided, and forgot about it for some months. Then we decided to move out of the flat. The day we were moving our furniture from the flat, the tile turned up, behind the bookshelf.

To this day John and I are puzzled by the inexplicable things that happened at 56 Huron Street.

A Real-Life Ghost Story

DAVID HUNTER

The real-life ghost story that David Hunter relates in this account is the kind of true ghost story which most people associate with Merrie Olde England. The fact that it took place in modern-day England may come as a surprise. What is doubly surprising is the fact that the events occurred not to a noble or dotty Britisher but to a Canadian couple, as down-to-earth as they come.

David Hunter is a specialist in computer applications who lives and works in Mississauga, Ont. He wrote the following account not for me but for the editors of a magazine. He read a real-life ghost story in the July 1969 issue of the *Reader's Digest*. It was titled "I Don't Believe in Ghosts, But...." It was signed Jhan Robbin. (The author's first name is spelled in this spooky fashion!) Robbin wrote about spending a scary night at the George and Dragon Inn, West Wycombe, Buckinghamshire, England. Inspired by this account, on a holiday in England, David Hunter and his wife, Kathy, decided to tempt fate. They would repeat Robbin's adventure—and perhaps experience—and sleep in the room frequented by the White Lady. And this they very nearly did!

"A Real Life Ghost Story" never did appear in the *Reader's Digest*. But it is being published here. It is hard to keep a good ghost story down!

◆◆◆

So you don't believe in ghosts? Neither did my wife, Kathy, until we stayed in a haunted room at the George and Dragon, an ancient English coaching inn beside the old London to Oxford road in the peaceful, rural village of West Wycombe.

Our adventure began while browsing through old *Reader's Digests* in a second-hand bookshop, when an article about a "haunting" caught my eye. As a British schoolboy who emigrated with my family to Canada in the 1950s, I had a healthy regard for such matters... but my North American wife just couldn't admit to the possibility of such things as ghosts existing. To her, creaks and bumps in the night were no more than natural house sounds, each with a normal explanation. The article, however, seemed too good to ignore, since in several months' time, we were planning a vacation in lovely rural Buckinghamshire, the part of England where the inn lay. What better way to test my wife's scepticism than spend a night in the haunted room?

The magazine article described how the author had been travelling from London to the famous university town of Oxford to do some research at a library there. During his drive from the city, he had broken his journey at West Wycombe and spent a night at the George and Dragon, unaware of its eerie reputation.

The village itself became infamous in the 18th century when the notorious Hell Fire Club, a gang of wealthy young men, met in the caverns and tunnels carved out of chalk underneath the sleepy, half-timbered houses. There they would wine, dine, and commit acts of debauchery with the local maidens.

According to the article, Sukie, one of the serving wenches from the inn, fell victim to the club members and met her death as the result of a cruel practical joke played by the rich young rakes. She had been led to believe that one of their number wished to marry her, and when she arrived in the caverns at the appointed hour, dressed in a wedding gown, ready for the ceremony, the drunken practical jokers had seized the young girl and attempted to ravish her.

She struggled and in her fury she slipped on the damp chalk floor and cracked her head on some projecting rocks. She slumped to the ground and blood matted in her hair. The subdued debauchers carried Sukie's unconscious body through the cavern tunnels and through a secret passageway to her bedroom in the George and Dragon where they left her to recover. In the morning, the inn servants found the girl, just as she had been abandoned, still dressed in her torn gown of blood-specked white, but dead from injuries.

Her ghost is said to haunt Room Number 5, the bedroom where her body was laid out after the incident. Apparently, she is a mischievous spirit who, to this day, roams the rooms and passageways of the inn, seeking vengeance on the bygone youths who caused her death. She pulls bedclothes off beds in the night, searching for her killers. Many of the local villagers have seen her staring out a window which may be seen from the rear of the inn. The window lies in the passageway just outside her former room. There, her forlorn apparition watches and waits for her murderers of two hundred years ago to appear in the courtyard below. Many modern guests, unaware of the haunting when they arrived at the inn, have left their accommodations in the middle of the night, rather than finish their disturbed sleep in "her" room.

I purchased the magazine and immediately wrote to the proprietor of the George and Dragon to reserve that room for our visit. Several weeks later, we received a letter confirming the arrangements. Room Number 5 was ours for the night of October 21st. In her letter, the innkeeper mentioned that her young niece had recently moved to Canada to work as a nurse at a nearby hospital. The family hadn't heard from her since she had left England, and our hostess asked us if we would mind locating the girl to make sure that all was well.

A phone call to the hospital quickly established contact. The young lady asked if we would mind visiting her and taking several small gifts back for her aunt and for other members of the family. We readily agreed, since it was a golden opportunity to meet her and get the inside story of the haunted inn.

During our visit, I asked the nurse if she would spend a night at the George and Dragon. "Absolutely not!" she replied. "Even my aunt doesn't sleep there now. The hauntings have become so bad that she rents a small cottage in the village at extra cost so she can sleep in peace at night."

Kathy didn't seem to be too impressed by this. But to me, things were becoming decidedly interesting. I planned to take along several cameras. On the advice of a photography buff, I loaded one with infrared film so that I could capture on film anything that moved in the darkened room during our stay at the inn.

Finally, we left Canada for our vacation. After several weeks touring the English countryside, we arrived on a cold, rainy afternoon at the George and Dragon for our night's stay. The inn was a tall building, three or four storeys high, and it had a slightly dilapidated, red-brick façade set back from the main road by a wide pavement of cobblestones. The building was once an old coaching stop. An archway ran through the centre leading from the main road to a courtyard and converted stables in the rear. I drove through into the yard and looked back towards a crooked, white-framed window above the arch. This was the landing window, the one from which the ghost could sometimes be seen staring malevolently down at the cobblestone courtyard, searching for her 18th-century tormentors. A cold shiver crept up my back.

We went inside and introduced ourselves to the owner. The lounge area was furnished in aged oak; burnished copper and brass artifacts from old coaching days hung from the chiselled beams overhead. Two large German Shepherd dogs lay curled up in front of the hearth, beside a blazing log fire.

As I registered at the Elizabethan refectory table which served as the front desk, our hostess said, "I'm sorry but we've had to change your plans somewhat. I'm putting you in the room next door to the haunted one. Something happened in Number 5 last week." She raised her hand to silence my unspoken query. "We would rather not talk about it, but we can't possibly let anyone sleep in the haunted room for a while." She sensed my disappointment. "Don't worry, though," she said, "your room, Number 6, is almost as bad."

She paused to lift the key from the wall rack behind her and passed it to me. "In the days before the building became a hotel, it was a private house belonging to a Roman Catholic family. During the religious persecutions of King James, they hid their priest in a false compartment underneath the floorboards of the room, which is now Number 6. Unfortunately, the family was arrested and the priest, locked in his hiding place, starved to death. His spirit has been reported from time to time roaming through the room, and in the 1880s, it is said, a coach traveller hanged himself from the beam just inside the door."

Kathy gave a smug smile as if to say she didn't believe in such nonsense. As I signed several traveller's cheques in payment for the night's lodging, the innkeeper curiously asked us not to mention the fact that we were staying on the haunted floor to anyone in the lounge or bar that night. "We used to welcome the publicity, but recently many strange things have been happening," she said. "Now the locals don't talk about the subject much. Too many guests have left in the middle of the night, and we are trying to play down the story a bit."

In the Residents' Lounge, we enjoyed a hot meal of roast beef, garden peas and potatoes, topped with lashings of thick gravy, after which our hostess invited us to visit the nurse's family in the nearby town of High Wycombe. They were pleased to have a firsthand report of their daughter and enjoyed the presents we had brought with us.

During the evening, I cornered three of the teenage family members and asked them about the hauntings. Modern youth would have no time for ghosts, I assumed. But I was wrong... they all maintained that the George and Dragon was badly affected by something and that under no circumstances would they spend a night there. In fact, we became heroes in their eyes for attempting such a feat!

After an enjoyable evening, the innkeeper drove us back to the hotel and we followed her up the wide main staircase of age-darkened oak to the second floor where our room, Number 6, could be discerned down a dimly lit passageway. Her dogs trotted at her heels until they reached the "haunted" landing. Instead of entering the passageway, they lowered their heads with their hackles raised, and growled.

"Don't worry about the boys," our hostess said in a matter-of-fact voice. "They never come onto this landing. Something seems to scare them off." I glanced at the famous window as we passed by, but nothing disturbed the quiet serenity of the darkening evening outside.

Our room was cold and forbidding. Its sparse furniture consisted of two single beds, an old dresser, and several chairs. Over one of the beds dangled a light bulb, with a pull-switch cord. Threadbare Oriental carpets of dark reds and browns attempted to hide the oak-planked floor, and old blackout curtains, left over from Second World War years, obscured the glow of the lighted inn sign which hung on the brick wall outside. Beyond, we could hear the muffled hum of traffic as it whizzed by on the busy Oxford–London road.

The dampness of the inclement October weather seemed to invade our very bones. We lit a gas wall-fire, but its heat just didn't seem to warm the room at all. Worse still, we normally book accommodations with a double bed. I hadn't thought to question the sleeping arrangements of Room Number 6, and the twin beds were an unwelcome surprise. Neither of us wished to sleep alone that particular night.

A Night in Old City Hall

AGATHA BARDOEL

Here is a gripping account of a night spent in Toronto's Old City Hall. The ghosts of convicted murderers are said to haunt the halls and chambers of the old and stately building, particularly Courtroom 33.

Agatha Bardoel decided to see for herself whether there was any substance to the tale. She did not do so alone, for she made sure she was had the companionship of her sister Frannie!

Agatha Bardoel's brave account appeared as "This Is a Ghost Story" in the *Toronto Star*, October 27, 1979.

◆◆◆

This Is a Ghost Story

We lie in our sleeping bags on the floor of Courtroom 33, terrified.

It is the middle of the night.

And ten feet away, in the prisoner's box where nearly twenty years ago two men were condemned to hang, a slow, steady knocking breaks the silence.

It is Old City Hall, one of Toronto's most haunted buildings, at 3:00 a.m. on a Saturday in October.

We came here, my sister Frannie and I, at 11:00 p.m. the night before with a photographer, hoping to get evidence whether the building is indeed haunted.

By 4:00 p.m. the unexplained events had driven us out in panic into the night.

Old City Hall. Five days a week during daylight hours, it teems with life. There are marriages. There is traffic court. There are minor criminal cases—women up on prostitution charges, men up for shoplifting. There are preliminary hearings for murder.

And until the mid-'60s, when a new court building opened on University Ave., there were the great murder trials.

The memory of those still hangs in the air, casting shadows on the rich oak walls, the doors, the rows of spectator seats, the jury box—and the small, rectangular prisoner's box that still stands before the judge's bench in Courtroom 33.

Here, where we now lie in our sleeping bags, the last two men hanged in Canada stood before the judge and heard how they would die. Arthur Lucas and Ron Turpin were tried for murder in two separate trials and hanged at the Don Jail, Dec. 11, 1962.

"Tough break," Lucas told the court calmly when the sentence was read.

Ten years earlier, in September, 1952, Steve Suchan and Leonard Jackson, members of the notorious Boyd Gang, were condemned to hang for the murder of a Toronto detective. They, too, stood in that prisoner's box.

They were hanged Dec. 16, 1952.

Beverly Janus, a Toronto teacher of parapsychology and writer of a weekly syndicated newspaper column called "The Psychic," believes that the spirits of the dead linger around areas where they have suffered great unhappiness or stress, that they "sear" their emotion onto the environment. They have no intellect, she says. They stay and do the same thing repeatedly until one day they disappear.

From 1900 to the mid-'60s, the courts at the Old City Hall saw several other murder trials that ended in death.

There were William McFadden and Ray Holtrum, hanged in 1921 for the murder of a druggist.

In 1942, Bill Newell was tried and hanged for the murder of his wife on Centre Island.

In 1948, Leslie Davidson was tried and hanged for the murder of Margaret Meredith.

Excellent credentials for a haunted building. And there have been many stories.

The night staff tell of cleaning women who have asked for transfers, unnerved by door handles turning, objects falling off shelves, groans in the night.

A night watchman claimed that his feet were rooted to the floor, held by unseen hands.

Judges have said they have felt their robes being tugged as they climbed the back stairs to the courtroom.

We took large sheets of film, taped to our bodies. Some psychics believe that apparitions will leave vague forms and shadows on the film, even in darkness.

We took a camera loaded with infrared film, which is said to be capable of photographing ghostly images in the dark.

And a tape recorder, with a blank tape, to record sound. Mrs. Janus said that when a tape recorder has been left on in an empty room, it has later been found to have voices on it.

None of it was any use to us. When the time came, we had no time for experiments. We just wanted to get away.

"You simply do not know what you're letting yourself in for," Beverley Janus told me the day before.

City Hall staff said more or less the same thing.

"We had to take one man off the night shift. He asked to be transferred, he was so frightened by the sounds he heard," said Jim Scott, superintendent of the building. "But you have to remember that this is one of the few large old buildings around with wooden joists.

"Of course the windows blow open, floors creak, doors close. Old buildings groan."

Maintenance worker Joseph Bonett insisted it is more than that. "When I'm alone on Sunday during the day, I won't move from my chair."

Bonett's office is on the ground floor. Above him, on the first, there are some courtrooms, some clerical offices.

"They start running, footsteps, and not just one or two. There are many of them and they run up and down the corridors, hard and fast."

Bonett says the sound of running feet goes on for a long time. He went up to investigate once, but there was nothing there. He has not been again.

Dennis McTernant, who was once maintenance foreman in the building but now works elsewhere, recalls one story he was told.

"One of our guys was up in one of the halls one night, walking around, about 2:00 or 3:00 in the morning.

"Suddenly he couldn't move. Something had grabbed a hold of his ankles and he was rooted to the floor. For fifteen seconds or so, he couldn't get loose.

"Then, just as suddenly, it was over.

"He swears he couldn't move."

McTernant says many of the cleaning women reported similar mysterious events. They'd be going along the halls and the door handles would begin to rattle and they'd turn, as if they were going to open. When they went into the room, there was no one there.

"One watchman we had swears that one night, when he was going through the courtyard, he saw a man standing on the tower in the northwest corner.

"He was dressed all in black, just standing there.

"The women were complaining to me that they'd put something on a desk or a shelf in one of the offices. Then they'd go back in half an hour and it'd be on the floor.

"A lot of them were really scared."

"Some of the women have asked for transfers out of there over the years. And we have transferred people," says John Carry, manager of operations. "They were upset by strange noises, doors closing after they had been propped open, that kind of thing."

Night watchman Charlie Dobrzensky led Frannie, photographer Doug Griffin and me up to the second floor.

"Some of the guys have been talking about it," Charlie said, "and some of them were making fun of it.

"But others said they'd heard things and they didn't think it was funny."

Dobrzensky opened the door; the photographer took his pictures and left.

We heard his footsteps echoing down the hall. Then there was silence. The darkness wrapped itself around us.

We pointed our flashlight at the clock on the wall. It was minutes after midnight. Suddenly the flashlight went out. I pressed down anxiously on the button. It flickered, then went out.

On the next try, it worked again. For what seemed like the first time inside the room, we breathed.

Of course it would go out, I thought. We're nervous as cats. I can hardly hold this flashlight.

In the centre of the room, illuminated only by the faint yellow light from the hall that filtered through the courtroom door, stood the small prisoner's box.

Our footsteps echoed as we walked over to it, opened the small swing gate and went inside. We sat down. Almost immediately, I felt very cold.

The rest of the room had been quite warm, so warm we already had taken off our sweaters.

"I feel terrible," Frannie moaned. "I don't understand it. I'm so anxious, like there's something awful that I've got to do, and I don't want to do it.

"And it's so cold, like you get by the lake at the cottage. There should be some water."

I had not told her I felt cold. And I had not told her that if there were ghosts, I was told we would feel cold. A drop in temperature, and a damp, clammy atmosphere often accompanies apparitions, psychics say.

We sat there for moments in silence. I asked her to stand and face the judge's bench, to grip the railing in front of her. Almost immediately there was a sharp rapping sound from the floor of the box under our feet.

It was then that I first began to feel uneasy.

We left the box and climbed into our sleeping bags on the floor, about ten feet away. We lay very still, talking quietly.

"We shouldn't have done this," Frannie whispered. Outside the window on Bay St., a siren wailed in the night.

To the left of the judge's bench is a small doorway that leads to a narrow hall and a small wooden staircase. It is the judge's private access from the street to the court chambers on the second floor. Then it runs on up to the third and fourth floors, where the attic is.

In the mid-'60s, two judges reported strange happenings on the staircase. One, now retired Provincial Judge S. Tupper Bigelow, told a Toronto newspaper he had heard light footsteps on the staircase and, on one occasion, felt a tugging at his robes.

Another, Judge Peter Wilch, followed the footsteps up to the top floor, which was then untenanted (court reporters now use it). There was no one.

Frannie and I walked quietly through the door and into the corridor.

The air was cold and the light from a single overhead light bulb showed that it was also clear.

The wooden steps creaked under our weight. We descended, then ascended right to the top. We heard nothing. "This feels good," Frannie whispered. "Let's sit for a while."

We sat in a corner of the stairway, occasionally looking gratefully at the light bulb. "Has someone been through here smoking?" Frannie asked after a while.

"There's some kind of a smoke through here. Look, you can see it on the light bulb, around it."

There was. It was getting misty. And it was clouding up against the window to the courtroom.

Frannie did not know that, like a sudden drop in temperature, a mist or fog also often accompanies an apparition. Sometimes it is wrapped around the apparition itself, sometimes it fills the room and there is no other phenomenon.

I sucked in some air. "Let's go," I said. "If there's someone there that wants to meet us, it can meet us on our own turf."

It was just after 3:00 o'clock. We lay quietly. Frannie had taken a long wooden stick with an iron hook on the end used for opening tall windows, and placed it between us on the floor.

The room had grown very cold. Echoes, groans and sights that are part of an eighty-year-old building hung in the background. The sound effects were continuous. We had become used to them; we were interested in this room, but not afraid. Over in the corner, the pale window leading to the judge's staircase kept its eye fixed on us.

I began to tell her stories about the courtroom that I had found in old newspaper clippings. I told her the background of some of the trials, how Suchan and Jackson had a showdown with Sergeant of Detectives Edmund Tong and Detective Roy Perry in a Toronto gunfight. How Tong had died, his spinal column severed.

And then, from ten feet away, from the prisoner's box, we heard it again. A steady rapping sound, not hard, not quick, but keeping pace with my words.

"Listen!" Frannie urged. I stopped talking, and as I did, the rapping stopped. "Did you hear it?" she said.

I resumed speaking, but very slowly, measuring out each word. "Tap... tap... tap... tap..." came back the rapping, keeping pace with each word.

We froze. In the vast room, our hearts beat thunderously. The blood ran to our heads. Sweat broke out on our hands.

Fear, in small doses, can be pleasurable.

But we were terrified.

It was a matter of leaving immediately, or no longer being able to, I thought.

We grabbed everything, half dragging, half kicking it to the doorway.

Frannie looked to the right, into the judge's hallway.

"My God, look at the smoke," she cried, digging her nails into my arm.

In under a minute, we were down the stairs and at the back door, then into the cold October night.

A few days later, I asked Building Superintendent Scott how the building was heated. I was trying to account for that fog in the hallway.

"Steam heated," he explained.

"Ah," I said, "that explains it."

I froze at his next words. "But we had not turned it on yet. Not when you were there."

Much to My Horror

ROSEMARY VYVYAN

Discovery Harbour (or Havre de la Découverte) is a component of the reconstructed Historic Naval and Military Establishments at the head of Penetanguishene Bay, Ont. The Officers' Quarters here is interesting for psychical as well as historical reasons. Few people are in a better position to talk about both than Rosemary Vyvyan, historical planner with Discovery Harbour. In response to one of my queries, and some goading, she prepared a personal account, dated September 21, 1995, of some of the distinctly odd events that have occurred here.

◆◆◆

The Officers' Quarters at Discovery Harbour in Penetanguishene has a curious past. Completed in 1836, the building has had an almost continuous history of use. Today the building has been restored to the 1840s period and is furnished to reflect the genteel living quarters of the officers who once lived there.

I have worked at this historic site since 1979, and over the years our costumed interpretive staff have spoken to me about the uneasiness they experience in the building. Many of these people have said they feel a presence in there with them. On several occasions, staff have reported an item (wine glasses seem to be a favourite) missing from the building, only to find it moved to another location therein.

There have been a number of incidents that have happened to me that have been puzzling. I say puzzling because I am very much a sceptic when it comes to believing in the presence of a spirit or spirits in a building in which I work. The most consistent occurrence has been the impression of someone sitting on one of the beds in the building. There is one bed that always looks as if someone has been sitting on it. I cannot count the times I have straightened the blankets on the bed, only to return the next day to see the impression there again.

Another incident occurred several years ago when I was instructed to turn off all the heat in the building to help freeze-dry a humidity problem over the winter. I did so. About a month later I had a team of restorationists come to the site to look at the building and give me further advice on its restoration. I explained to them about the deliberate non-use of the furnaces. Much to my horror, when I took the group into the building, the furnace was blasting out nice warm air. To this day I have no idea who turned the furnace on and why.

It was during this same time that I removed all of the fragile furnishings from the building. In the spring, when I went to refurnish the building, I was missing one box of furnishings. I searched the site for the box of things. All efforts were to no avail. You can imagine my complete shock when I went into the Officers' Quarters one day and the box, full of the artifacts, was sitting in plain view at the top of the stairs.

We attribute these strange goings-on to Private James Drury, who froze to death on New Year's Eve in 1839, at the back kitchen of the building.

The Haunting School

RON HLADY

H aunted houses in Canada are legion, or at least reports of haunted houses are legion. Haunted schools, primary or secondary, are few and far between. But here is one.

At the time of writing this account, Ron Hlady was a Building Preservation Technician with the Edmonton Public Schools Archives and Museum. He wrote this account of his experiences in the building in which he worked. "The Haunting of McKay Avenue School" originally appeared on a page reserved for "ghost stories" in the *Edmonton Journal*, October 30, 1988.

◆◆◆

The Haunting of McKay Avenue School

I don't live in a haunted house but I do work in a haunted school.

McKay Avenue School is the museum and archives for Edmonton public schools. The big, old brick building and the original 1881 School House are on the same lot at 10425 99 Avenue.

I've worked here since 1984. During this time I have been made aware of the presence of more than one ghost. These phantoms have never tried to frighten me but on several occasions they have interfered with my work. They've unlocked doors that I've locked, turned on and off the boilers, removed pictures from the wall, and scraped furniture across the floor of the room above me when I knew I was the only one in the building.

Once I'd swear they had a party. Another man and myself spent the last part of a working day setting up a room in the school for an early morning audio-visual presentation. We pulled all the blinds down and stapled them to the sills, lined up chairs in neat rows, and locked the building on our way out.

We were the last to leave that day and the first to arrive the next morning. You can imagine our surprise when we discovered the blinds were up, some right off the windows and lying on the floor. The chairs were knocked over and strewn around the room. We had to really rush in order to redo the room in time for the meeting.

Former staff and students frequently visit the building and many of them have spoken of hauntings and ghosts. With all these strange goings on I decided to bring a Ouija board.

One ghost, Peter, was quick to identify himself and he maintains that there are half a dozen other spirits floating around. Peter's a very personable character and has "told" me quite a bit about himself. He won't reveal his last name but he has explained that he was a labourer during the construction of the 1912 addition. He was killed in a fall from the roofs. It was winter and the ground was frozen. The only place he could be buried was under the floor of the school. Apparently his spirit has roamed the building ever since.

Lately things have been quieter at work. The odd drawer that was shut will be wide open. Pictures may be off the wall or tilted, but I actually wonder if Peter's presence is still as strong as it was.

I asked two young psychics who operate "Second Sight" to come through the school. They confirmed there are a number of ghosts in the building, and the woman was continually drawn to the southwest corner of the addition. Could this possibly be where Peter fell from? I'll probably never know, but that corner does overlook the 1881 School House.

The building was used as a storage shed during the construction of the addition, and so Peter would've been in and out of there frequently.

Sometimes when I go out there, a cold shiver passes through me.

It originally opened on Jan. 3, 1882. Peter claims to have died on Jan. 3, 1912. I was born Jan. 3, 1951. Quite a coincidence, isn't it?

It Had to Be a Dream

KAREN P. COLAUTTI

T his letter is an account of nocturnal disturbances that occurred to Karen P. Colautti, a college student, soon after she moved into Apartment 3A at 425 Sherbourne St. in Toronto. The letter, dated September 14, 1995, is reproduced here with minimal editing. Today Ms. Colautti lives on Sherbourne St., but not at the apartment building in which the disturbances occurred!

What to make of her experience? Psychical researchers and channellers talk about pools and whirlpools of psychic energy. Psychologists and parapsychologists discuss hypnagogic and hypnopompic states of consciousness, "borderline" experiences that occur in the state between sleeping and waking or between waking and sleeping. Folklorists have documented visits of the "old hag," a form of succubus or incubus that ravishes sleepers. Everyone, it seems, has an immediate appreciation of nightmares and the terrors of the night.

One interesting feature of Ms. Colautti's account is that it is open-ended. It comes to no conclusion. If someone devoted the time to research the occupant history of Apartment 3A, it might be found that an event occurred between those walls that places these nocturnal disturbances in some credible—or incredible—perspective.

◆◆◆

Dear John,

I have owned a copy of *Extraordinary Experiences: Personal Accounts of the Paranormal in Canada* for a few years now. I am writing to relay one of my extraordinary experiences to you. Perhaps you will wish to use it in one of your future works.

In 1989, I was nineteen years old, in my last year of college, and I had just moved into a bachelor apartment at 425 Sherbourne St. in Toronto. The building I had moved into was once, I assume, some sort of boarding house that had been renovated into an apartment building. There were two entrances into my unit. One was from within the building itself, and one from the wooden fire escape—*yes! wooden!*—that led up from the ground. I shared the escape's landing with my neighbour. We have our own doors that led into our separate apartments.

For two years I had been living outside of my parent's home, so I was used to "being on my own." I had adjusted to new sounds and bizarre shadow formations, etc. (As a student I made many changes of residence.) The first few months I lived there, nothing seemed to be out of the ordinary. The fourth month or so, I was awakened very late at night by what sounded like footsteps coming up the wooden fire escape. (Yes, wooden!) I thought at first that it must have been my neighbour returning from a late night out, but I did not hear him unlock and open his door, nor did I hear any footsteps retreat down the stairs back into the night. Thinking that it surely must be some lunatic out for blood, I got a knife from the kitchen and I put it under my pillow. Then for some strange reason—stress-induced narcolepsy?—I promptly fell back to sleep.

Over the next couple of months, this happened many times. I never really gave much thought to it during the day. Actually, after putting the knife back in the drawer the morning after, I didn't even remember it had happened, until it happened again.

Over the next few months things progressed. I started to hear footsteps coming up the escape, enter my apartment, and then stop. Then they would come up the escape, enter the apartment, go through the living area, then stop. The next time they would come up the escape, enter the apartment, go through the living area, pass into the hallway, then stop. Then they would come up the escape, enter the apartment, go through the living area, pass into the hallway, go back into the living area, turn in circles, then stop.

I would be paralyzed with fear every time I experienced one of these "episodes." I would try to scream, "*No! No!* Get out—*stop!*" But for the life of me, I could not get the words out. I would be thinking to myself, "Please, Karen, just go back to sleep. Just go back to sleep and everything will be okay." Then I would fall back into a deep sleep.

Convinced that what I was experiencing had to be dreams, or games that my mind, sound asleep but conscious, was playing on me, I told one of my close friends that I was having some really odd dreams, and I explained them to her. She said that these did not sound like any dreams to her. There was too much order to them. They progressed too smoothly. She reminded me that I had never reported recurring nightmares in the past. Still, I was convinced that they *had* to be dreams. It was all so terrifying to me. I did not want to believe that this could be happening in reality.

Still, I kept her up to date on what was happening. She would ask, "So, have you had any more of *those* dreams?" Yes, indeed I had. The footsteps continued. They did not stray from the aforementioned routine, until one night. That night, after the footsteps turned their circles, I heard them approach me. Then I sensed something was sitting on the edge of the bed. I felt panic. The time after that, they followed the same routine, but instead of something sitting on the bed, it felt like something was lying down beside me. Again I felt panic, extreme panic. I prayed that I could just fall back to sleep, and I always did, quite promptly. Except for relaying these occurrences back to my friend, I didn't think about them during the day. Since nothing odd happened during the day, I figured that it *had* to be a dream.

The next episode was the most frightening episode of all. In fact, it was the most frightening thing that I had ever experienced in my life. Again, the footsteps followed the regular routine. But this time, after turning in circles, they came towards me, and it seemed they stopped, as though someone was kneeling at my bedside. I sleep on a mattress with a box spring that sits directly on the floor. I could hear breathing, very loud, deep breathing, as if through a nose rather than a mouth. My hands were resting on the pillows, up over my head. The next thing I remember was my wrists were being grasped in someone's hands. That did not seem to bother me as much as the breathing, which was so loud. I remember thinking, "Stop breathing! Just make that breathing stop!" It felt like someone's head was right there behind my own. With my hands still being clutched over my head, I decided the best way to stop that horrible breathing sound was to place my fingers up the nose of whoever or whatever was making the noise. I remember making an attempt to do this, thinking, "Stop the breathing, just stop the breathing, go back to sleep, and all this will stop." Then I fell back to sleep.

I called my friend the next day to tell her about this development. Apparently she had told her boyfriend about my experiences. I could hear him in the background yelling, "That's it! She's moving out of that place! Get her out of that place!" They scared the pants off me with stories about people being raped by ghosts, etc., so I agreed that I would move. And I did move away shortly thereafter.

I'm still not fully convinced that what happened to me was real. But I never experienced anything like it before I lived in Apartment 3A. And since I've moved, I've yet to experience anything like it again.

I've meant to do research on the building and the area, but I've never gotten around to it. I guess, perhaps, I'm afraid I may discover something to confirm my fears that none of it really was a dream.

Karen P. Colautti

My Experience at 90 Sumach Street

I have always felt that radio studios have an atmosphere that is all their own. The air seems alive with waves: the voices and even the personalities of the talented performers who have projected their characterizations while broadcasting and recording in these studios. The walls contain the words. Radio studios have this quality, but not television studios. Television seems to me to be more an operation than a procedure, so there are no reverberations left in the air to be caught within the walls. If that is so for words, perhaps it is also so for spirits.

Here is an account of the haunting of some buildings operated by the Canadian Broadcasting Corporation. The account was written by an ex-CBC employee who submitted it to Matthew Didier, one of the founders and organizers of the Toronto Ghost and Hauntings Research Society. Readers and fans of the fantastic who have access to the Internet will find the World Wide Web to be the World *Wild* Web—a treasure trove of the mysterious! The address of the TGHR website is *www.torontoghosts.org*. Matthew forwarded this account to me with the permission of the writer, who remains nameless by choice. The original posting was dated October 28, 1999.

◆◆◆

Back in 1989 I worked for the CBC as a security officer. I was given the job to patrol and check on other guards at fourteen CBC buildings around Toronto.

My experience at 90 Sumach St. was on the fourth floor. Near the stairwell the area was always cold. As you went up and down the stairway, you could feel the cold getting colder as you reached the fourth floor, and it was getting warmer as you walked away from the fourth floor. I knew one of the commissioners who worked there and heard the stories.

One night he set up a voice-activated tape recorder to record what he thought was voices. I checked on him around 1:00 a.m. and that's when he told me. He was going to put the recorder on after I left. No one was in the building except for him after I left and until I returned at 5:00 a.m. I asked if he recorded anything and he told me that he had something or someone on the tape. He would not let anyone hear it until he was able to identify what it was.

Another CBC building that was strange was the Annex on Jarvis St., the old white house in front of the TV building. At the very top floor there was a light that would keep coming on. At night, the only way to get into the building was with security. A key and a combination was needed, yet this light would be turned on. I can't remember how many times I had to climb the stairs to turn the light off. (The switch would be turned on.)

If you worked the night shift in the Radio Building, and if it was quiet, sometimes you could hear a faint moan being made by a girl. Rumour has it that it was once an all-girls' school and one girl hanged herself, and it was her ghost.

Another was the building at 1140 Yonge St. The commissioners would tell me stories of one of the dressing rooms. The door would closed and lock, lights would go on and off, wall outlets would lose power for no reason.

Hope this info could be of help to you.

Night Sounds

SANFORD BROOKS

Here is an unusual account, dated September 1995, and written by Sanford Brooks, a young Toronto writer whom I have yet to meet. "Night Sounds" was published in the October 1995 issue of *Toronto's Midtown Voice*. The account is unusual, for the present collection at least, because it is really someone else's story, not really the author's. However, it is a good yarn, one that smacks of verisimilitude. Brooks has an unusual, lively, and haunting tale to tell.

◆◆◆

There is an old saying: "If you listen to the October wind you can hear the cries of a thousand souls."

A few years ago I went to a Halloween party held at one of Danforth Avenue's local bars. As I sat at the bar waiting to be served, I looked up to see that my bartender was Viki, a woman whom I knew from when she used to be a waitress at another bar in the area. We smiled and exchanged our greetings. After she brought me a beer, we engaged in some small talk. Our conversation soon shifted to the crowd of people, all of whom were attending this evening's Halloween festivities.

"Check out how many people are here tonight. This place is packed!" I observed.

"That's for sure! I'll get some good tips tonight," Viki said, as she scanned the room.

"So, how come you aren't wearing a costume?" I inquired, as I sipped my beer.

"I'm not really into Halloween. It kind of gives me the creeps."

"Halloween is supposed to give you the creeps. I mean, after all, that's part of the fun. Right?" I replied.

"Well, a couple of years ago I had a really weird experience that's sort of left me with bad vibes," Viki said in a dour tone.

"Sounds like you've got a ghost story to tell. I'm listening."

"The last bar that I worked at," Viki began, "had an apartment for rent above it. My boss saw the ghost of one of the tenants who apparently lived there many years ago. That incident is why I'm not too keen on Halloween. I quit shortly afterwards."

Viki's story began the night of October 30th, 1990. Viki and her boss, Martin, were closing up the bar after a long and busy evening.

"Martin, I'll lock up," Viki said as she placed the last of the stools on top of the bar.

"Do you mind? My feet are killing me," Martin asked as he slipped on his jacket.

"No. Not at all. You go home," Viki assured.

"Thanks, love. Remind me to give you a raise," Martin said, flashing a smile.

"Promises, promises," Viki replied in a mocking tone.

"Well, good night. See you tomorrow," he said as the door slowly closed behind him. Viki reached behind the bar and retrieved a spare key ring. Buttoning up her coat, she grabbed her purse and headed for the back door. As she turned off the lights, the bar was plunged into darkness.

Outside, the cool air pricked her skin. Flipping through the keys, she eventually found the one that would lock the door. Viki was about to lock the door when she suddenly froze. Listening intently, she thought she heard the sound of a moan coming from inside the darkened bar. Unnerved, Viki hurriedly locked the door. In her car driving home, Viki dismissed the sound as probably being just the *October wind*.

The next day, October 31st, Viki wasn't due to start work until 6:00 p.m., when she would begin her evening shift. Viki was surprised when she received a phone call from Martin.

"Hello?" Viki answered.

"Viki? It's me. You left the door open. This morning, as I was about to open up, I found the door open."

"No way! I absolutely locked the door as I was leaving!"

"So you didn't leave the door open?" Martin stressed.

"No," Viki replied firmly. "Don't tell me you've been burgled."

"I don't think so. Except..." Martin's voice trailed off.

"Martin. What?" Viki sensed something was not right.

"It's crazy. I thought it was my eyes playing tricks." Martin sounded shaken. "After I found the door open and I looked around I started to take the stools off the bar...."

Tense, Viki urged, "And?"

"I heard this moan," Martin continued, "and saw this old woman in her nightgown, with dark, hollow eyes and flowing white hair, moving towards the back of the bar."

Viki was relieved. "Did you call the police?"

"Viki, the woman was floating above the floor. She had *no feet!* When she reached the door she just... *disappeared!*"

Viki's stomach was in knots. Realization set in as she knew that the moan she had heard was from the ghost of that woman....

I remained silent for a moment before I spoke. I was stunned.

"That's a creepy story. I understand why you quit."

Viki paused, then slowly answered, "That incident made me a true believer in ghosts."

The Gibraltar Lighthouse Experience

ELOISE Y.

Life changed in a small way for Eloise Y. as the result of our first meeting. The psychic, who lives in Toronto's Parkdale district, shared with me some of her impressions of that part of the city.

I published them in the book *Mysteries of Ontario*. I recommended her services as a medium to the producers of a children's show on TVO, the Ontario educational television channel. Eloise Y. was agreeable, and she charmed the producers and produced a lively show about the ghost that haunts the city's oldest still-standing site, Gibraltar Lighthouse. She kindly wrote up for me this account of her experience, Halloween 1995.

◆◆◆

Dear John,

What a delight to have been graciously recommended by you for the TVO children's show *Off the Hook*. I am truly honoured. The producers of the show decided on the Gibraltar Lighthouse on Hanlan's Point. Originally they were to have met at the Keg Mansion. However, we all agreed that the Keg might prove to be much more disquieting than the island, just in case the legends of rape and murder surrounding the old mansion might be more validated. It was a lovely experience at the lighthouse for me. I had hoped you might make an appearance there yourself. I would have loved you to see what I saw.

Speaking of what I saw, the following paragraphs are an account of what transpired for me on a psychic level. I had made a point not to research anything you or anyone else had written about the lighthouse before going; quite a difficult thing to do for an old magpie like me. Nor had I the luxury of growing up in Canada, where I might have heard school-day whisperings of the debacles and debauched goings-on there. My approach, then, was fresh and untainted.

Here then my Gibraltar Lighthouse experience:

Early last week I received a phone call from the researcher for a TVO children's programme called *Off the Hook*. The show is aimed at the 11 to 14-year-old ages with a mixture of fun and problem-solving expeditions called "missions." The researcher explained that, since Halloween was approaching, the producers would like to do a light-hearted piece on the pros and cons of the existence of ghosts. They were looking for a psychic who has had some experience with sensing spirits in alleged haunted places, and, since I had been referred to her by you, an accepted and respected authority on the subject, asked if I would be willing to take part in a small segment of the programme where the "mission" was to go and seek out a real live (?) ghost. Being a theatrical sort myself, I jumped at the chance, but not before agreeing on two conditions: that under no circumstance would I agree to taking a youngster on a haunting that would have possible malevolent vibrations without exploring it first, and that the spirits and the workings must be viewed with some respect. These being agreed upon, we set forth on the particulars of the day of the shoot.

On Thursday last, accompanied by my husband, we left for the ferry dock at Bay Street Quay to board the last ferry of the day to Hanlan's Point, where we would be met by private shuttle to take us to the lighthouse. Since we arrived almost forty-five minutes early for boarding I took the opportunity to psych out the area. I had no idea in which direction the lighthouse stood, but began sensing some sort of pull from the southwest of the island. Now, normally, I try not to do preliminary research or meditations on a haunting, rather personally preferring to save the pieces of research for later, then piecing information together in a puzzle-like fashion. In fact, when the TVO researcher asked me if I needed any special preparation I replied in my usual piquish manner that a walk around the outside of the building along with a strong cup of coffee and a cigarette will be just fine. I am grateful to report that this time I was most obliged.

Standing just a few feet from the turnstile where I was observing other ferries coming in to shore, I noticed two men debarking from a boat that had just landed. They were both fairly tall and painfully slim, lanky perhaps, dressed in identical bluish Navy pea coats, khaki coloured pants and long rubber boots. It struck me ever so clearly that these two must be deckhands. On their heads were caps that I can only describe as those worn by fishermen or sailors in the Maritimes, perhaps a hundred or so years ago. These caps were touched ever so lightly toward me as to say "Hello" as they sauntered away. From one of these men I got the clear message of "They're waiting for you on the other side, Miss." I was both dumbfounded and delighted that these two spirits, friendly in an understated manner, heralded what was to be an interesting evening.

Though it had been raining the entire afternoon ever since our departure, for a brief moment the sun peeked out from behind the dull slate clouds as if it was guiding me. I turned to my husband and said, "White with blue and red, now it is all red but it used to be blue and red and John, John wants to tell his story." Bless his heart, my psychically dead husband is used to these little outbursts from me and enjoys the adventures as if he is watching an episode of *Miss Marple*. I said nothing further until we reached the lighthouse.

The five-person crew, the young cast member, and several members of the Parks and Recreation from the island were there to meet us. I was then informed that neither the cast member nor I was to go inside the lighthouse until after dark as they wanted to catch the surprise element on camera, so I walked around the outside of the building and in surrounding property for a while. First I was shocked to notice how very small the structure was and that it was completely landlocked. I sensed a great deal of frustration emitting because of this fact but could not as yet tell if it was coming from the spirit of a person or from the building itself. Walking up the dirt path around the building the first thing I said was, "Drunken brawls, men, aggressive drunken men." I wouldn't know until much later how important that feeling was to the legend of the lighthouse keeper himself. At one point soon after, I had inquired of the Parks and Recreation manager if there had been any small structure behind the lighthouse, say a meat-smoking pit, or an outhouse perhaps. He told me astonishedly that there, indeed, had been a small one-room house about seventy or so feet from where we were that at one time had been used as a home for lightkeepers. It had been demolished about forty or fifty years ago, he replied, quite astonished. I knew it had been there because I smelled cooking flesh on the very spot where it stood.

What intrigued me next were the small grassy patches behind the lighthouse, toward the canal, and what is now some brush and landfill. I saw someone wounded, crawling toward water, bleeding and disoriented. Next I had a vision of a canoe, perhaps of Native origin, some soldiers passing through on the thickets to our left and the soft rustling sound of someone trying to hide in the thicket. Only a few of these things noticed me at all, and nodding their heads for me to go back to the front of the lighthouse, they carried on with their business. By dusk, I heard no sounds at all and felt very clearly that the soldiers had aborted their tasks, retreating into the silent night. The crescent of the moon could be seen climbing overhead as I received my instructions for the after-dinner-break shoot which would be my entrance into the lighthouse for the first time.

We were driven over to another section of the island to have a supper break inside the offices of the Parks and Recreation Dept. The TVO crew, much to my delight, had their own stories and beliefs of ghosts to share with me. All of them were believers in one form or another, all of them sharing the latest inside scoop about ghost and other paranormal activities being the current darling subject of the television industry. By the end of the hour we were calling this episode the "L-Files." My one concern was the young man, LaVel, whose mission it was to enter the lighthouse and find a ghost. A bright and personable young boy of 14, he was visibly frightened and kept asking me if everything was going to be fine. He and the rest of the crew had heard all the legends of the lighthouse keeper. I had asked them not to tell me until I was done with my exploration. The director, a wonderful woman named Kathie Lee Porter, and I took LaVel aside and promised him that I would enter first with the crew in tow and without him. If I sensed anything at all remotely unnerving or frightening, I would tell Kathie Lee and she would cancel the shoot and take the story to a different angle. What I didn't tell anyone but Terry, my husband, was that I had already begun communicating with "John" and had told him I would not tolerate any ghostly theatrics coming from him. The sense I got at first was that he just wanted to finish up his work for the night and settle into a nice evening with a meal and a pipe. What he couldn't understand was why all these people milling about didn't "just bloody well come in already" and get about their business and leave him alone. What amused me greatly was his confusion about my presence. He could sense as well that I had come for a "secret purpose." The purpose, so "John" thought, was that I had been sent over by an innkeeper from the mainland to keep him "company" for the evening. Apparently, he thought I had been selected for this work since I was a mature and buxomly woman with a "bloody fat ass" which would warm him quite nicely on a chilly October evening. I kept this information for the adults alone. We were, after all, taping a children's show.

Upon returning to the lighthouse I realized something about the structure. I believe it was built not to guide ships to a safe harbour, but rather to warn and send signals to the mainland, possibly by runners, of approaching enemy ships. I did not sense at all that this was a particularly honourable job and that our ghost friend "John" had somehow been promised a job that had not lived up to its expectations. Throughout the entire evening's experience was a nagging feeling of despondency and sadness mixed with some sort of anger at being duped somehow.

Now it was time for me to enter the lighthouse. It was completely dark outside save for the glow of a beautiful first-quarter moon shining down on clear skies and the invasive, intrusive lights of a video crew. Just before knocking (I always knock or announce myself in some way) I saw our ghost come down the stairs and wait just inside the door for me. "Come in if you're comin' in," is what I heard from him. I could feel what he looked like but at this point I could not see what he looked like. I was sure I would after a while spent with him.

The stairs leading up to the top of the lighthouse are small triangular wooden steps with unannounced treacherous turns. The walls are brick whitewash with cobwebs and insect exoskeletons hanging like cotton floss from every imaginable crevice. I did not sense anything but physical decay and sadness until I made my way to the third of five small landings on the stairs. I was beginning to have some difficulty in seeing the physical stairs and began experiencing some psychic vertigo, both first clues for me that I am near something. Anger, frustration, anger and great loss is what I felt. The poor man is prevented somehow from doing his work. Perhaps there is here a discussion about being laid off, concerns about money and management, future employment and the future itself. I heard voices with foreign accents and tempers flaring, complete consternation over conditions and the overwhelming sense of frustration a man feels when all he wants to do is work hard at the only job he knows and cannot. As I approached the top of the last landing leading to the metal door above, the door which leads to the actual room where the light was kept, I could not only see and feel "John" very clearly but the two companions with him. "There are three men here," I said on camera, "two English or Upper Canada and one is dark and swarthy, possibly Spanish or Portuguese," since I heard that accent being spoken. Here were three highly intoxicated disgruntled old seafarers who, because their services were no longer required by the government, were losing their jobs. What we had here was 19th-century downsizing! At one point the anger was so pervasive that I believe I uttered an audible "Yech!" on camera. I began hearing the same words over and over again and seeing the repetitive actions of this ghostly trio picking up and putting things down on an invisible table, spitting, drinking and smacking each other's backs in an aggressive but congenial way. It was very clear to me now that I was seeing an event that was stuck in a loop. Although I saw muskets and knives, pistols and daggers, none had yet been used. I could see the energy of the anger going toward the weapons but it would rise just above it and then wane. Again, I was given a nod of a head and I knew it was time to descend the rickety stairs. I felt for this lighthouse keeper. I wanted to stay and speak with him. I wanted to encourage him to manifest deeply and clearly so I could aid him in some way in his dilemma. At this time the TVO crew was a little unnerved and was quickly agreeable to my suggestion that it was time to leave. On the descent, with a camera and audio crew behind me I received the loveliest moment of the evening.

About the fourth or third landing down on this 50-odd-foot tower, I happened to stop and gaze out the little windows and touch some of the brick around it. Something drew me to a part of the white wall opposite me. I looked up and saw, as clear as any photograph or perfectly painted portrait outlined in a cameo frame, "John." Handsome and seasoned and in his very best, as if reading my mind, he was showing me exactly what he looked like. I was so pleased as I gazed at this gift from a ghost. He was more handsome than I imagined, with a facial structure I likened to that of Gregory Peck, with a full dark moustache, large dark eyes, a strong bottom lip, and a determined chin. Neither smiling nor frowning, but rather saying, "Here it is, girl. You wanted to know what I looked like. Well, here I am." I pointed it out to the cameraman and audio man behind me. "Look, look, there he is!" I tried outlining where he was on the wall by first curving my finger and then describing every brick piece by piece until I was sure they too would see it. "Don't you see him?" I asked with great excitement. "Well, sort of, I guess," was the response I got. When I reached the bottom I ran outside to where Kim the researcher and Terry were waiting for us. I was so gleeful at this point that I went for another run with them up the stairs to the lighthouse to show them my wondrous gift from a very willing and co-operative spirit. At first I thought I had been mistaken as to which landing this apparition made itself known. I arrived at the very top of the lighthouse, stopping at each landing I thought was the spot, before I realized, much to my sadness, it was gone.

When all the excitement had waned, the crew, the Parks and Recreation workers, and Terry told me all the versions of the missing lighthouse keeper and the terrible hauntings of Gibraltar Point Lighthouse. I had heard them for the very first time. This is what I think happened:

There was no murder on that dreaded night. Poor John and his cardplaying cronies, probably seamen with no jobs, engaged often in roughhousing, arguing over ships, armies, and women. There hopelessness drew others with similar fates to the company of the lighthouse keeper. One fateful night, with some new invited men, the unknown variables, the drunkenness and despair escalated to the point of no return. Worried about money, John and his friends were either caught cheating or accused the newcomers of cheating. A fight began, weapons were raised, John ran down the stairs, possibly bruised from a wound. Being very intoxicated he fell down at the entrance to the lighthouse. His friends, though I would hardly refer to them as such, and the newcomers left him for dead. Fearing for their own lives or fearing punishment, they fled in terror. John, in a drunken stupor, headed for the canal out near the lake, fell and was discovered by either some friends disguising themselves as Natives, or Natives found him, and quietly and secretly took him somewhere to be healed of his wounds. John never recovered. His friends concocted a story of his "mysterious" disappearance to the authorities, who sent out soldiers as a search party for him and would-be assailants.

Nothing was ever found. The human bones found near the lighthouse? Relics that were placed there I think, perhaps a cruel prank, but more likely, someone buried John where any hard-working keeper would want to be... near his beloved lighthouse.

The time loop I saw was nothing more than John's wish to right a wrong; wishful thinking, if you will, to undo a foolish but costly deed. Oh, he is there, alright, wanting to work, tired of the tourists who bother him and needing to clear his name and find some friends. But what he mostly wants is a bottle of stout, some pipe tobacco, and a roast pork sandwich.

There it is then, John Robert. Thank you again for making the referral which allowed me this wonderful experience.

Let's get together soon. I am anxious to share my most recent findings about the house at the corner of Jarvis and Gloucester.

> Terry sends his regards.
> Happy Samhain.
> *Eloise*

Hunting Henry's Ghost

The Royal Canadian Legion Hall on Royal York Road, below the Queensway in Toronto's west end, has been known since the 1960s as a haunted site. Donna Dunlop and other folksingers who have performed there have felt the presence of its ghost or spirit.

Kathryn Newman is a freelance journalist whose face lights up when she hears the word "ghost." For an article for a community newspaper, she asked me to recommend some haunted sites to visit in the city's west end. I drew her attention to the tradition that the Legion Hall is reputed to be haunted by the ghost of a young soldier, named Henry, whose spirit is trapped in the hundred-year-old building. Kathryn was plainly attracted to the idea of Henry, so she resolved to devote one night of her life to seeking him out. She did so and described the experience in this lively account.

◆◆◆

Ghosts have always been a part of my life.

As a young child I would sit at my grandmother's knee and listen to her weave stories of haunted spectres and eerie happenings. At the end of each story, she would tell me that when you are dealing with ghosts, you have to be ready for the unexpected.

As a freelance writer, I have learned to expect the unexpected. However, no amount of stories, training, or experience could have ever prepared me for spending a night in "the haunted Legion Hall" on Royal York Road.

Originally the structure was built and named Eden Court by Edward Stock. The Stock family was one of the first families of settlers to populate the area which is now considered part of the Bloor West Village in the west end of Toronto. In its heyday the building was an attractive house with a sprawling porch, veranda and beautiful gardens.

There is a shadier side to the Stock House. During the 1930s it was used as a gambling hall and meeting place for the criminal element. Gangster Abe Orpen owned the building, and when it was renovated in 1966, bullet holes were found in the doors.

When Harry MacIsaac, the assistant steward at the Legion, informed me that permission had been granted for me to spend the night looking for the ghost of Henry, I almost jumped right out of my skin. The veterans and staff at the Legion had named the ghost Henry after a boarder who at one time resided in the attic.

I immediately recognized that I needed someone to accompany me on my adventure. It would have to be a person who could verify any ghostly phenomena and not jump to conclusions. My first and only choice was Sylvia Peda. She had a background in journalism, and we had worked together on many stories. Armed with notepads, a tape recorder, pens, talcum powder, and a flashlight with new batteries, we stepped through the Legion door into the unknown.

Bill Lazenby, president of Branch 217 Legion Hall, escorted us through the building and up onto the third floor. This was the floor that had the reputation of being the most haunted.

"There is something I should tell you. The light switch is at the end of the hall, and you have to walk down in darkness to turn it on. The only escape is by the main staircase. If you are cornered, you have had it."

Thankfully, the president turned on the switch for us and wished us luck. We were on our own.

Sylvia smiled one of the sly smiles that she is most famous for. With a gleam in her eye, she reminded me that we would probably be found with our heads at the bottom of the stairs, our faces frozen in hideous expressions of terror.

Despite Sylvia's bizarre sense of humour, I was glad that she was with me. I would not want to be in this place alone. Besides, when the atmosphere became too weird for my liking, I could always send Sylvia into the darkness to switch on the light.

We had to decide whether we wanted to conduct our investigations in the dark. After much discussion, we both decided that it might be wiser to leave the light on for the time being. While we were debating the issue of the light, we both became aware of a noticeable chill. It became intensely cold, and then Henry turned out the light. We tore down the stairs sensing Henry at our heels. It was then that I realized that I had left some of my equipment upstairs.

The second floor is set up as an entertainment area. Small tables are scattered along the side of the large room. At the back is a stage. We felt comfortable there. We convinced ourselves that we were safe and that nothing could happen on this floor. We relaxed.

We needed to gather our thoughts. "There is so much history here," Sylvia commented.

"Yes," I responded. "But it's more than that. When you think of what could have happened here with the gambling. Hey, maybe Henry's still up there in the wall," I chuckled uneasily.

There is a fine line between fantasy and reality. It was important to try to restrain my imagination. We needed facts, and we both knew it was time to go back upstairs and face Henry head on.

With courage and determination, we marched up the stairs. A ghostly green glow shone in the hall, and the doorway to the third floor was cloaked in darkness. Somewhere between the second and the third floor, I lost my courage. But it was my turn to brave the hall and turn the light on. I tried not to notice the room getting colder. I switched on the light and then I heard footsteps and thumping right behind me.

Sylvia sprinkled talcum powder on the floor, and we ran for our lives. This time I remembered my equipment. A cold breeze passed by us in the entrance on the second floor. We stood for a few seconds, trying to determine its direction, and then we returned to the safety of our table in the entertainment area.

Traditionally, the witching hour is the time when spirits are said to be most active. As the clock on the second floor ticked towards midnight, I wondered just how much more activity I could endure in one night.

For the next half-hour we listened to the building creak and moan. Cold breezes invaded our space. Unusual noises and whispers were heard coming from the second-floor bar. I experienced itching on my hands and feet. It felt like I had been exposed to fibreglass.

Sylvia became so cold that she was forced to put her winter jacket on. Then, at 12:30 a.m., she was touched on the head by an unseen entity. It took her several seconds to recover from her encounter with the ghost.

We began to discuss our next move, and just as we were about to enter the stairway hall, the toilet on the third floor flushed by itself. Sylvia and I grabbed hold of each other's arms for support. We held our breath. "I didn't know ghosts went to the bathroom," Sylvia commented.

The hours ticked away. We began to discuss our departure. We had seen enough ghostly phenomena to last a lifetime, and we both sensed it was time to go. It was important to leave the building the way we found it. That meant all the lights in the building needed to be shut off.

For the last time we climbed the stairs to the third floor. I felt the ghost's presence ahead of me. I was not nervous. In fact, I sensed a sadness. Sylvia did not sense the same thing. Her sense was one of a spectre who was lost, caught between worlds.

White powder footsteps had formed in the talcum which we had sprinkled on the floor. The steps started on one side of the room, travelled in one direction, and stopped suddenly. I flipped the light off, and darted through the hallway, and down the stairs. I did not look back.

One by one we turned off lights until we reached the rear door of the second floor. That was the way out. I felt relieved to be outside the building. It was good to feel the cold fresh air. I turned, and waved goodbye to the upper back windows of the building. I knew somehow that Henry was watching us leave.

As I drove the car to the front of the building, I decided to stop to take a few pictures. Sylvia and I climbed out. I was fiddling with my camera, when a circular flash of blue light shone from behind the centre curtained window on the third floor. Several seconds later the curtains on the second floor parted ever so slightly.

Upon reflection, Sylvia and I both believe that this was Henry's way of saying goodbye. One thing is for certain. Whoever Henry is, he gave us an experience neither of us will ever forget.

Trick or treat.

PART V
WARNINGS AND WHATNOTS

Every collection of ghost stories and eerie tales must include room for a section of "whatnots." These are items that are not easily worked into other sections. They belong together because they are essentially unclassifiable. So in this section the reader will find (in no particular order except chronological) discussions of wizards, prophecies, premonitions, strange abilities, warnings, guides and ghouls, If nothing else, expect variety in the world of ghosts and spirits!

Guidance

"The woods are full of creepy things." So runs a line from a child's song. At least one of these "creepy things" is a spiritual sentinel, a guardian angel of sorts.

There is certainly a guardian in this anonymous account. "My Ghostly Guide" is reprinted from the *Ottawa Free Press*, January 15, 1891.

◆◆◆

My Ghostly Guide
A Lumber Merchant's Story

In January 1853 I was engaged as assistant clerk in a large lumbering camp in the woods about a hundred miles north of the Ottawa River. Our main shanty was by the side of an outlet of the Red Pine Lake about two miles from the south side of the lake itself, a sheet of water of oblong shape, about a mile and a half wide and five miles long. There was a fairly good road from the edge of the lake to the shanty, and from the north or opposite side of the lake, a road had been made for some miles through the forest, to a point where a smaller camp had been established, and where a number of our men were engaged in making timber. From the main shanty to the smaller one was probably twenty miles. One day my chief, Mr. Simpson, sent me off with some instructions to the foreman in charge of what we called the Crooked Creek camp. I started with my snowshoes on my back and moccasins on my feet, at a brisk pace. It was a bright clear day. The road to the lake had been well worn by teams, and as there had been a thaw covered with frost, the ice on the lake was hard and smooth. The road from the lake to the Crooked Creek camp was rather rough and narrow, and a stranger might have difficulty in following it. However, I knew the route well, and arrived at my destination in good time, just as the men were returning from their work, with axes on their shoulders. I spent the night in the camp, being asked innumerable questions, and hearing all the petty gossip the men had to relate. It must be remembered that these shanty men go into the woods in October or November and excepting in rare instances hear nothing whatever from the outside world until they come out in the spring. Next morning I executed my commission and about ten o'clock started back for the main camp. I had not travelled more than half the distance when a snowstorm set in. In the woods the flakes fell down steadily, and I had no difficulty in keeping the road. It was about sundown when I reached the edge of the lake. The snow had reached the track across the ice and there was nothing to guide me to the entrance to the road to our main camp on the opposite shore. Out on the lake the storm was blinding, but I did not doubt my ability to reach the other side and find the road. So I started across the lake. When less than half a mile from the edge of the woods the snow was so thick that I could see neither shore. Moreover it was getting dark and exceedingly cold. If I should lose my way on the lake and have to spend the night there I would certainly perish. What was to be done? I turned in my tracks and managed to reach the North Shore again, stopping in the shelter of some bushes to recover my breath. Should I stay there all night? To tramp back to Crooked Lake camp was my first decision, but on reflection I remembered that any person travelling that road at night was liable to be attacked and eaten by wolves. Moreover I was hungry and fatigued. While I was thus communing with myself, jumping up and down and slapping my hands to keep myself warm, I saw a man dressed in a grey suit with a tuke on his head and a scarf around his waist, about 200 yards out on the lake, beckoning to me to follow him. I at once jumped to the conclusion that Mr. Simpson had sent one of the axe-men to meet me and guide me across the lake. So I ran with all my might towards him, calling to him at the same time. When I came close to the spot where he had stood, I looked around. He was not there, but a lull in the drift showed him some distance further on, still beckoning me to follow. No reply came to my calls to the man to wait for me, but every few moments he would appear some distance ahead beckoning me towards him. I could not tell what to make of the man's eccentric behaviour, but thought it possible he was angry over being sent to look me up, and was taking this method of evincing his displeasure. At last I saw him on the shore, pointing towards the woods, and reaching the spot where he had been standing I found myself at the point where the road to our camp left the lake. The road was easy to follow, and I hurried forward, still somewhat puzzled over the refusal of my guide to wait for me; and wondering also why he had not brought a horse, and sled. I reached the camp just as the men had finished their supper, and everybody was surprised at my return. Mr. Simpson said he supposed that even if I had started from Crooked Creek camp in the morning I would have turned back when the snow storm came on. Somewhat bewildered I asked which of the men it was that guided me across the lake and pointed out the road to the camp. "Why did he not wait for me?" I asked in a rather injured tone. The men looked at one another in amazement. Not a man had been out of the camp that evening. Every man had returned from work at the usual time and remained in camp until my arrival. We were nearly seventy miles from the nearest settlement and there was no camp nearer than the one at Crooked Creek. Every person in the camp became restless and nervous. That man who guided me across the Red Pine Lake was not a being of flesh and blood, was the general conclusion of the shanty men and my description of his disappearances and reappearances tended to strengthen their theory. The experience was such an inexplicable one that very few of the inmates of our camp slept that night. I was grateful for my rescue, and it was evident that whoever my guide was it was not my destiny to be eaten by wolves or frozen to death in attempting to cross Red Pine Lake in a snowstorm.

Prophecy of Death

ere is a grim reminder that the Grim Reaper is out in the fields forewarning his victims! "Singular Occurrence" appeared in the *Morning News*, Saint John, N.B., July 26, 1854. The original story was published in the *Times*, Centreville, N.S.

◆◆◆

Singular Occurrence

The following is from the Centreville *Times*:—

"Under the obituary head in today's paper will be found the death of Mr. Jacob Reese. On the day of his death Mr. Reese was engaged in seeding oats, and towards evening was startled by a voice apparently at his elbow, saying, 'You may sow but shall not reap!' He looked around, and seeing no one, continued his work of seeding, attributing it, as he afterwards stated, to his imagination.

"At every step, however, the warning was repeated, and at last, unable to bear it, he proceeded home to his wife. He was persuaded by her that it was only imagination, and finding that he had no fever, and did not complain of any unusual indisposition, she induced him to return to his field. There, however, the same solemn warning voice attended him at every step—'You may sow, but you shall not reap!' and in a state of extreme agitation, he again ceased work and went home. He took an early supper, was shortly after attacked with a swelling in the throat, and before sunrise next morning was a corpse."

Another Prophecy
of Death

Here is another grim, grizzly forecast of one's mortality. It offers, in addition to the bad news, a fair amount of domestic detail. "A Warning of Death" appeared in the *Lethbridge News*, 2 Nov. 1892.

◆◆◆

A Warning of Death

A curious incident, of recent date, was related to the writer a day or two since by a friend to whom most of those concerned are personally known. A young lady, sister of Mr. A., an artist of some repute, whose family live in Toronto, came down to breakfast one morning recently and related a singular vision, which had impressed itself more vividly on her mind as she was accustomed to perfectly dreamless slumber.

She had awoke at about seven, and finding by her watch that it was not yet time to rise, had dozed off, waking again very shortly after, and in the interval dreaming this dream. She saw running down the main street of Toronto, as if much agitated and in a great hurry, her friend, Miss M.C., a young lady of about her own age, and subsequently her sister-in-law.

Her friend was dressed in what appeared to be wedding or ball attire, and had orange blossoms in her hair and on her dress. A waterproof cloak was over her head and shoulders, apparently donned in haste or want of a handier covering. Miss M.C. proceeded with great rapidity down the street until, reaching the train terminus, in her hurry she slipped and fell in the mud; and rising again she disappeared from her friend's sight amongst a number of people who were entering a car.

This was the dream; and later on the A. family were informed that Mr. J., stepfather of Miss M.C., had met with sudden death just before four o'clock that morning through falling out of a window at an hotel where he was staying some miles from Toronto, he being a commercial traveller, and that his stepdaughter, Miss A.'s friend, who had been at a ball, was arriving home late, found a telegram awaiting her, had hurried off to take the train for the scene of the accident at the same hour, and habited precisely as seen in the dream.

Now comes the second part of the story. A few miles from the town, where Mr. J. met with his terrible death, was a lonely farm kept by a woman with her son and daughter, who were on friendly terms with the traveller, and knew of his stopping at the hotel. The daughter was dressing at a very early hour in order to get her brother's breakfast ready, he being in a stable close by, when a loud triple knock was heard at the front door. The girl promptly jumped into bed again, and excused herself to her mother, who was lying in another room, for not answering the summons, as she was not dressed.

"Then," said the farm-wife, "the loud knocking being here repeated, 'I will go myself,'" whereupon she wrapped herself in a cloak and went down to the door. The farmhouse clock struck four as she went, and just as her fingers were on the handle of the door the three loud knocks were given for a third time with such emphasis as to startle her and elicit the remark, "Dear me, they're in a great hurry, to be sure." But when a moment later the door was opened no one was to be seen. A thorough search was made over the farm premises without discovery, and the son visited a neighbouring farm, it being thought that somebody might be ill there, but found all asleep.

At breakfast the mother said that she had been thinking of Mr. J. all the morning, and could not get it out of her head that some harm had befallen him. The feeling became so strong that, against the wishes of the others, she had the horse harnessed and drove to the town, and on reaching the hotel, found there Miss M.C., who, coming downstairs to greet her, said: "Then you have heard already. How kind of you to come in my trouble."

A Canadian Wizard

In the rural areas of Ontario and Quebec in the 19th century, there may not have been covens of witches, but there was no shortage of self-initiated witches and warlocks, clairvoyants and psychics, or at least wise old men and women as well as eccentric women and peculiar men, whom others said were conversant with the spirits of "the vasty deep" or possessors of the so-called Black Arts.

Here is the wizard Bisonette, of whom history records hardly any more than what is known in this article, and in others like it, from the columns of daily and weekly newspapers. "A Canadian Wizard" appeared in the *Ponoka Herald*, future Province of Alberta, January 17, 1902. In accounts like this one are preserved some of the lore—and recipes—that permit the casting of spells.

◆◆◆

A Canadian Wizard
Some Tales of the Dead Bisonette of Sicotte, Quebec
An Escapade of His College Days
Drove Him to the Backwoods—
Credulity of Settlers Drove Him to Practise Witchcraft—
A Rival Witch—What He Did with His Large Earnings

Bisonette of Sicotte township is dead. As a professional wizard he had a large and widespread clientele, composed chiefly of the unlearned and ignorant, but comprising also some of the higher social rank. In the days before the railway, to reach his little mica-covered house in the woods, many people took the laborious drive of eighty-five miles from Ottawa. And the post offices within a radius of thirty miles, delivered to Bisonette much mail matter, some dainty missives, and many a registered letter.

Many of the inquiries he received were concerned with matters of health. To such inquiries Bisonette was not an altogether bad adviser. He was a medical student in Montreal in his young days, but an escapade drove him from college to the backwoods. Some surprising cures of men and beast when out of pure kindness he helped his neighbors in the time before doctors settled in the locality, and the credulity of the settlers led him on to practising witchcraft, in which he finally came himself to believe.

Much of his correspondence and most of his local business had to do with charms. These in the shape of meaningless incantations, sprigs of herbs, dried insects, bits of dried skins, ambiguous texts of Scripture, and sentences borrowed from books upon the Black Art, of which he had a curious collection, were sold to all who wanted them. His prices were always nicely graded to the customers.

Some forty miles lower down the river lived a rival of Bisonette's, a Mrs. Benham. This woman was popularly supposed to have more power on water than Bisonette, who excelled upon dry land. One day some log drivers came to her house and partook of such food as she had, but went away without paying for it. Just as their boat pushed out into the swift current the sorceress demanded her money, when the men jeered and flatly declined to pay. The next moment their boat stopped, and, in spite of their rowing, remained stationary until they humbly besought the powerful lady to allow them to return to shore and settle their bill. At least so the story runs.

Mrs. Benham died of pneumonia one night twelve or fourteen years ago. That same night Bisonette was in attendance upon a sick horse. He knocked his head against its forehead, and then told those present to leave the stable, as he felt he was about to have a bad struggle with a rival witch, who was at work upon the suffering brute.

As the men left they declared that they saw a black cat enter the stable, and the candle in the lantern was burning low and with a blue flame. They heard the sound of a conflict between a dog and a cat, from the house, where they remained until the witch came in, his face scratched and bleeding, and exclaiming that the horse was saved at last, but

Mother Benham was so badly hurt that she could not live till morning.

The doctor explained that the woman had died quite naturally from lung trouble in his presence.

A man, driven to desperation by rheumatism, made a laborious visit to Bisonette. The advice showed the wizard's acquaintance with negro voudouism. The patient was to take a two-inch augur and a two-inch plug four inches long and go at midnight into a certain bush there by moonlight to hunt up a brown ash tree. He was to bore six inches deep into this and within the hole place a lock of his hair and then breathe hard into it thirteen times. Then as quickly as possible he was to drive in the plug and let no one know where the tree was situated. The visitor received no palpable benefit, but was assured that the disease would never reach his heart unless that plug was withdrawn.

Philtres are still used by the love-lorn in that region. Many a mother believes that her lad was inveigled into marriage by a love dose secretly administered, and many a young lover slyly slips the potent drops into the sought-after one's cup. One philtre which a maiden bewailing the death of her lover acknowledged having administered was rather surprising. A tree toad, a black smoke, a horned pout, a bat, thirteen hairs from a black cat's tail, and a lock of the damsel's hair were put into a covered oven, and baked to a black crisp in the sand. The ashes were rubbed fine and divided into twelve parts, of which seven were left in a church, four were put in a bag and worn over the heart, and one was to be surreptitiously administered to the victim.

What became of all the money Bisonette made the local folk could not imagine. There are only three who know that all he could spare from a bare existence went by way of expiation for a crime committed against a too-confiding friend in the old days, when he was innocent of any coquetting with the Black Art.

"Ghost Case"

J ust when you think you have heard and read everything there is to hear and read about ghosts and hauntings, you come across a case that is outlandish and in its own special way ridiculous.

Such a case is the one that appears here. It concerns the real estate value of a property that is said to be haunted. It is no mean consideration if the "price" of a ghost is a drop in the monetary value of its haunt. The subject is not lacking in contemporary interest because real estate agents are wary of listing properties that have been "scarred," "slurred," or "tainted" in any way. Any slight on its esthetic appeal may have a negative effect on the asking price and hence its retail value. "$1,000 for a Ghost Story" was published in the columns of the *Winnipeg Free Press*, April 9, 1907.

◆◆◆

$1,000 for a Ghost Story
Court of Appeal Grants Appeal of Plaintiff
and Gives Her Damages

The following is the copy of the judgement in the "ghost case" delivered by the court of appeal yesterday morning:

Nagy vs. Free Press Co.

Richards, J.A.:

A reporter employed by the defendant company discovered the following entry in what is known as the "occurrence book" at the police station in Winnipeg.

"Second house east of Main Street on St. John's Avenue is believed by some people to be haunted at night between 11 and 12 midnight.

There are parties of men hanging around the house, also in basement, awaiting the appearance of the spook. This house is at present unoccupied. The Northern Fuel company are the agents of this house."

He then wrote the following for publication in the *Manitoba Free Press*, a newspaper published by the defendant company:

A North End Ghost

"There is a ghost in the north end of the city that is causing a lot of trouble to the inhabitants. His chief haunt is in a vacant house on St. John's Avenue, near to Main Street. He appears late at night and performs strange antics, so that timid people give the place a wide birth.

"A number of men have lately made a stand against ghosts in general, and at night they rendezvous in the basement and close around the haunted house to await his ghostship, but so far he still remains at large."

The article so written was passed on by one of the defendant's sub-editors and allowed by him to be printed in the defendant's paper, and it was printed and published in the morning and evening editions of Oct. 23, 1905, and in the weekly issue of Oct. 25, 1905.

An article somewhat to the same effect as the one published by the defendants appeared in the *Winnipeg Telegram* newspaper, and it appears that there were rumours of some kind to the same effect before either of these papers published anything concerning the property, though it does not appear to what extent such rumors had existed prior to such publication.

Closely following the publications by the defendants a number of people congregated in the evenings, and at night, about a house owned by the plaintiff, which is the house described in the above article. The crowds so assembled did damage to the house, and the plaintiff was compelled to employ people to stay in the house to prevent greater injury being done. This continued for several weeks; a crowd of people assembling every evening. Finally the plaintiff herself moved into the house for the purpose, she says, of protecting it.

At the time of publication of the article in question a physician named Kelly had agreed to buy the house for $11,000, intending to use it for a private hospital. He had paid down $250 on account of the purchase money, and had agreed to pay $4,750 more in cash on Oct. 24, 1905. He saw the article in question in the evening edition of the defendants' paper, and then refused to make the payment of $4,750, or complete the purchase. He broke off negotiations and forfeited the $250 already paid.

The plaintiff brought this action claiming damages for injuries alleged to result from the publication of the article in the defendants' paper.

In dealing with this case unusual questions have to be considered. While there are many people who have no belief in ghosts, there are many superstitious people who do believe in them, and many such, including especially many domestic servants and children, are likely to be terrorized by the thought of phantoms being in their neighborhood.

It is claimed by the plaintiff that the publication in question was malicious. I see nothing to support that contention. On the contrary, I take it to be evident that the publication was meant to be merely jocular, and I have no doubt that neither the reporter nor the sub-editor for a moment thought that the article would be taken seriously by anyone.

It seems to me further that we must assume that men of education, such as the reporter and sub-editor must have been, would know beyond a doubt that ghosts do not exist except in the imaginations of superstitious people, and, therefore, would know that the publication was untrue. In a case where a party publishes an article knowing it to be untrue, it seems to me that he takes the risk of such consequences as will naturally arise from that publication.

The evidence shows that the report of the house being haunted did attract the crowd of people that did the damage, and did put the plaintiff to expense in connection with guarding the house.

Part of the claim is for damages for loss of the sale to Dr. Kelly. In his examination as a witness the doctor stated that, but for this report he would have completed his purchase. In his cross-examination he made several statements which, if not explained by other parts of his evidence, would appear to mean that his real reason for abandoning the purchase was not because of the story that the house was haunted, but because he wanted to go to Vancouver, and had changed his mind about buying the house. This learned trial judge took that view of his testimony.

I have carefully read Dr. Kelly's evidence, and with much deference it seems to me that the learned judge misapprehended its meaning as to the cause why the doctor refused to complete his purchase. What Dr. Kelly meant, I think, by the expression relied on by the learned judge, was only that he had no belief in ghosts, and therefore so far as he himself was concerned he was not influenced one way or the other by the thought of such phantoms; but his evidence does seem to me to show that what really influenced him in abandoning the purchase was the thought that, owing to the large percentage of people who were superstitious, and to the fact that the minds of sick people are easily influenced, he might lose intending patients for the private hospital which he meant to carry on in the house, because of such patients being afraid to live in a house said to be haunted. The evidence of the doctor was in no way discredited or contradicted, and therefore following the cases of Coghlan vs. Cumberland, 1898, 1 Ch. 704, and Creighton vs. the Pacific Coast Lumber Company, 12 M.R. 546, it is the duty of members of this court, sitting in appeal, to review that evidence, and to deal with it, as regards its effect, as fully and freely as the trial judge has done.

It is contended by the defendant that an action of this kind does not lie; and apparently neither side has been able to find any law report of a similar action having been brought. It seems to me, however, that under the statute of Westminster, 2, 13 Ed. I., chapter 24, there is no doubt of the right to bring the action. It has been further contended that if such an action does lie the plaintiff must prove three things: first, that the statement was false; second, that the article was published with actual malice; and third, that special damage resulted which is attributable to the article complained of and to it alone.

As to the first point, it is urged that the plaintiff has not proved that the article is untrue, and that the house is not haunted. It is, of course, impossible to prove such a matter by evidence in the ordinary way. The very nature of a ghost, as understood by superstitious people, is that of a phantom appearing at rare intervals. Unless, therefore, we hold that courts should take judicial cognizance of the fact that ghosts do not exist, the falsity of the statement could never be absolutely proved. I think that the members of the court may, and as educated men should, assume that there are not such things as ghosts, and that therefore the statement is necessarily false.

I do not agree with the contention that malice must be shown to enable the plaintiff to succeed. It seems to me that people who publish an article knowing it to be false, as I assume that both the reporter and the sub-editor must have known it in this case, must be held to have done so without reasonable justification or excuse, and to render their employers, the defendant company, liable for the natural results of such publication, even though, as in this case, that result was quite unforeseen by those causing the publication, and though no malice whatever existed.

In using the word "malice" I refer only to what is ordinarily understood by that expression. Judges have in many cases used it as meaning only the absence of reasonable justification or excuse, and have attempted when so using it to distinguish it from real malice by calling it "legal malice." I see no need for its use in the latter sense, as such use only creates confusion.

As to the third question, I think special damage is shown in two respects; first, as to the physical injury done to the property, and the cost incurred by the plaintiff in protecting the house from injury by excited superstitious people. The fact that superstitious people would be likely to assemble at the house; and when so assembling would be likely to make trouble, is something that would have occurred to the reporter and sub-editor had they taken time to remember that, while they themselves and other people of the educated class, would only treat such a report as jocular and harmlessly contemptuous, the more ignorant of humanity would through reading it be naturally and readily aroused to commit such overt acts as happened in this case. Secondly, as stated above, I also think that the effect of the article was to cause Dr. Kelly to refuse to complete his purchase of the house, as a result of which the plaintiff lost the sale for $11,000. That result also seems to me a most natural one, and one which a reasonable man starting such a report would readily have foreseen had he known of the intent to buy the place for a hospital for sick people, or even for a dwelling house, and had he further taken a moment to think of the effect of the article on ignorant people. It is well known to everyone that many children, servants and others are particularly affected by stories of this kind.

A great deal of the real value of a house is that its use may be enjoyed as fully and with as little hindrance and annoyance as possible. Anything real or imaginary which interferes with that enjoyment is therefore a serious drawback to the value. It is to be expected that a man who is himself entirely free from belief in disembodied spirits will refuse to buy an otherwise acceptable house which is reported to be haunted, because though he would have no fears, he knows that it will be difficult to get servants to live in it, and that young children or sick people living in it would be terrorized if the report came to their ears.

The reasonable and inevitable result of such a publication seems to me to be, to greatly decrease the desirability of the house for purposes of habitation, and thereby to lessen its selling value.

With regard to the quantum of damages I find it difficult to arrive at an opinion. It is one of the many cases where they could be estimated more satisfactorily by a jury than by a judge. Still in this case the trial judge was, and the members of this court are, in the position of a jury, and though the quantum of damages cannot be accurately arrived at by any course of reasoning, we must, as far as we can, put ourselves in the position of jurors and deal with the question in some such way as we think a jury of reasonable men would. It is not shown that all members of the crowds who used to be at the house did so because of the publication in the defendants' paper, but there is evidence that some of them did, and a jury would therefore be justified in holding that at least a portion of the damage resulted from the publication in question. As to Dr. Kelly's refuse to complete the purchase, the evidence seems to me, as already stated, to show that it was caused by the publication in question.

On thinking the matter over carefully as to the amount that should be assessed for damages, and allowing some part of the loss to be due to the publication in the *Telegram*, and to rumours otherwise started, it occurs to me that $1,000 is the nearest that I can come to the sum at which a jury would assess such damages as should be given against the defendant.

No case for a new trial has been made out. In my opinion the appeal should be allowed with costs, the judgement for the defendants in the court of King's Bench should be set aside, and judgment entered there for the plaintiff for $1,000 with costs of the action.

This is eminently a proper case to be appealed to the supreme court, owing to so much that is involved being new in law. If the defendants decide to so appeal there should be a stay of executions till one month after that appeal shall be finally disposed of.

Mr. Justice Phippen delivered a judgement agreeing with Mr. Justice Richards, that the appeal should be allowed and judgement entered for plaintiff for $1,000 and costs. Mr. Justice Perdue delivered a dissenting judgement, holding that the judgement appealed from should stand, and the plaintiff's appeal should be dismissed with costs.

◆◆◆

Judge Perdue's Decision
Appeal in His Opinion Should Be Dismissed
and Judgement Stand

Judge Perdue's decision was as follows:

The plaintiff alleges that she was the owner of a house on St. John's Avenue, Winnipeg, and that the defendant falsely and maliciously printed and published concerning that house the following article:

A North End Ghost

"There is a ghost in the north end of the city that is causing a lot of trouble to the inhabitants. His chief haunt is in a vacant house on St. John's Avenue, near to Main Street. He appears late at night and performs strange antics, so that timid people give the place a wide berth.

A number of men have lately made a stand against ghosts in general, and at night they rendezvous in the basement and close around the haunted house to await his ghostship, but so far he still remains at large."

By way of showing special damage, it is alleged that sales which were being negotiated with several persons were broken off by reason of the article. The plaintiff's cause of action is alleged in the statement of claim alternatively in several different ways, but they all come down to practically the same thing, the wrongful publication of a false statement concerning the plaintiff's property resulting in damage to her.

There is no direct precedent for this action to be found in the English or Canadian courts. It is an action in the case akin to slander of title and to actionable disparagement of goods. These actions are well known and frequently discussed in reported cases. It is well settled that an action will lie for written or oral falsehoods maliciously published concerning a man's goods, where such falsehoods are calculated in the ordinary course of things to produce, and where they do produce actual damage.

"When a defendant either knows or ought to know that special damage will happen to the plaintiff if he writes or speaks certain words, and he writes intending that such damage shall follow, or recklessly indifferent whether such damage follows or not, then if the words be false and if such damage does in fact follow directly from their use, an action on the case will lie." Odgers on Slander and Libel, 4th ed., p. 73.

If an action will lie under such circumstances, where a man's goods are disparaged, there seems no valid reason why an action should not lie where the false statements are made in regard to his house or his real estate, which cause direct damage to him by preventing him from selling or leasing the premises. Since the argument of this appeal, the attention of the course has been drawn to the report of a case of Barrett vs. Associated Newspapers (Limited), which appeared in the *London Daily Times* of 7th and 8th March. That action seems to have been brought in respect of a statement in the *Daily Mail* newspaper that the plaintiff's house was haunted. Mr. Justice Grantham, before whom the case was tried, allowed it to go to the jury, apparently directing the jury that if they thought there was evidence of malice, they were to assess the damage plaintiff had suffered. The jury returned a verdict for the plaintiff, and judgement was entered for him.

Assuming that the plaintiff has disclosed in her statement of claim an actionable injury, it will be necessary to consider what she must establish in order to succeed. The present action is analogous to one of slander of title. The same necessary elements must therefore be established as would be necessary in an action for slander of title, before the plaintiff can succeed in this action. By authorities extending over a very long period, it has been established that to succeed in such an action the plaintiff must prove (1) that the statement is false; (2) that it was spoken or published maliciously; (3) that special damage was occasioned.

It would be difficult to establish conclusively the falsity of the statement complained of. One witness, Pugh, who passed a night in the house, said the statement was false, but on cross-examination he said he would not swear that there were not ghosts there. Upon the argument, the plaintiff's counsel asked the court to assume that the statement was false. But the court could do so only upon the ground that such a statement is repugnant to common sense and common knowledge, so that no proof of its untruth would be necessary. If the statement were admitted to be of that nature, it is difficult to see how anyone was deceived by it. The article complained of is not defamatory per se. It can only be actionable if it was intended to be believed and was believed by some third person who was influenced by it to the detriment of the plaintiff. This has an important bearing upon the consideration of the question of malice, which I shall next consider.

In some of the earlier cases it was held that to support an action for slander of title, actual malice must be shown. This view, however, has long been overruled. In Pater vs. Baker, Maule, J. expressed the opinion that there must be an intent to injure the plaintiff which might be inferred by the jury, and this view seems to be supported by the subsequent cases relating to slander of title.

It is distinctly stated by Coleridge, C.J., in Halsey vs. Brotherhood, that there must be in such an action an element of mala fides and a distinct intention to injure the plaintiff. The ingredient of mala fides or intent to injure may be described in various ways, but its presence is always necessary in one form or another and constitutes legal malice as referred to in the cases.

In view of the many decisions in which the word "malice" and "maliciously" have lately been discussed and criticized and the old meaning and effect of these words so greatly modified, one must approach with some diffidence the discussion of the meaning now to be given to these words as used in the reported decisions relating to slander of title and analogous actions.

In Bromage vs. Prosser, 4 B. & C. at p. 247, it is said that "malice" in its legal sense means a wrongful act done intentionally without just cause or excuse. This definition is approved by Lord Watson in Allen vs. Flood (1893) A.C. at page 94. He goes on to say: "In order to constitute legal malice, the act done must be wrongful, which plainly means an illegal act subjecting the doer in responsibility for its consequences and the intentional doing of that wrongful act will make it a malicious wrong in the sense of law."

In Brown vs. Hall, 6 Q.B.D. 333, Brett, L.J., with the sanction of Lord Selborne, thus expressed his view: "Wherever a man does an act which in law and in fact is a wrongful act and such an act as may, as a natural and probable consequence of it, produce injury to another, and which in the particular case does produce such an injury, an action on the case will lie." In Mogul Steamship Company vs. McGregor, 23 Q.B.D., Bowen, L.J. said "'maliciously' means and implies an intent to do an act which is wrongful to the detriment of another. The term 'wrongful' imports in its turn the infringement of some right." These last two statements of the law are approved in

Allen vs. Flood and in South Wales Miners' Federation vs. Glamorgan & Co. (1905) A.C. p. 250.

Now, I take it from these various definitions of legal malice that in so far as it relates to actions like the present, the conclusion may be reached that the statement complained of must be wrong, and it must be made with the knowledge that it will cause, or is likely to cause, injury to the plaintiff. There must be some mala fides, or improper motive, whether it be one of positive intention or of mere recklessness, coupled with a knowledge such as a reasonable person should possess that the statement is calculated to cause injury.

It cannot be pretended that the defendant in publishing the article in question intended or contemplated any injury to the plaintiff or her property. It is not as if the statement were that the house was badly constructed and unfit for occupation. If it was untrue to the knowledge of the party making it, it must properly be held to be a wrongful act, and an intention to injure might be inferred. But nothing derogatory to the house is stated in the article in question. To speak of a house as being the chief haunt of a ghost, or to speak of the house as haunted, would not, in the minds of reasonable men living in the present age, be considered as likely to produce an injury to the owner. There was evidence produced to the effect that some persons still believe in, or have a fear of ghosts. But the number of those actually affected by such a fear must be small, and we must consider the effect of the words with regard to the way they would be received by men of ordinary reason and intelligence, and not by the ignorant and superstitious. I think that any man of ordinary intelligence who read the article in question would see that it was an attempt to treat humourously an absurd rumor that had already got abroad.

It is said that in any event there was no justification or excuse for the newspaper publishing the statement. It may be that the falsity of a statement that is injurious implies malice, but in such a case the falsity must be distinctly proved. The Court cannot be asked to assume the falsity of the words, and from that to deduce the malice. That would be to assume two out of the three necessary elements, and nothing would remain except the consideration of the damages. It is true that in some of the cases we find the expression "without just cause or excuse" used as equivalent to "maliciously," but such use has occurred in actions for disparaging him in his trade. A disparagement of goods or a statement damaging a man's trade are acts calculated to do immediate injury by interfering with the sale of the goods or the profitable carrying on of the trade. If the statement was not unlawful, as, for instance, puffing one's own goods and comparing them with another's to his disadvantage, no wrongful act has been done, and the presence or absence of malice seems to be immaterial. But if the statement is prima facie injurious, as for instance where persons are warned against buying a certain patented article, then it is for the defendant to show that he had just cause or excuse for making the statement. I cannot, therefore, come to the conclusion that absence of "just cause or excuse" is equivalent to "malice" in the present case. The article which the plaintiff complains of is not prima facie injurious, or likely to cause injury.

If the statement is harmless on the face of it, it is for the plaintiff to show how it became harmful and she must also show that the defendant when publishing it knew it was calculated to prove harmful, and that it was published either with intent to injure, or recklessly, whether injury would be caused or not.

It appears to me that intention to injure must be established either directly or by reasonable inference to support an action like the present. Intention is not an element in civil actions for slander or libel, for it is not necessary in such cases to allege malice or to prove it unless the defendant claims privilege. But this is not an action for slander or libel in the ordinary sense and is not governed by the same rules. In actions on the case for wrongful injury, motive or intention is an essential element.

If the defendant must show "just cause or excuse," was there any such? The defendant company is engaged in the business of printing and publishing newspapers. The publisher of a newspaper undertakes to furnish its readers with news respecting current matters of interest. That is an important part of his business. Shortly before the publication of the article in question a rumour that the house in question was haunted appears to have been started. The house was unoccupied at the time and some persons hearing the rumour visited, or hung around, or went through the house, moved by idle curiosity to ascertain the cause of the alleged manifestation, or possibly to see if some trick were being played, and to detect its perpetrator. The police became aware of the rumour and of the actions of these persons, and an entry of the matter was made in the "Occurrence Book" kept at the police station. A reporter on defendant's staff read this entry and reproduced it in the form in which it was published, treating it in a quasi-humorous or serio-comic style. In publishing the article the newspaper only repeated as a matter of news the rumour that had already been circulated, that was evidently rather widely known, and to which the attention of the police had been directed. A newspaper would be justified in publishing under these circumstances such an occurrence, as a piece of news, first guarding against publishing anything defamatory. In the article in question nothing improper is said about anyone, nothing improper is said about the plaintiff's house, but only incidentally and inferentially is it brought into the article in describing the vicinity where the alleged ghost was seen, and where persons had been congregating to watch for it. It is clear that there was no intention on the part of the defendant to do a wrong to the plaintiff and that it never entered into the mind of the reporter, or of anyone else concerned in the publication, that the article would be likely to injure any person.

I think the plaintiff also failed to prove that she sustained special damage resulting directly from the statement complained of. This she is bound to prove. In the statement of claim plaintiff averred special damage in that the publication of the article caused the breaking off of negotiations for sale of the property to three separate persons. The evidence failed completely in respect of two of these. Mr. Hodgins' offer had been declined by the plaintiff before the occurrence complained of, and in any event it appears to have been contingent upon his selling his own property. Mr. Hagel does not appear to have ever opened negotiations for the purchase of the house. The only evidence of importance in respect to his branch of the case is that referring to the transaction with Dr. Kelly. After reading the evidence of that gentleman I must confess that I consider it very contradictory and too inconsistent to justify the finding of damage upon it alone.

Dr. Kelly had purchased the house and had paid a deposit of $250. He refused to complete the purchase. In his evidence in chief he stated that his main reason for refusing to complete the transaction was the report in the *Free Press*. But in cross-examination he stated that that was the reason he gave for not buying, that the real reason was he had changed his mind. He admitted it was not the ghost that prevented him from buying, but it was the change of mind. Then he said the cause of his change of mind was the report about the ghost and the other cause was that he wanted to go to the coast, that he could not say which was the real cause. Then immediately afterwards he stated that if it had not been for the report he would have completed the deal. He also on cross-examination made several admissions that were damaging to his evidence in chief and which cast much doubt upon his whole testimony. He admitted having said that the reputation the house had of being haunted did not influence him.

Upon evidence such as this it would not be safe to found damages, where damages are the gist of the action. The learned trial judge refused to believe the statements of the witness that were favourable to the plaintiff, and to disbelieve those that favoured the defence. He saw the demeanor of the witness, and refused to find upon his testimony, that the statement in question had caused the breaking off of the sale. In this I think he came to a proper conclusion, and this Court should not interfere with his finding upon such evidence. His finding under such circumstances should be treated in the same manner as if it were the verdict of a jury. It rested upon the plaintiff to establish by clear evidence that she had suffered damage directly caused by the article in question, and in the opinion of the trial judge she failed to do this. The other claims for damages for wages guarding the house, buying extra furniture, maintenance of house, car fares, etc., are not such as could, under any circumstances, be recovered in an action like the present.

The trial judge also points out that the rumour in question was current before it was entered in the police court book, and that it was published in another newspaper. This adds to the difficulty of finding damage directly traceable to the defendant's publication.

Evidence was put in to show a general depreciation of value by reason of the publication of the article. Damage is the gist of an action like the present. "The necessity of proving actual temporal loss with certainty and precision in all cases of this sort has been insisted upon for centuries." "Where the special damage alleged is that the plaintiff has lost the sale of his property, it is necessary for the plaintiff to prove that he was in the act of selling his property either by public auction or private treaty, and that the defendant by his words prevented an intending purchaser from bidding or completing": Odgers on L. & S., 4th ed., p. 76, citing Tasburg vs. Day, Cro. Jac. 484; Law v. Harwood, Sir W. Jones, 196. In Ratcliffe vs. Evans, which was an action brought for maliciously publishing an untrue statement about the plaintiff's business, proof of general loss of trade was held to be admissible to support the action. This was upon the ground that a general loss of business had resulted as distinct from the loss of this or that known customer. Such reasons can have no application here. It must be shown that an actual sale was prevented. Evidence of opinion as to depreciation of value, caused by the statement, is not sufficient. No lasting injury was shown to have been caused. A rumour like the one in question is soon forgotten in this community.

In my opinion the judgement appealed from should stand and the appeal should be dismissed with costs.

They Would Hold Long Conversations

V.G.

The time is the Great War. A Canadian soldier in France is at the point of death. He addresses dying words to his wife, his dear wife who lives in faraway Saskatchewan. At that very moment she is at work in a restaurant in Regina…and she hears him!

We owe the account of this crisis apparition to V.G., a native of Regina. V.G.'s full name has not been preserved. Her account was included by Winifred G. Barton in her collection *Psychic Phenomena in Canada* (1967).

◆◆◆

I had my fourteen birthday in 1917. Shortly after I started to work as a waitress in a small restaurant not far from home.

The hours were long but at certain times during the day business was slack; then the cook and I would sit in the kitchen, chatting, as I peeled potatoes and she baked pies.

The cook, Elizabeth, would be a woman in her early forties at this time. She was a warm-hearted, out-going person, and frequently told me stories about her home life, her family, and, above all, her husband's activities in the trenches in France.

As she rarely received letters I wondered aloud how she could possibly know so much, in such detail, about how he was getting along. To which she replied that two or three times each week she would meet her husband in dreamland and they would hold long conversations. She said his chums knew about this too, and sometimes he would give them messages from home. I believed everything Elizabeth said simply because she spoke in such a candid way.

Several months later, just as our rush hour was subsiding, I came bursting through the swinging dutch doors loaded with a tray of dirty dishes, to find Elizabeth clutching onto the edge of the table. Her face looked ghastly. I poured a cup of tea and persuaded her to sit down and tell me what had happened.

She finally explained that in the middle of serving up the mashed potatoes she had heard her husband's voice calling to her. "I've had it, Liz," he had said, "I'm a goner…." The plate she was holding had crashed from her nerveless fingers as the message was repeated twice more.

It was nearly a month before Elizabeth received the official notification, but during that period she was quite convinced of what had happened even though she had two letters from her husband postdated to the day of the incident I have related.

Madame Curry's Prophecy

JOHN E. WALL

The author of this remarkable account of a family's own prophecy is John E. Wall, an editor and writer who lives in Altona, Man. Wall has a special interest in anomalous phenomena, especially events of a Fortean nature, particularly those that involve cryptozoology (the study of hidden or unknown beasts) and pre-Columbian history. He has contributed articles to *Cryptozoology* and *The ISC Newsletter*. The account here comes from a letter that he wrote in the early 1990s.

◆◆◆

When my mother was a girl—she may have been a young teenager at the time—she and her mother travelled by train from their home in Glenboro, Man., to Winnipeg, for a day's shopping.

The exact day or even time of year this occurred, I do not know. I do remember, however, my mother telling me that the war was on at the time. Therefore, it could not have been earlier than 1939; it may have been as late as 1941. My mother could have been as young as eleven or as old as thirteen. Whatever her age, the incident I am about to relate impressed my mother so much that she never forgot it.

After spending some time shopping, my mother and her mother decided to rest and have a meal in a Chinese cafe at or near Winnipeg's famous Portage Ave. and Main St. intersection. It was here that they met a tea-leaf reader who called herself Madame Curry. That was not her real name. Possibly she named herself after the Curry Building, in or near which the restaurant was situated. This building still stands and houses a number of stores.

After their meal my grandmother and her daughter decided to have their tea-leaves read. To do this, one downed one's cup of brew to the last drop and inverted the cup over a saucer; a sharp bang of the cup against the saucer and the tea-leaves would come tumbling down. This was done, and Madame Curry proceeded to tell her customers' fortunes by studying the patterns that the leaves made on their saucers.

My mother did not remember the prophecy uttered by Madame Curry for her mother, but she clearly remembered her own. She would one day, predicted the tea-leaf reader, meet a tall, dark-haired man having the initials J.W. She would marry this man and they would have three children, all boys. Their family would move frequently, and after being married to this man for thirty-five years and some days, her husband would die.

In 1951, my father met my mother in a cafe in Glenboro, where my mother was working as a waitress. A year later they married. He was tall (six feet or over) with dark brown hair; his name was John Wall. As a requirement of my father's employment with the Interprovincial Pipeline Company, my parents and their children—three boys—moved frequently in Manitoba and Saskatchewan, finally settling in Outlook, Sask., where my father became ill with cancer. He died in a Saskatoon hospital one day short of his sixty-sixth birthday. Thus my parents' marriage ended after thirty-five years and five days. Everything that the tea-leaf reader had predicted, possibly forty-five years earlier, had come to pass.

But the irony was not complete. I happened to mention this prophecy to my aunt, who lives in Altona, one evening as I paid her a social call. She asked me what Madame Curry looked like. I described her to my aunt the way my mother had described her to me—a large, loud, buxom woman with white hair. "That sounds like Harry Smith's wife," said my aunt. "She used to live in Plum Coulee."

Mrs. Sharry Smith, my aunt related, had the gift of second sight, prophecy, or so she claimed. Every so often she would go to Winnipeg to read people's fortunes. She lived in the village of Plum Coulee, where my father, his two sisters, and their mother also lived. Mrs. Smith had a loud voice that she used to good effect when calling her children in for supper—one could hear her all over the block. Mrs. Smith was Madame Curry.

I later had independent corroboration of Mrs. Smith's powers from the widowed manager of the Co-op store in Glenboro. She had also had her tea-leaves read by Madame Curry, who had accurately predicted her husband's death as well.

Whether or not the foregoing constitutes the entirety of the tea-leaf reader's prophecy, I do not know. In any event, it is now too late to make further inquiries. My mother died suddenly and without warning of a pulmonary embolism two and a half years after my father's death. Yet she was able to see the fulfillment of Madame Curry's prophecy, uttered half a century or more ago.

"La Paloma"

JEAN CARTWRIGHT

It has long been accepted that birds are portents of well or ill. Doves are symbols of peace, crows are harbingers of death. I am indebted to Calgary researcher W. Ritchie Benedict for the following story. It originally appeared as "The Unexplained...By Jean Cartwright As Told to Inez Hosie, Regina, Sask." in *News of the North*, Yellowknife, N.W.T., 24 June 1964.

◆◆◆

This is a true incident that happened in Ontario.

My grandparents used to move into Toronto from their farm for the winter months, as grandmother was troubled with rheumatism and had to have warm quarters during the cold days.

They always managed to get a suite of rooms on the second floor of a large house on Balliol Street, which was owned by a friend. The farm, being only a hundred miles east of the city, enabled us to go two or three times during the winter to visit our grandparents, who were always glad to see us, and hear the news about the farm.

It was during the last visit we made at that house, while we were sitting in the front room chatting away, our attention was drawn to a beautiful white pigeon which alighted on the sill outside the window, tapped on the window, then flew away.

My grandfather remarked that it was strange that a pigeon would come into the city like that. Soon it returned again, flapped its wings against the window pane, remaining on the sill for a few minutes.

While the bird sat on the sill my sixteen-year-old sister, Wilma, began to sing her version of "La Paloma." "If at thy window pane a beautiful dove comes winging, treat it with kindness, for it has come to bear your soul away."

The incident was forgotten for the time being, as our parents prepared to leave for their return to the farm. Our grandparents invited us two girls to stay a couple of days longer, which we were delighted to do, as we planned on doing some shopping.

On the following two days the pigeon came to sit for a brief while on the window sill and to tap on the window pane, and at all hours of the day Wilma persisted in singing the same words from "La Paloma" until it grated on us, and grandfather asked her to stop it.

On the third day, we opened the window to let fresh air into the apartment. Alighting on the sill the bird boldly entered the apartment and, unafraid, flew to the top of the glass cupboard, where it sat undisturbed.

We all felt just a little awe at its presence. Certainly its behaviour was not that of an ordinary pigeon. After sitting on the cupboard for a few minutes, it found its way outdoors again through the still-open window.

The third day after the pigeon's initial visit, we prepared to leave, so grandmother accompanied us downstairs to say farewell to the folks below, as she had become friends with them.

We visited for half an hour and then returned to grandmother's rooms above. As we entered the door, grandmother called out to grandfather, "Do you think we were gone long?" There was no answer and we heard no sounds.

So we walked into the front room and there slumped over the easy chair was grandfather. We shook him, but he didn't wake. Grandmother became hysterical and Wilma rushed downstairs and phoned a doctor. As the people below hurried up and tried to calm grandmother, the doctor arrived and pronounced him dead.

Friends of ours moved into the same suite, where they lived for several years after. I asked them about the white pigeon, if it ever returned, and they said they had never seen it. It had never returned. White or any other coloured pigeons had never been seen near or in the vicinity of that particular house since grandfather's passing.

Scared to Death?

A.R. ELKINGTON, P.R. STEELE, D.D. YUN

The subject of the following letter is not a ghost story at all. Instead, it is a self-fulfilling prophecy. It is also a testimony to the power of a curse, or at least to the willingness of people to believe in the effectiveness of such a suggestion.

The letter appeared in the correspondence column of the *British Medical Journal*, No. 5,457, August 7, 1965. It concerns the death of woman following routine surgery at North West River Hospital, Labrador. The hospital, founded in 1915 by the International Grenfell

Association, was located at North West River, northeast of Goose Bay, Labrador. The hospital is no longer in operation.

The physicians who signed the letter appealed to "any reader who has had experience of a patient dying under similar circumstances." Two replies were published in No. 5,461, September 4, 1965. The first was contributed by J.C. Barker of Shelton Hospital, Shrewsbury, Shropshire, England. Barker noted that "one is left wondering why a fortune-teller should impart such devastating information to so young a child which was to make such a terrible and lasting impression upon her." He wondered whether "it is possible that were she a hysterical manipulative type her psychological symptoms, stress incontinence and reaction to it, leading to surgery and its attendant complications, might have resulted from her own unconscious efforts to predetermine her demise at the appointed time, having reflected endlessly upon the admonitions of her soothsayer." He concluded, "Perhaps the boundaries of western psychiatry should now begin to be extended to include some of the phenomena of extra-sensory perception."

The second reply was contributed by A. Fry, of London S.E. 25. He noted that "the case may represent a version of voodoo death." He observed, "A persistent state of fear can end the life of man," and then drew attention to the influence of a persistent state of fear on the sympathetic nervous system and its role in the control of the patient's blood supply. He concluded, "'Scared to Death' is not an idle saying. A feeling 'I am afraid I am going to die' may actually result in death. The anxiety is not removed even when the patient is anaesthetized. Although asleep, the patient is still suffering from anxiety."

I am pleased to be able to offer this verbatim account to my readers and I am a little relieved to be able to do so because the story has haunted me for some time. I learned about it from the book *Arthur C. Clarke's World of Strange Powers* (London: Collins, 1984), written by John Fairley and Simon Welfare, for the popular Yorkshire Television series, one of the few series on television that seriously considers claims of the supernatural and the paranormal, to the point of examining what evidence exists, whether pro or con, and regarding it both sympathetically and unsensationally.

At a reception in the 1990s, I met with a medical doctor from Labrador and described what I knew of the incident to him. He replied that he had worked at the North West River Hospital in the late 1960s. I asked him about the case. He said it was familiar to him and that everyone on staff at the hospital regarded it as deeply puzzling. He had no further light to shed on where I could learn more about the incident.

Fairley and Welfare concluded intelligently: "It may be remembered in this connection that fear serves biologically as a defence mechanism which, among other effects, leads to an enhanced activity of the adrenalin glands." They added, "The surgeons in the above case drew the conclusion that death was likely to have resulted indirectly from the stress created by the prophecy. While the present case hopefully involves a reaction of exceptional severity, the self-fulfilling pressure on those who profoundly believe in the fortune-tellers' powers is probably far from negligible; and the number of predictions that have been made to come true in this manner no doubt continue to swell the number of adherents."

◆◆◆

SIR,—We would like to report a case of an apparently healthy middle-aged woman dying with massive adrenal haemorrhage, following a relatively minor operation, who was subsequently found to have had forebodings of death.

Mrs. A.B., aged 43, mother of five children, was admitted to North West River Hospital, Labrador, on 18 March 1965. She had been complaining of severe stress incontinence for several months. She had been treated during the past three years for anxiety which responded well to reassurance and mild sedation with phenobarbitone, 30 mg., three times daily. There was no relevant past medical history. On examination she was found to be in good health. Vaginal examination revealed a moderately large cystocele and urethrocele. On 19 March anterior colporrhaphy was performed under general anaesthesia. The premedication was pathidine, 100 mg., and atropine, 0.65 mg.; induction with intravenous thiopentone, 400 mg., and Flaxedil (gallamine triethiodide), 40 mg.; maintenance with nitrous oxide, oxygen, and a trace of trilene, accompanied by intermittent intravenous pethidine to a total of 80 mg. The operation, which lasted less than one hour, was straightforward with minimal blood loss. Her blood-pressure remained around 120/70 throughout the operation, and pulse and respiration were normal. She regained consciousness before leaving the theatre. One hour later she became shocked and her systolic blood-pressure fell to 70 mm. Hg. She remained conscious, but shortly afterwards complained of severe pain in the left hypochondrium. Methedrine (methamphetamine) was immediately given, 15 mg. intravenously, and 15 mg. intramuscularly, and the foot of the bed was raised. As the blood-pressure showed no response Aramine (metaraminol), 10 mg., was given intramuscularly. An infusion of dextran, 500 ml., with hydrocortisone, 100 mg., was started. Despite continuous infusion with metaraminol and hydrocortisone no improvement was obtained and intranasal oxygen was required as the patient became cyanosed. The pain was partly controlled by injections of morphine, 16 mg., given on three occasions. The E.C.G. was normal. Her condition deteriorated and her temperature rose to 103.6° F. (39.8° C.) by midnight, when she became comatose. She died at 5 a.m. on 20 March.

At post-mortem examination the adrenal glands showed extensive haemorrhage. Petechial haemorrhages were found in the stomach, ileum, liver, and in the skin of the nose. There was no other pathology.

Subsequently we learned that this patient had had her fortune told at the age of 5 years, when she was informed that she would die when she was 43 years old. She had told her daughter for many years that she would die at this age. Her 43rd birthday was one week before operation. On the evening before operation she told her sister, who alone knew of the prophecy, that she did not expect to awake from the anaesthetic, and on the morning of operation the patient told a nurse she was sure she was going to die. These fears were not known to us at the time of operation.

We would be grateful to hear from any reader who has had experience of a patient dying under similar circumstances. We wonder if the severe emotional tensions of this patient superimposed on the physiological stress of surgery had any bearing upon her death.—We are, etc.,

A.R. Elkington.
P.R. Steele.
D.D. Yun.
Grenfell Labrador Medical Mission,
Ottawa, Canada.

Mackenzie King's Ghost

PERCY J. PHILIP

D id Mackenzie King return from the dead? Did his ghost converse with his old friend, newspaper correspondent Percy J. Philip, on a bench at King's estate at Kingsmere in the Gatineau Hills?

William Lyon Mackenzie King (1874–1950), who served as the country's longest-running Prime Minister, was a closet spiritualist. What is known for certain is that he was fascinated by spiritualist theory and practised spiritualist methods. He consulted mediums, engaged in table-rapping, and took omens seriously. All this was done in private or in secrecy. It was only following his death that the closely guarded secret of his spiritualistic interests became common knowledge.

Mackenzie King played favourites among the newspapermen who covered political events on Parliament Hill. One of his favourite journalists was Percy J. Philip, widely travelled war reporter and veteran Ottawa correspondent for the *New York Times*. Two years following the Prime Minister's death, just prior to his retirement, Philip paid a sentimental visit to Kingsmere, King's stamping ground in the Gatineau

Hills north of Ottawa. He sat down at a bench…and proceeded to converse with the late Mackenzie King.

"I Talked with Mackenzie King's Ghost" is reprinted from the December 1955 issue of *Fate Magazine*. Here is the strange but true story of how one man was affected by the legacy…the spirit, if you wish…of William Lyon Mackenzie King.

◆◆◆

On a June evening in 1954 I had a long conversation with the former Canadian Prime Minister William L. Mackenzie King as we sat on a bench in the grounds of his old summer home at Kingsmere, 12 miles from Ottawa. It seemed to me an entirely normal thing although I knew perfectly well that Mr. King had been dead for four years.

Of course, when I returned to Ottawa and told my story nobody quite believed me. I myself became just the least bit uncertain as to whether it really had happened, or at least as to how it had happened. Did I fall asleep and dream? Was this due to paranormal circumstances which cannot be explained?

Of one thing I am sure. Mr. King himself would believe me. He once held similar conversations—almost daily in some cases—with persons who had left this world. He talked with his father and mother regularly and with great men and women of the past. His diary, in which he recorded his spiritual experiences, as well as his political activities and contacts, gives detailed accounts of these conversations. Unfortunately it is not likely to be published in full because his will provided that certain parts should be destroyed. His literary executors feel bound to carry out these instructions.

It was not until after his death that the Canadian people learned that their bachelor, liberal Prime Minister communed with the dead both directly and, occasionally, through mediums. When it did become known—in a rather sensational way—it shocked many.

Yet the Prime Minister made no secret of his beliefs and practices. To friends who had lost dear ones he wrote in this manner: "I know how you feel. It seems as though you cannot bear to go on without that wonderful companionship and affection. But let me assure you that love still exists. A bond as strong as that is not broken by death or anything else. Your father is still near you. If you can be still and listen and feel, you will realize he is close to you all your life. I know that because it is so with my mother and me."

That quotation is from one of the many hundreds of letters of condolence which Mr. King wrote with his own hand, for he was punctilious in such matters. At funerals he always spoke similar words of comfort to those bereaved. Otherwise, although he made no secret of his beliefs, he did not parade them.

Once, at Government House, about Christmas time in 1945, he told the Governor General, the Earl of Athlone, that he had spoken with President Roosevelt the previous night. "President Truman, you mean," said the Governor. The Earl saw that some of his staff were making signs from behind Mr. King's back, evidently trying to convey some message. He was puzzled but, being a good constitutional Governor General, he kept quiet and did not again correct the Prime Minister when he repeated, "Oh, no, I mean the late President Roosevelt."

The occasion of the incident was the showing of the Noel Coward film, *Blithe Spirit*, which Mr. King found "most interesting."

"It is difficult to imagine the life after death," he said, chatting gaily. "Probably the best thing to do is to regard it as a continuation of the one we know with the same processes of growth and change until, eventually, we forget our life and associations on this earth, just as old people tend to forget their childhood experiences."

His Excellency, who was a brother of the late Queen Mary and a soldier by profession, muttered, "Yes, yes, probably." He obviously was shaken. He had been chosen by Mr. King to be Governor General of Canada and it made him nervous to learn that his Prime Minister was receiving advice from extra-mundane sources.

"Good God," he exclaimed when his staff explained why they had tried to shush him, "is that where the man gets his policies?"

Having an open mind about the occult and being inquisitive by nature, I later managed to turn several conversations with Mr. King to this subject. Once, especially, when we were crossing the Atlantic to Europe, he talked freely about his beliefs and experiences as we walked the deck.

"If one believes in God and a life after death," he said, "it is inevitable that one must believe that the spirits of those who have gone take an interest in the people and places they loved during their lives on earth. It is the matter of communication that is difficult. For myself I have found that the method of solitary, direct, communion is best. After my father and mother died I felt terribly alone. But I also felt that they were near me. Almost accidentally I established contact by talking to them as if they were present and soon I began to get replies."

These and other things that the Prime Minister said to me at different times came back to my mind as, on that June evening, I drove up the Kingsmere road and was reminded by a sign that the estate of Moorside, which Mr. King had left to the Canadian people in his will, lay just ahead.

It is a beautiful place. There are 550 acres of woodland and clearings, through most of which everyone is free to wander at will. A little stream with a waterfall flows through it down to the valley below. Mr. King accumulated it almost acre by acre, adding steadily in his methodical way, to the original lot he had bought when he first came to Ottawa at the beginning of the century. His quick temper seldom flashed more hotly than when he discovered that some neighbour had sold a parcel of land without giving him a chance to buy. Adding to his estate became a passion with the future Prime Minister. There he loved to receive visitors and also to be alone.

In buying the land Mr. King showed his Scottish shrewdness. But the building of the "ruins" was a perfect example of that romantic daftness that sometimes bewitches the supposedly hard-headed Scot. The direction sign now set up for tourists calls them "ruins" but the uninformed must wonder what they once were. There were doorways and windows, a fireplace, a row of columns, which Mr. King called the cloisters, coats of arms carved in stone, bits and pieces of the old Parliament Buildings, the mint, banks and private houses all built into an artistic enough wholly whimsical suggestion of a ruined castle. Somehow, perhaps because the surroundings with outcrop rock and pine are so fitting, they escape being silly.

On that evening there were no other visitors. The air was clear and cool. I sat down on a bench beside the ruins and thought about the strange little man who loved his hill-top home so dearly. I suppose I was in what I called a receptive mood. Although I had not then read it, I was following the instructions in that letter from which I already have quoted, to "be still and listen and feel."

I became conscious that I was not alone. Someone sat on the park bench beside me.

There were no sighs, groans and lightning flashes such as mark a spirit's arrival on the Shakespearian stage. There was, if anything, a deeper peace. Through a fold in the hills I could see a stretch of the broad Ottawa Valley. I tried to concentrate on it and keep contact with the normal but the presence on the bench would not be denied.

Without turning my head, for somehow I feared to look, I said as naturally as I could, "Good evening, Mr. King."

In that warm tone which always marked his conversation the voice of Mr. King replied, "Good evening, Philip. I am so glad you spoke to me."

That surprised me. "I was thinking of you," I muttered.

"Oh, yes," he replied. "I knew that. But one of the rules which govern our conduct on this side is that we are like the children and must not speak unless we are spoken to. I suppose it is a good rule because it would be very disturbing if we went around talking to people. The sad thing is that so few of them ever talk to us."

Here I think I should say that the reader must decide for himself whether or not he believes this story. It puzzles me greatly.

"I suppose," I said, or I think I said, resuming the conversation, "that we are just a bit scared. You know how hard it is to speak into a dark, empty room."

"That certainly is a difficulty for many people," Mr. King said. "But the room is never really empty. It is often filled with lonely ones who would like to be spoken to. They must, however, be called by name, confidently, affectionately, now challenged to declare themselves."

"Your name," I said, "must often be so mentioned in this lovely place you bequeathed to the Canadian people."

"Oh, yes, mentioned," he said. I glanced at him and seemed to see his eyes sparkle as they did in life, for he had a great deal of puckish humor. "But between being mentioned and being addressed by name, as you addressed me, there is a great deal of difference. I have heard things about my character, motives, political actions and even my personal appearance and habits that have made me laugh so loudly I thought I must break the sound barrier. And I have heard things about myself, too, that have made me shrink."

In the evening silence I had the sensation of being suspended in time and space as the quiet voice went on. "There are things that I said and did that I could regret but, on this side, we soon learn to have no regrets. Life would be meaningless if we did not all make mistakes, and eternity intolerable if we spent it regretting them."

He paused and I thought he looked at me quizzically. "By the way," he said, "Do you still write for the *New York Times*?"

When I said that I had retired, he chuckled. "But still," he said, "I think I had better not give indiscreet answers to your questions."

I asked several but he answered with the same skill as marked his replies to questions in the House of Commons and at meetings with the press, divulging nothing. It was I who was the interviewed. He was eager for news and it surprised me then, as it does now, that he seemed not to know fully what was happening in the world. The dead, I discovered, are not omniscient. Or perhaps what we think important is not important to them.

We talked of the development of Canada, of housing and new enterprises like the St. Lawrence Seaway. "My successor has been lucky," Mr. King said. That was as far as he went in any personal reference. "Canada has been very prosperous. I hope it will continue to be so. But you cannot expect good times always. It is adversity that proves the real value of men and nations."

The conversation drifted to the international scene, to philosophic discussion of forms of government, of the balance between Liberty and Authority, the growth and decay of nations and of systems. I cannot tell how long it lasted but I noticed that the sickle moon was getting brighter. I mentioned the time, fumbling for my watch.

"Time," said Mr. King, "I had almost forgotten about time. I suppose I spend a great deal of time up here. There is so much beauty and peace. I gave it to the Canadian people but in a way I have preserved it for myself. It is good to have some familiar, well-loved place to spend 'time' in, until one gets used to eternity."

We both rose from the bench—or at least I did. When I looked at him, as I then did for the first time directly, he seemed just as I had known him in life, just as when I had talked with him once at this very spot.

"I think you told me once that you are Scottish born and a wee bit 'fey,'" he said. "It's a good thing to be. We have two worlds. Those people who think their world is the only one, and who take it and themselves too seriously, have a very dull time. Do come back and talk with me again."

I muttered words of thanks and then, following the habit of a lifetime, stretched out my hand to bid goodbye. He was not there.

The Power of Suggestion

PETER STEELE

The following article was written by Peter Steele, a physician who practises in Whitehorse, Y.T. It appeared as "A Testament to the Power of Suggestion" in the *Medical Post*, May 30, 1995. Dr. Steele has consented to its appearance here.

◆◆◆

I'm a very conventional doctor—no iridology, a touch of homeopathy, little chiropractic—but I have had remarkable success with charming warts. My apogee of success was a child of nine who had forty-seven painful verrucae on the soles of his feet.

We went through my routine, with the essential connivance of the parents, of going to the bank to withdraw one new penny for each wart, going down to the Yukon River and throwing each of the pennies over the shoulder while saying the magic word: *Tikkitikkitembonaserembo-beriberibushkidankerwallamannapannakofemaskoshotz* (which I have printed out on a label stuck on a wooden tongue depressor for the child to learn at home).

Since I started, I have had at least fifty successes, mainly with children between the ages of six (when they can understand my mumbo-jumbo) and twelve (after which they think I'm a jerk). I attribute this to their sug-gestibility in a matter I think is mostly attributable to self-hypnosis.

I find it marvellous that in these days of hi-tech science the charm-ing of warts is so completely inexplicable. But I have a theory, completely empirical. Warts are small tumours caused by the human papilloma virus. Tumour behaviour can be modified by the immune system, and the immune system can be triggered by hypnosis.

I suggest that in charming warts we are inducing a state of self-hyp-nosis, whether it be by juice of celandine, frog legs under a full moon, or by my magic word. It is interesting that the only adults with whom I have had success are highly suggestible.

The mundane scientific fact is that it doesn't matter what your incanta-tion, potion, or sacrifice, you must believe to trigger your immune system to alter the metabolism of the papilloma virus in your skin. Then, Presto!

Dr. Peter Steele,
Whitehorse, Yukon

The Most Beautiful Woman in the World

ROBERT HOSHOWSKY

Robert Hoshowsky is a freelance writer who lives in Toronto. "The Most Beautiful Woman in the World" is an amazing ghost story. It has all the qualities of imaginative fiction, yet the author maintains that it is a complete and accurate depiction of what he saw early one morning when he went out jogging in North Toronto. It first appeared in the October 1992 issue of the neighbourhood weekly *Toronto's Midtown Voice*—the Halloween issue.

◆◆◆

A long time ago, before it became fashionable, I was a jogger. Not just a block or two, but five, ten, even fifteen *miles* each and every night. Initially, I was joined by friends. The three of us huffed and wheezed our way through the labyrinth of streets and alleyways known as North Toronto a couple of hours after dinner, long after the sun had dipped below the horizon and the food in our stomachs had settled enough so we wouldn't puke. With our lungs straining for the next breath, we savoured every second of our run with youthful enthusiasm.

After a while, however, one friend after another dropped off and sought other pursuits. Tyler discovered the joys of poker, and became forever lost to gambling away his pocket change after class. Dwight formed a heavy metal band, and pretended to bite the heads off stuffed parakeets in the high-school auditorium during lunch. Since I had no musical abilities whatsoever, I kept running, alone.

One night, feeling especially adventuresome, I decided to try twenty miles. No stopping, not for pain or traffic lights. This was in August, and there are surprisingly few people awake at three in the morning.

Dressed in a ratty old muscle shirt and shorts that looked like they'd been washed ten thousand times, I was ready. And, up until the time I saw her, I was having a pretty good run. She was about half a mile away, on the other side of the street. I rubbed the sweat from my eyes and kept on running. At first, I thought she was a disheveled housewife, wandering around looking for her cat. That is, until I noticed a few little things.

Her bare feet weren't touching the ground.

I stopped so suddenly that I nearly fell flat on my face. The "housecoat" she was wearing was a nightgown, a very old-fashioned one, adorned with a high lace collar and white material that reached to her ankles. Her hair was loose, and hung around her slender shoulders in thick black ropes.

What shocked me the most was her body. It was translucent, not like anything I had seen before. With every passing second, sections of her appeared and disappeared at the same time. She seemed just as astonished to see me as I did her, looking at me like I was intruding on her territory. Yet she was striking, with firm, high cheekbones and a lovely oval face. She couldn't have been more than thirty.

Her entire appearance suggested nobility, as if she had just drifted off the canvas of a Pre-Raphaelite painting. Long, slender hands, the supple neck of a swan, and enormous dark eyes which seemed to occupy most of her exquisite face. I fell in love with her in an instant, despite the fact she was a ghost. Never before have I wished so hard for one thing: for this woman to be truly *alive*, with warm human flesh and the breath of the living, not the wind of the dead. By the way she was dressed, she had been that way for at least a hundred years.

As I walked towards her, I felt my knees turn to water and stopped, not out of fright but of fear—of myself. We stood on opposite sides of the road staring at one another for an eternity, a supernatural breeze blowing the nightgown around her naked form. She was trapped, a prisoner caught in the never-world between life and death; a place I could not enter, and a land she could never leave.

I turned and ran, stopping only when I reached the top of the hill. The instant I turned to look at her, she swirled around, her body slowly disappearing into the darkness. The look of sadness hadn't left her eyes, and won't until the day I am dead, when we can meet again, not as strangers, but lovers.

She was, and forever will be, the most beautiful woman I never met.

The Pedlar's Ghost Story

A pedlar takes refuge in a derelict cabin in the woods, where his life is threatened by a menacing, ghostly hand! This lively piece of writing appeared under this title in the *Toronto Telegram*, October 20, 1870.

◆ ◆ ◆

Several years ago, I was engaged in the business of peddling among the frontier towns of Canada. The route over which I was accustomed to travel usually occupied me about six weeks; and so scattered were the settlements which I visited, that not infrequently I was obliged to encamp for the night in the woods. I carried my goods in a pack upon my back, and was accompanied in my journey back and forth by a huge mastiff hound—one of the most intelligent brutes I ever saw, and devotedly attached to me. Of course I was armed. In addition to a pair of good revolvers and a knife, I carried a cane, which I used as a staff in walking, but which I could, upon occasion, instantly convert into a most deadly weapon. It was charged with a heavy load of buckshot, and was quite as effective as a blunderbuss.

Much of my journey lay through a rough country just beginning to be broken up by the pioneers; and often for miles I had to travel through forests which none but the trapper, or men engaged in some business like my own had ever visited.

One afternoon I was seated on the bank of a little stream, resting from my walk; and being warm and tired, I proceeded to bathe my face.

While thus engaged, I noticed a little path, which led from the water's edge up into the forest. I knew at a glance that it was made for deer and other animals coming down to drink; and, impelled by curiosity, I determined to follow it up for a short distance. I had passed less than a quarter of a mile, when I suddenly came upon an opening in the woods, of several acres, in the centre of which stood a good substantial log cabin. Going to the door, I pushed it open, and took a survey of the premises. There were but two rooms in the building—one on the ground, and a loft overhead, which was reached by a short ladder. At one end of the lower room was a huge fireplace, strewed with ashes and a few pieces of charred wood; while at the other, in one corner, a pile of fir boughs were lying, showing that some traveller had made it a stopping-place for the night; but it must have been long before, for the branches he had gathered for a couch were dried and dead.

Glancing at my watch, I saw that it was half-past five, and the sun was nearly down. Thinking myself fortunate in securing so good a camping-place, I proceeded to gather some dry sticks and kindle a fire. Dry wood there was in abundance, for directly in front of the cabin stood a pine tree, which the lightning had shivered, scattering splinters and boughs for rods in every direction, and I soon had a cheerful fire blazing and snapping on the hearth. Then, gathering a few armfuls of fir boughs for a bed, and extemporising a rough seat, my dog and I betook ourselves to supper. He seemed to be as well pleased with the situation as myself, and after eating the food I gave him, went and stretched in the door-way—for it was a pleasant spring evening—and composed himself for a nap, while I, filling my pipe, indulged in a smoke and a reverie.

For a long time after my pipe had gone out, I sat watching the fire creeping up the dried wood, now burning steadily, and now leaping with burning flame, as it caught at some part more combustible than the rest. At length, tired with my day's journey, I nodded and fell asleep, but was soon awakened by the growling of my dog. Rising and rubbing my eyes, I went cautiously to the door, and looked about me. Everything was quiet, and the full moon, just peering over the tops of the forest trees, streaked the clearing here and there with patches of mellow light.

"What is it, Brave, old fellow, eh?" said I, speaking to the dog.

He wagged his tail, whined, and snuffed the air uneasily. Satisfied that something was wrong, I cocked a pistol and went out into the moonlight, closely followed by the dog. I went round the cabin; there was nothing to be seen. I peered into the shadows of the woods about me—all was still, save that the branches now and then swayed to and fro with the evening wind.

Satisfied that there was nothing within the opening, yet feeling a little uneasy, I entered the cabin, replenished the fire, and was about to close the door, when, as if in answer to a threatening growl from the dog, there came a quick, sharp blow against the side of the building, similar to that which could be produced by striking with a piece of board. With a short, savage bark, Brave sprang out of the open door, while I, with a pistol in readiness for instant use, followed. There was nothing to be seen, although I made a most careful search, and everything was as quiet as before; but there was something very strange about it, for the dog came to me with a half whine, half growl, his hair bristling, and he sniffling the air and looking uneasily overhead. A thought struck me. Had not some persons been in the cabin, and, seeing me coming, concealed themselves in the chimney, and were they not now, with some object in view, trying to frighten me? Impossible! for the smoke from the resinous pine I had burned would soon have driven them out, or suffocated them in their hiding-place.

"Brave," said I, "we are a couple of fools; there is no one here, and everything is all right; if it isn't we'll make it right in the morning."

As I spoke these words I reached the door, and was in the act of entering, when, without the least noise, with a motion silent as death itself, a huge bird, black as midnight, came swooping past so close that it almost brushed my face with its wings. On that instant the dog sprang, and though his motion was as swift as lightning itself, and I could swear that he grasped it in his jaws, yet I heard them clash together with a snap like a steel trap, while the bird, swooping upward, settled itself on a branch of the withered pine.

"Born in the woods, and scared by an owl." I repeated to myself; but looking at the dog, I saw that he had slunk into the cabin, and was shivering with fright.

Almost angry at his actions, I commanded him sharply to come to me, and he obeyed, though reluctantly.

"Now, Brave," said I, "you are too wise and old a dog to be scared by a paltry owl, though he is a big one. He'll be giving us some of his precious music presently; and as I don't care about that kind of a serenade I'll drive him back into the woods."

So saying, I picked up a handful of stones and began trying to frighten away my unwelcome visitor. But the more I wanted him to leave, the more he wouldn't go; and though on several occasions I was sure I struck him, still he never altered his position or budged an inch. Now, when I begin to do a thing I like to carry it through; and so, without thinking what the consequences might be, I drew one of my pistols and fired at the strange bird. The report rang sharply out upon the night air, and went echoing through the forest and over the hills for miles and miles away. Half frightened at what I had done, and provoked that he did not stir, I fired again and again. How strange it was that I could not hit that bird! Did I miss my aim? I am a good shot—it was almost light as day, and he was not over twenty feet distant.

Going into the cabin, I reloaded my pistol, and being now fully aroused and provoked at my want of success, I determined that this time at least he should not escape me. I got my cane, adjusted it, took deliberate aim, and fired. The piece was heavily loaded, and the discharge almost deafened me; but when the smoke had cleared away and I looked upwards, the bird had gone.

"I thought I'd settle you that time," I muttered.

Gone! Yes it was gone—but where? I looked into the air above me, on the ground around me; I peered into the tree to see if perchance it had lodged in any of the branches; I listened, that I might hear it flutter, if but wounded; but there was no sound save the wind moaning through the dead branches of the tree above me, that stood withered, scalped, and ghastly, like a thing accursed.

Partially satisfied in that the bird had disappeared, and musing on the strange occurrence, I took my way into the cabin, reloaded my piece, securely fastened the door, and calling my dog close to me, lay down on the branches to sleep, resolving that I would suffer no more mysterious sounds or strange birds to annoy me. With my faithful dog at hand, and my arms in readiness for use, a feeling of security came over me, and I fell into a sound slumber.

I must have slept for several hours, for when I woke the fire was burning but feebly, and its flickering, dying flames cast weird and grotesque shadows on the wall. But what was the strange presence in the room that made my flesh creep and the perspiration to stand in cold drops upon my brow? There was nothing that I could hear; yet a strange sense of impending and appalling danger almost paralyzed me. It came at length, as I knew it would—a wailing sound, at first faintly heard, but swelling louder and louder until it deepened in its hideous intensity to the pitch of an unearthly yell; then again all was still.

I sprung to my feet; there was nothing in the room but my dog, who stood with burning eyes and bristling hairs glaring at the opening in the loft overhead.

"By all the beings of earth and air!" I shouted, "I'll see this thing out, if it cost my life!" And kindling the fire to a roaring flame, I seized a blazing brand in one hand and a pistol in the other, and climbed to the loft above.

I searched in every nook and corner where even a mouse might hide. I went round it again and again; I descended to the open air and peered into places which I had examined a dozen times before. Nothing was changed. The old pine still stretched its long, gaunt arms in the moon-light, and the wind sighed and moaned like the wail of a wandering spirit through its shivered boughs.

I entered my cabin, took up my pack, and resolved to pass the remainder of the night beneath the open sky; but a feeling of pride prevented me; and closing the door once more, I flung myself upon my bed.

Suddenly, as I lay pondering on the mysterious manifestations, a livid gleam, like lightning, shot from the loft overhead; and that yell came once more—not as at first, slowly and indistinctly, but sharply and fearfully sudden; then it died away like a death groan. The fire, which was burning brightly, with a sudden hiss went out, and the room was left in utter darkness. Then a little vapory ball of light appeared at the opening in the lift; it grew brighter and brighter, till the room was as light as day; and from the centre of that vapory ball, a hand appeared—a hand! with moving fingers that seemed searching the air for something they found not. It moved towards me; at first the hand alone, but soon a wrist, and then an arm appeared, lengthening, lengthening, and slowly stretching out to grasp me. Great heaven! was there no end to that arm? My dog was crouched beside me, but not in fear now; his eyes were fixed with a steady glow upon the moving hand, and every nerve was braced for a deadly spring; and when at last it had reached so frightfully near that I might have reached it with my hand, and I might have touched it, and I shouted, "Take him, Brave!" the noble creature leaped, with panther spring, from the ground beside me. There was a growl, a crash, and a smothered fall, and then I was caught in a vice-like grasp. I struggled to free myself, but in vain; and when at last a pair of clammy arms were passed close to mine, I gave a shriek of terror and despair, and felt my senses leave me.

I knew no more till I woke up to find my faithful dog locking my face and whining piteously, and I lay on the bank of the stream where I had stopped to rest.

'Twas only a dream after all, but so frightfully real did it appear, that it was hours before I recovered my strength or composure of mind.

It was the last trip I ever made upon the route, for I never could shake off the impression left upon me by the dream. I believe it to have been a warning of danger ahead, and I shudder now, and ever shall, as I think of that afternoon nap in the woods of Canada.

Warned of Danger by a Ghost

On a dark and stormy night, a traveller who is returning home approaches a fork in the road and is surprised to behold old Angus cautioning him to take the longer route rather than the shorter one. He accepts the advice and returns home safely...to discover that old Angus has been dead for six weeks! This tale appeared under the title above in the *Canadian Statesman*, December 24, 1889.

◆ ◆ ◆

Warned of Danger by a Ghost
The Meeting on the Road and the Spectre's Words of Guidance
The Shade Was "Not Wrapped Up for Driving"
and Refused the Invitation to Ride, as "Walking Was Warmer"

Such a glorious night! The snow sparkled like diamond dust, and the sleigh runners squeaked as they passed over it, with frosty sound so dear to the heart of the true Canadian.

The moon had risen, and it was as bright as day. The horse's breath seemed to fill the air with clouds, and his coat already began to sparkle with frost. Oh, it was good to be home again! "Canada for the Canadians." Is it any wonder we love our beautiful country with such passionate devotion?

From these high and patriotic thoughts I was aroused by coming to a turn in the road, a fork. Now there were two roads to the village from this point, one leading down a long, steep hill, at the bottom of which an aboideau, or primitive bridge, built of fire trees and brush, with alternate layers of earth and stones—a sort of earthwork, in fact— spanned a deep treacherous little creek, in which the ice piled in huge blocks in winter, and, as it was an estuary of the river, it was a dangerous spot when the tide was high. Taking this road would cut off more than half a mile of my journey, so I decided to try it, despite a curious reluctance on the part of my horse. The road certainly did not look as if it was travelled much, but just at the turn the snow had drifted off, leaving it nearly bare. So I forced the unwilling nag into the roadway and jogged on cautiously.

The spot bore an unpleasant name, and a still more unpleasant reputation. It was called "Ghost's Hollow."

Fifty years ago, in the old days when the province was thinly settled and a weekly stage coach was the only means of communication between the different towns, the horses of a heavily laden coach had taken fright at the top of the hill, and dashing down at mad speed gone over the aboideau. The tide was full in at the time and the creek filled with great floating blocks of ice. There were none to help in that lonely spot, so every one had been drowned, and the superstitious country people insisted that on wild winter nights any one standing at the top of the hill and listening intently could hear the muffled sound of sleigh bells, the shouts and the splashing and struggling of the horses. Certain it was that, when the tide was very low and the wind high, the water rushing through the sluices under the aboideau made an eerie, gurgling sound that was not by any means cheerful. I could hear it now with painful distinctiveness, though there was no wind. And my thoughts travelled back to my boyhood and to old Angus McDonald, a queer old Scotch farmer, with whom I had been a favourite, who had taught me how to make fox traps and to shoot rabbits, to believe in omens and to be frightened in dreams.

He was a superstitious old fellow, who declared that he had the gift of second sight, and who had always insisted that to hear the sound of the groans and struggles in "Ghost's Hollow" was a sure forerunner of coming misfortune to the one hearing them.

I smiled to myself as I remembered it, and made a mental note that I would tell Angus the first time I saw him, and ask him what he made of the omen now.

The horse stopped so suddenly that I nearly fell over the dashboard! And directly in front of the sleigh I saw a man plodding slowly along through the snow. I could have sworn that he was not there half a minute before, and yet he could not have come out of the woods without my seeing him. "Holloa!" I called. He turned slowly, and I saw that it was old Angus himself.

"Why, Angus, old fellow," I said, "what in the world are you doing in this lonely spot? Jump in and I'll drive you home. I was just thinking about you."

"Many thanks, Walter, for yer offer and yer thoughts, too; but it's a cold night, and I'm not that wrapped up for driving; walking's warmer," he answered.

"But what brings you out here on such a night, Angus?" I persisted. "Your rheumatism must be better than it was, or you would not run such risks."

"Ay, the rheumatism's not that bad, I was seein' to the fox traps, an' then I heard the bells an' knew someone was going down the hill, so I came out to warn them. The 'bito's' all down, Walter, an' you'd get an ugly fall amongst those ice cakes if ye went over; turn back, boy, an' go the long way."

"But, Angus," I cried, "I don't like to have you here."

"I'll do well enough, lad; I'm going home now, good night."

"Good night," I answered reluctantly, "I'll see you tomorrow."

He made no answer and I turned the trembling horse, who pranced and snorted and tried to bolt until he realized that he was going the other way. When I looked back Angus was gone.

Once on the main road again we went like the wind, and soon the lights of home shone out, and in a few minutes more I was in the hall being shaken hands with, and kissed and questioned, passed around from one to the other like a sort of cordial, exclaimed over and commiserated because I had not any tea, and reading a welcome in Maggie's sweet eyes that was more "truly sustaining," as the old ladies say, than all the tears in the world.

"Walter, dear," said Maggie, "you have not been taking care of yourself. You look terribly worn and pale."

"Never mind, Maggie," I answered, "I am going to rest and get strong again now."

The boys were both home for the day.

Jack was in the civil service and Will was in a bank, both younger than I, and already winning their own way in the world, I thought with a sigh.

Then mother came in to tell me my supper was ready, and everyone came into the dining room to see that I was taken care of. Maggie poured out hastily made coffee, and if I could only have shaken off a curious feeling of languor that would creep over me, I should have felt as if I were in Paradise, after my long months of solitude.

"By the way, Walter," said Jack suddenly. "How did you happen to come the marsh road, as of course you did, or you would not be here—

you know you always take the old coaching road because it was a little shorter. Was it by chance, or did they tell you at the hotel that the aboideau was down?"

"I believe they did tell me," I answered. "At least the hostler called after me, but I did not hear him. So I took the coach road, and if it had not been for poor old Angus McDonald I should be floundering among the ice cakes now instead of sitting here. I met him before I had more than started down the hill, and he told me about the 'bito,' as he called it."

For a full minute after I spoke there was a dead silence. Then Jack opened his mouth to speak, but was checked instantly by a look from father. Maggie grew very pale, and then flushed uneasily, and mother said something hurriedly about my having missed the train, and how disappointed the girls had been.

Something had evidently happened, for everyone seemed constrained, but made nervous efforts to talk, so I was glad when the meal, which had begun so merrily, came to a close.

I went back to the parlour with the girls and tried to feel as I did when I first came in, but it was of no use, and, hearing Jack's footstep crossing the hall, I slipped out and stopped him.

"Look here, Jack," I began, "did I say anything out of the way at supper?" "No! Oh, no," said Jack, uneasily; he had evidently received private instructions to hold his tongue, and he found the task a hard one.

"Very well," I answered shortly; "if you don't choose to tell me, I'll go out in the kitchen and ask the servants. They will tell me fast enough. Now what was there in my saying I had seen old Angus to startle anyone so?"

"Well, if you will have it, there was a good deal. Angus died six weeks ago. I can't imagine how we forgot to write you about it—Walter!!!"

I can't tell much about what happened after that, for the reason that I don't know. Jack says I just staggered and fell, as if I had received a blow. And when I was able to take any interest in what was passing around me it was nearly the last of January, and I had lost count of time for many weeks.